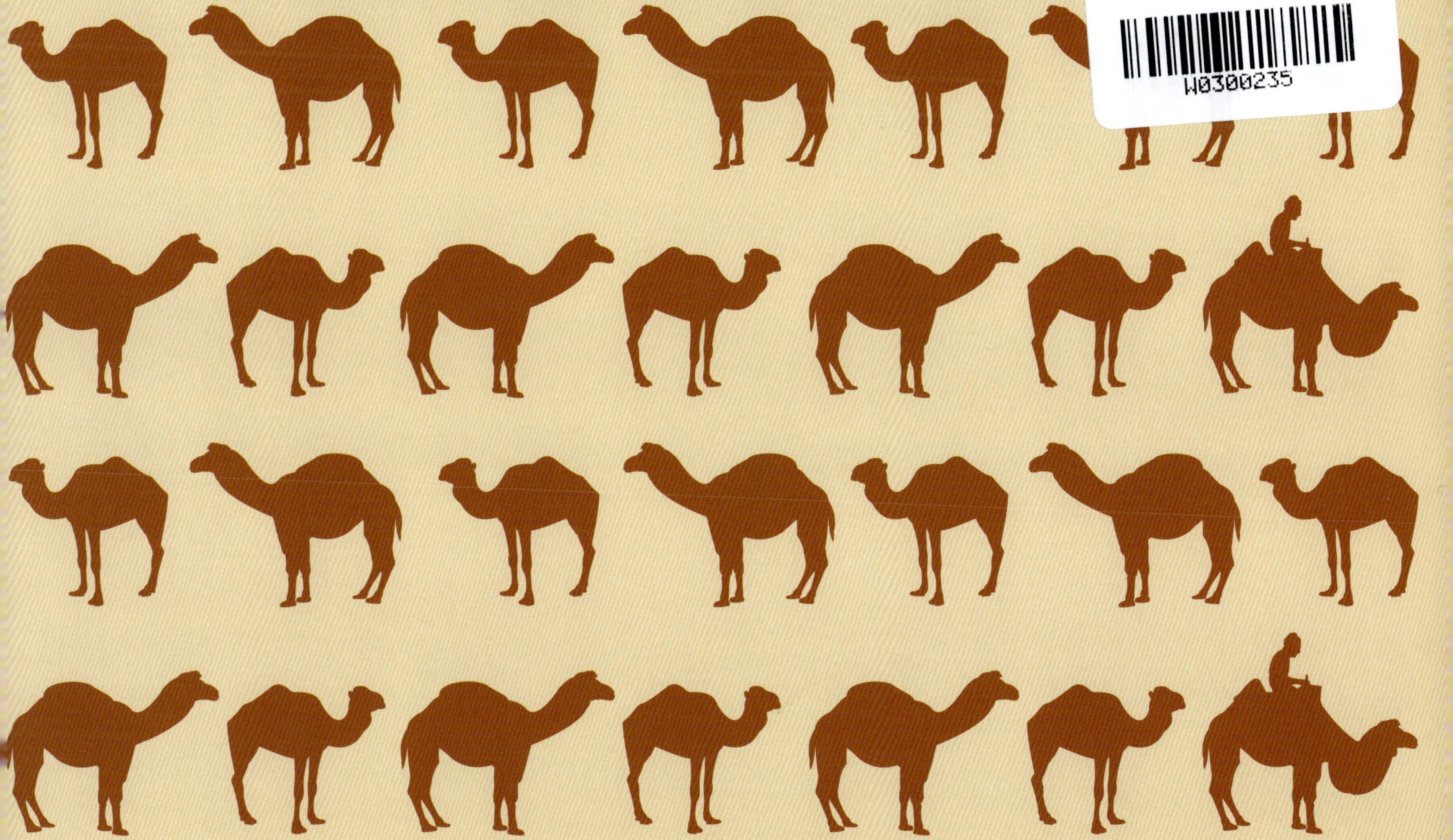

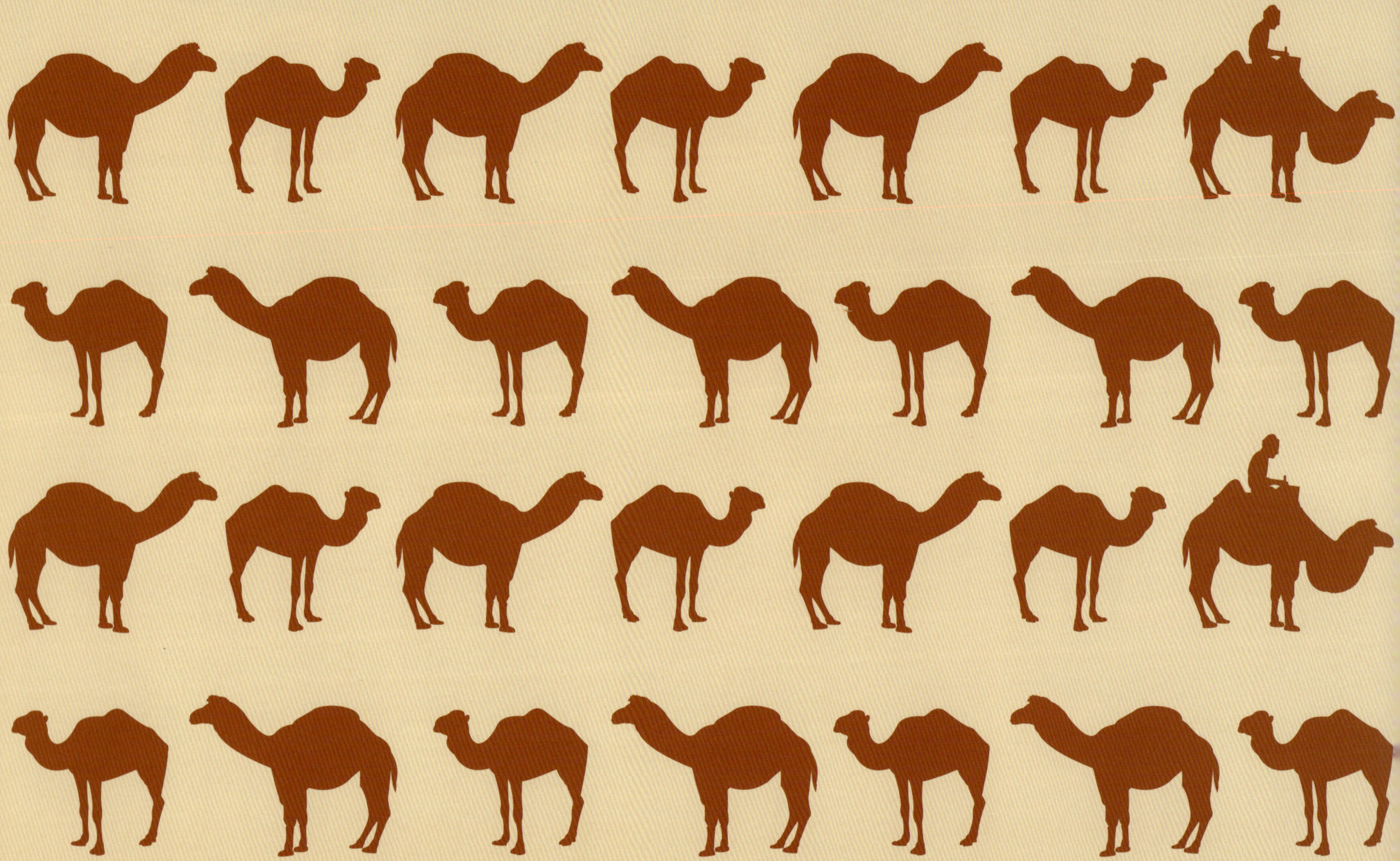

HANS GASSER

SAHARA PANORAMA

Text by Iris Lemanczyk

EDITION**PANORAMA**

SAHARA

Bahr bela ma – Meer ohne Wasser – nennen Karawanenführer die Sahara. Ozeangleiche Weite, schiere Unendlichkeit. Meere aus Sanddünen mit Oasen als Inseln. Land ohne Schatten. Wüste der Wüsten. Die Sahara reicht über 6000 Kilometer vom Atlantik im Westen zum Roten Meer im Osten, dehnt sich über 15 Breitengrade hinweg, 2000 Kilometer vom Mittelmeer nach Süden, eine schwer überwindbare Barriere zwischen Europa und Schwarzafrika. Mit neun Millionen Quadratkilometern ist sie größer als Amerika. Groß wie ein Kontinent. Sahara. Wüstenkontinent.

Hohe Sanddünen, rot, gelb, ockerfarben, über die der Wind stetig Sandkörner vorantreibt, so sieht das klassische Idealbild eines grandiosen Wüstenpanoramas aus. Tatsächlich sind nur etwa zwanzig Prozent der Sahara von Sand bedeckt. Zwischen den Sandmeeren liegen steinerne Hochplateaus, bizarre Granitgebirge, Ebenen, die bis zum Horizont reichen, vulkanische, mehr als 3000 Meter hohe Gebirge – Hoggar, Air, Tibesti –, undurchquerbare staubgefüllte Becken, Kieswüsten und palmenbewachsene Oasen, Symbole für das Leben. „Diese Wüste lebt, das sage ich euch. Diese Leere, dieses Schweigen (...) sind bewegter als Volksgedränge auf offenem Markt“, schrieb der Schriftsteller und Pilot Antoine de Saint-Exupéry.

Die Wüste lebt. Nicht nur durch Pflanzen, deren Samen eine 50-jährige Dürre überstehen, oder die Tamariske, den genügsamen Baum, der in der Sahara am häufigsten vorkommt, auch durch Nagetiere, die ihr ganzes Leben ohne

SAHARA

Bahr bela ma – the sea without water – is what caravan-drivers call the Sahara. The vastness of an ocean, sheer infinity. Seas of sand dunes with oases for islands. A land without shadows. The father of all deserts. The Sahara extends over 3,700 miles from the Atlantic in the west to the Red Sea in the east, encompassing over 15 degrees of latitude, 1,200 miles from the Mediterranean and on southwards, an almost impassable barrier between Europe and black Africa. With an area of 3.5 million square miles, the Sahara is larger than America. As large as a continent itself. Sahara, the desert continent.

High sand dunes, red, yellow, ochre, with the eternal sands being driven over them by the wind, this is the classical image of a grandiose desert panorama. In fact however, only about 20% of the Sahara is covered by sand. Between the sand seas lie rocky upland plateaus, bizarre granite mountains and plains that stretch to the horizon, volcanic mountains over 10,000 ft. in height – Hoggar, Air, Tibesti – impassable dust-pans, deserts of gravel and palm-fringed oases, symbols of life in this arid wasteland. “This desert is alive, I tell you. This emptiness, this silence (...) are more lively than the jostling crowds in a street market”, wrote the author and pilot Antoine de Saint-Exupéry.

The desert lives. Not only in the form of plants, whose seeds can survive a 50-year drought, or the Tamarisk, the frugal tree which occurs most frequently in the Sahara, but also in the form of small rodents which survive their whole

SAHARA

Bahr bela ma – mer sans eau –, c'est le nom que les conducteurs de caravane donnent au Sahara. Aussi vaste qu'un océan apparemment sans fin. Avec des mers de dunes de sable au milieu desquelles les oasis ressemblent à des îles. Une étendue sans aucune ombre. Le désert des déserts. Le Sahara s'étend sur plus de 6000 kilomètres de l'Atlantique à l'ouest jusqu'à la Mer Rouge à l'est, sur 15 degrés de latitude et 2000 kilomètres de la Méditerranée vers le sud, formant ainsi une barrière quasiment infranchissable entre l'Europe et l'Afrique noire. Avec neuf millions de kilomètres carrés, il est plus vaste que les Etats-Unis. Aussi grand qu'un continent, le Sahara est un continent de sable.

Le vent qui amoncelle inlassablement sur les hautes dunes des grains de sable rouges, jaunes et ocres, voilà à peu près l'image classique idéale d'un grandiose panorama désertique. En fait, le sable ne couvre que vingt pour cent du Sahara. Entre les mers de sable, on trouve de hauts plateaux rocheux, des massifs granitiques aux formes bizarroïdes, des plaines qui s'étendent jusqu'à l'horizon, des chaînes montagneuses volcaniques de plus de 3000 m d'altitude – Hoggar, Air, Tibesti –, des bassins infranchissables emplis de poussière, des déserts de graviers et des oasis plantées de palmiers qui symbolisent la vie. « Je vous jure que le désert s'est animé. Je vous jure que cette absence, que ce silence sont tout à coup plus émouvants qu'un tumulte de place publique » a écrit l'écrivain et pilote Antoine de Saint-Exupéry.

Le désert vit, non seulement à travers les plantes dont les

SAHARA

"Bahr bela ma" –Mar sin agua– así llaman al Sahara los guías de las caravanas. Y efectivamente este desierto tiene una amplitud que recuerda al océano, aparentemente ilimitada. Y mares de dunas de arena entre los cuáles los oasis parecen islas. Un país sin sombra. El desierto de los desiertos. El Sahara abarca más de 6000 kilómetros desde el Atlántico en el oeste al Mar Rojo en el este. Con sus 2000 kilómetros desde el Mar Mediterráneo hasta su extremo sur, el Sahara constituye una casi infranqueable barrera entre Europa y el África negra. Con sus nueve millones de kilómetros cuadrados es más grande que América. Tan grande como un continente. Sahara. El desierto-continente.

El viento no ceja jamás de arremolinar sobre las altas dunas los granos de sus rojas, amarillas y ocres arenas. Esa es aproximadamente la clásica imagen ideal que tenemos del grandioso panorama del desierto. La verdad es que sólo un veinte por ciento de la superficie del Sahara está cubierta de arena. Entre los mares de sílice hay mesetas pedregosas, sierras graníticas de fantásticas formas, planicies que se extienden hasta el horizonte, cadenas montañosas volcánicas de 3000 metros de altura, intransitables cuencas rellenas de polvo, desiertos de grava y oasis cubiertos de palmeras que simbolizan la vida. "Este desierto vive, os lo aseguro. Ese vacío, ese silencio (...) albergan más movimiento que todo el ajetreo de un mercado". Así describía sus impresiones sobre el desierto el piloto y escritor Antoine de Saint-Exupéry.

SAHARA

Bahr bela ma – mare senz'acqua: i carovanieri definiscono così il Sahara. Estensione oceanica quasi infinita. Mare di dune sabbiose con oasi, anziché isole. Terra senza ombre. Deserto dei deserti. Il Sahara si estende dall'Atlantico, a ovest, al Mar Rosso, a est, per 6.000 chilometri e 15 gradi di latitudine; dal Mar Mediterraneo si espande per 2.000 chilometri verso sud, formando una barriera difficilmente superabile tra l'Europa e l'Africa Nera. Con nove milioni di chilometri quadrati è più grande dell'America. Grande come un continente. Sahara, continente desertico.

Alte dune, color rosso, giallo e ocra, sulle quali il vento sospinge costantemente granelli di sabbia: è questa la classica immagine ideale di un grandioso panorama desertico. In realtà, solo il venti percento circa del Sahara è coperto di sabbia. Tra un mare di sabbia e l'altro si ergono altipiani di pietra, bizzarre montagne di granito, pianure che si estendono fino all'orizzonte, montagne vulcaniche che superano i 3.000 metri - l'Hoggar, l'Air, il Tibesti - bacini invalicabili e pieni di polvere, deserti di ghiaia e oasi ricoperte di palme, simbolo di vita. „Questo deserto vive, ve lo dico io. Questo vuoto, questo silenzio (...) sono più movimentati della folla al mercato" scrisse lo scrittore e pilota Antoine de Saint-Exupéry.

Il deserto vive. E non sono solo le piante, i cui semi sopravvivono ad una siccità lunga cinquanta anni, a renderlo vivo, o il tamarisco, l'albero senza grandi pretese più diffuso nel Sahara, ma anche i roditori, costretti a resiste-

eine Wasserquelle auskommen. Die Wüste lebt durch das Kamel, den Überlebenstechniker schlechthin. Kein anderes Tier ist so perfekt an seinen Lebensraum angepasst. Ein Weltmeister im Wassersparen. Kamele schaffen es, bis zu zehn Tage ohne Wasser auszukommen. Ihr wolliges Fell isoliert gegen die Hitze und verringert die Verdunstung beim Schwitzen. Schadlos kann ihre Körpertemperatur auf 46 Grad Celsius steigen. Durch die langen Beine befinden sich die lebenswichtigen Organe hoch über dem gleißenden Wüstenboden. In ihren Höckern ist ein Fettreservoir für Notzeiten angelegt. Beim Anzapfen dieser Energiereserve wird auch das im Fett chemisch gebundene Wasser freigesetzt. Ein Kamel ist in der Lage, innerhalb von 15 Minuten 200 Liter Wasser zu saufen.

Ohne Kamele wäre menschliches Leben in der Wüste nicht möglich. Von den Tubu, einem Nomadenvolk, das sich völlig an die lebensfeindlichen Verhältnisse im kargen Tibestigebirge angepasst hat, sagt man, dass sie drei Tage lang von einer Dattel leben können. Am ersten Tag essen sie die Haut, am zweiten das Fleisch und am dritten den Kern.

Leben in der Sahara ist ein ständiger Kampf ums Überleben. Zweieinhalb Millionen Menschen stellen sich diesem Kampf, 60 Prozent davon als Oasenbauern, der Rest als Halbnomaden oder Nomaden. Die Tuareg sind wohl die bekanntesten.

Tuareg! Das Wort allein genügt, um die Handelskarawanen seit Menschengedenken in Angst und Schrecken zu versetzen. Raubritter der Wüste oder auch wegen ihrer indigoblauen Kleidung blaue Reiter genannt, sind sie eigentlich selbst Karawanenführer, Vieh- oder Kamelzüchter und in

lives without any source of water. The desert also lives in the form of the camel, the ultimate survival expert. No other animal is so perfectly adapted to its environment. A world champion in saving water. Camels are able to survive without water for up to 10 days. Their woolly hide provides insulation against the heat and reduces loss of moisture by sweating. Their body temperature can rise to 46° C without any harmful effects. Their long legs keep their vital organs high above the gleaming desert floor. Their humps contain reserves of fat for times of need. When drawing on these energy reserves, the water chemically bonded in the fat is also released. When replenishing its reserves, a camel can drink over 40 gal. of water within 15 minutes.

Human life in the desert would be impossible without camels. People say of the Tubu, a nomadic people who have adapted completely to the hostile conditions in the barren Tibesti mountains, that they can survive for three days on a single date. On the first day they eat the skin, on the second day the flesh, and on the third day the stone.

Life in the Sahara is an unending struggle for survival. Two and half million people face this struggle, 60% of them by cultivating the land surrounding oases, and the rest as semi-nomads or nomads, of which the best-known are probably the Tuareg.

Tuareg! The word alone has been enough throughout living memory to bring fear and terror to the trade caravans plying the desert. Known as the robber knights of the desert or the blue knights, because of their indigo-blue clothing, they are themselves actually caravan drivers, cattle- or camel-herders, and can be found in Algeria, Libya,

semences survivent à des périodes de sècheresse de cinquante ans, ou les tamaris, arbre peu exigeant et très répandu dans le Sahara, mais aussi à travers les rongeurs qui peuvent survivre sans jamais voir une source d'eau de toute leur existence. Le désert vit aussi grâce au chameau, le spécialiste de la survie par excellence. Aucun autre animal n'est parvenu à s'adapter aussi parfaitement à son habitat. Un vrai champion en matière d'économie d'eau qui arrive à survivre jusqu'à dix jours maximum sans ce liquide vital. Son pelage laineux le protège de la chaleur et réduit la perte d'eau entraînée par la sudation. La température de son corps peut monter sans problème jusqu'à 46° C sans que l'animal en souffre. Grâce à ses longues jambes, les organes vitaux se trouvent loin au-dessus du sol incandescent du désert. Ses bosses contiennent un réservoir de graisse qui, par réaction chimique, peut se transformer en eau et dans lequel l'animal puise en cas de besoin. Un chameau est capable de boire jusqu'à 200 litres d'eau en l'espace d'un quart d'heure.

Toute vie humaine serait impossible dans le désert si les chameaux n'existaient pas. On dit des Toubou, peuple nomade qui a su parfaitement s'adapter aux conditions de vie hostiles dans les montagnes arides du Tibesti, qu'ils peuvent survivre trois jours avec une seule datte : le premier jour, ils mangent la peau, le deuxième, la chair et le troisième, le noyau.

La vie dans le Sahara est une lutte constante pour la survie pour les deux millions et demie d'individus qui le peuplent. Soixante pour cent d'entre eux vivent de l'agriculture dans les oasis, les autres sont des semi-nomades ou des nomades, comme les Touareg, qui sont assurément les plus connus.

El desierto vive. Y no sólo en las plantas cuyas semillas pueden sobrevivir períodos de sequía de 50 años o en los tamariscos, los duros árboles que con mayor frecuencia se pueden encontrar en el Sahara; sino también en los roedores que consiguen sobrevivir toda su existencia sin ver jamás una fuente de agua. Pero el desierto también vive en el camello, el especialista de la supervivencia por excelencia. Ningún otro animal ha conseguido adaptarse tan perfectamente a su hábitat. Un auténtico campeón en el ahorro de agua que consigue sobrevivir hasta diez días sin el húmedo elemento. Su lanosa piel le aísla del calor y reduce la pérdida de agua por la transpiración. Su temperatura corporal puede elevarse hasta los 46° C sin que el animal sufra daños. Gracias a sus largas patas los órganos vitales del animal se encuentran a mucha altura del ardiente suelo del desierto. Sus jorobas contienen una reserva de grasa para los períodos de necesidad que, al ser metabolizada, deja libres en el organismo las moléculas de agua que estaban fijadas químicamente en la grasa. Un camello puede beber en 15 minutos hasta 200 litros de agua.

Sin camellos no hubiera sido posible la vida humana en el desierto. De los Tubu, un pueblo nómada que se ha adaptado completamente a las terribles condiciones de las áridas montañas del Tibesti, se dice que pueden sobrevivir tres días con sólo un dátil. El primer día se comen la piel, el segundo la carne del fruto y el tercero el hueso.

La vida en el Sahara es una continua lucha por la supervivencia. Dos millones y medio de personas afrontan esa lucha, de las cuales un 60 por ciento viven de la agricultura en los oasis y el resto como nómadas y seminómadas. Los tua-

re tutta la vita senza una fonte d'acqua, o il cammello, esperto di sopravvivenza per eccellenza. Nessun altro animale si è adattato al suo spazio vitale con simile perfezione. Il cammello è campione del mondo di risparmio d'acqua. Riesce a farne a meno per dieci giorni. Il suo pelo lanoso è termoisolante e riduce l'evaporazione durante la sudorazione. La sua temperatura corporea può raggiungere 46 gradi Celsius senza riportare danni. Grazie alle sue lunghe zampe gli organi vitali restano in alto, lontani dal luccicante terreno desertico. Nelle sue gobbe l'animale accumula una riserva di grasso per i periodi di necessità. Quando il cammello vi ricorre il suo organismo libera anche l'acqua presente nella sua struttura chimica. Un cammello è in grado di bere 200 litri d'acqua in 15 minuti.

Senza cammelli l'uomo non potrebbe vivere nel deserto. Si dice che i Tubu, un popolo nomade che si è completamente adattato alle condizioni ostili della misera montagna Tibesti, possano vivere tre giorni cibandosi di un solo dattero: il primo giorno ne mangiano la buccia, il secondo la polpa, il terzo il nocciolo.

Nel Sahara la vita è una continua lotta per la sopravvivenza. Due milioni e mezzo di persone ne accettano la sfida: il 60 percento è costituito dai contadini delle oasi, il resto da seminomadi o nomadi. Tra questi i più conosciuti sono i Tuareg.

Tuareg! A memoria d'uomo è sempre bastata la sola parola per spaventare le carovane commerciali. In realtà gli stessi predoni del deserto o cavalieri blu, così chiamati per i loro abiti blu indigo, sono carovanieri e allevatori di bestiame o cammelli. Vivono in Algeria, Libia, Nigeria, Mali

Algerien, Libyen, Niger, Mali und Burkina Faso anzutreffen. Sie lieben ihre Freiheit mehr als die Sicherheit, Imohar nennen sie sich selbst – die Freien. Frei wollen sie auch bleiben, so wie sie es schon immer waren. Darum nehmen sie sich manchmal auch die Freiheit, ihre Autonomieansprüche gewaltsam durchzusetzen. Oder sich zu nehmen, was anderen gehört. Die Freiheit stößt an ihre Grenzen. Seit dem Ende der Kolonialzeit regieren nun Männer in den neu gebildeten Hauptstädten, die den Tuareg oftmals misstrauten, wodurch uralte Konflikte zwischen Sesshaften und Nomaden wieder aufbrachen. Konflikte, die bis heute nicht gelöst sind. Konflikte, die noch immer dafür sorgen, dass das Wort Tuareg mit Schrecken besetzt ist.
Eigentlich sind die Tuareg Muslime, sie suchen ihren Trost aber im Glauben an die versunkene Oase Gewas, ihrem Symbol für die Sehnsucht nach einer vollkommenen, paradiesischen Welt voller Reichtum und Überfluss. Ein imaginärer Gegenentwurf zur kargen, gnadenlosen Wirklichkeit des Lebens in der Wüste.
Auch heute noch stellen Tuareg die Salzkarawanen, die Tarhalamt, zusammen. Im Herbst ziehen sie los, in Gewaltmärschen von täglich 16 bis 18 Stunden versuchen die Karawanen die wenigen Brunnen zu erreichen. Nur der Sonnenstand bietet Orientierung, da Wegmarken fehlen. Die Oasenbewohner erwarten die Karawanen voller Ungeduld, sie sind angewiesen auf die Hirse und den Zucker, die ihnen die Tuareg bringen. Dafür tauschen sie die wichtigsten Oasenprodukte – Salz und Datteln – ein. Zurück müssen die bereits geschwächten Kamele 150 bis 200 Kilogramm Salz schleppen. Oftmals erreichen sie nur mit letzter Kraft die Weiden.

Niger, Mali and Burkina Faso. They love their freedom more than safety, and indeed call themselves the "Imohar" – the free. And they want to remain free, as they always have been. They therefore sometimes allow themselves the freedom to violently assert their claims to autonomy. Or to steal the property of others. This freedom is now coming up against its boundaries. Since the end of the colonial era, men now reign in the newly-formed capital cities who often mistrusted the Tuareg, resulting in the repeated outbreak of ancient conflicts between settlers and nomads. Conflicts which still remain unresolved today. Conflicts which ensure that the word Tuareg is still synonymous with terror.
The Tuareg are actually Muslims, who take comfort in their belief in the submerged oasis of Gewa, their symbol of the longing for a complete paradise, full of wealth and bounty. An imaginary antithesis to the barren, pitiless reality of life in the desert.
The Tuareg today still assemble the salt caravans, the Tarhalamt. They move off in the autumn, in forced marches of 16 to 18 hours per day in an attempt to reach the few wells along the way. There are no signposts – the Tuareg navigate by the angle of the sun. The oasis-dwellers impatiently await the arrival of the caravans, since they rely on the millet and sugar that the Tuareg bring them. These are obtained by barter for the most important oasis products – salt and dates. The already weakened camels have to make the return journey carrying 350 – 450 lb. of salt, often reaching their grazing with their last reserves of energy.
People have been transporting goods through the Sahara for thousands of years. In the beginning with oxen, horses

Touareg ! De mémoire d'homme, ce seul mot a toujours suffi pour épouvanter les caravanes chargées de marchandises. On les appelle les chevaliers pillards du désert ou encore les « cavaliers bleus » en raison de leurs vêtements bleu indigo. En réalité, ce sont aussi des chefs de caravane, des éleveurs de bétail ou de chameaux que l'on rencontre en Algérie, en Lybie, au Niger, au Mali et au Burkina. Préférant leur liberté à leur sécurité, ils s'appellent eux-mêmes Imohar – hommes libres. Et ils veulent le rester, libres, comme ils l'ont toujours été. C'est la raison pour laquelle ils prennent parfois la liberté d'imposer leurs velléités d'autonomie par des moyens violents. Ou de prendre simplement ce qui ne leur appartient pas. La liberté a ses limites. Depuis la fin de l'époque coloniale, les hommes qui président aux destinées des états dans les nouvelles capitales se méfient souvent des Touareg, faisant ainsi resurgir des conflits séculaires entre les sédentaires et les nomades. Des conflits qui n'ont toujours pas été résolus aujourd'hui, des conflits à cause desquels le mot « Touareg » fait encore peur.

Bien que de confession musulmane, les Touareg cherchent un réconfort dans leur foi en l'oasis perdue de « Gewas », symbole de leur nostalgie d'un paradis parfait, un monde de richesse et d'abondance. Sans aucun doute l'opposé imaginaire de la réalité dure et sans pitié de la vie dans le désert.

Aujourd'hui encore, les Touareg organisent les caravanes de sel, les Tarhalamt. En automne, ils se lancent avec leurs caravanes dans des marches forcées de 16 à 18 heures par jour, pour tenter de rejoindre les rares puits. Pour s'orienter, ils se réfèrent à la position du soleil car les repères sont inexis-

reg son seguramente los más famosos. ¡Tuareg! Desde que existe memoria tan sólo esa palabra basta para atemorizar a las caravanas comerciales. Se los llama los jinetes-bandidos del desierto o también "los jinetes azules" debido a sus vestiduras de color azul índigo. En realidad ellos mismos son guías de caravanas y también se los puede encontrar como ganaderos y criadores de camellos en Algeria, Libia, Níger, Mali y Burkina Faso. Aman más su libertad que su seguridad y por ello no es de extrañar que se llamen a sí mismos "Imohar", los libres. Y así quieren seguir, libres, como siempre fueron. Por ese motivo a veces se toman la libertad de imponer con violencia sus ansias de autonomía. O de adueñarse de la propiedad de otros. La libertad llega a sus límites. Desde el fin de la época colonial gobiernan en las nuevas capitales hombres que, a menudo, desconfían de los tuareg. Ello da lugar a que vuelvan a encenderse los antiquísimos conflictos entre nómadas y sedentarios. Conflictos que permanecen hasta hoy en día sin solución y que siguen siendo responsables de que la palabra "tuareg" no pierda su pavoroso efecto.

Aún hoy los tuareg siguen organizando las caravanas de sal, los tarhalamt. En otoño salen con sus caravanas realizando marchas largas de entre 16 y 18 horas diarias para alcanzar las pocas fuentes. Para orientarse utilizan la posición del sol en el cielo, ya que no hay marcaciones de camino. Los habitantes de los oasis esperan llenos de impaciencia a las caravanas, pues necesitan el mijo y el azúcar que les traen los tuareg. A cambio truecan los principales productos de los oasis: sal y dátiles. A la vuelta los camellos, ya debilitados por el viaje, tienen que transportar a

e Burkina Faso. Amano la libertà più della sicurezza; chiamano se stessi Imohar: i liberi. E liberi vogliono restare, come sono sempre stati. È per questo motivo che qualche volta si prendono la libertà di imporre con la forza le loro rivendicazioni di autonomia. O di prendersi ciò che appartiene agli altri. Libertà vissuta al limite. Spesso gli uomini che hanno regnato nelle nuove capitali dalla fine dell'età coloniale hanno diffidato dei Tuareg, facendo riaffiorare così antichi conflitti tra i residenti e i nomadi: dissapori rimasti irrisolti fino ad oggi e a causa dei quali la parola Tuareg assume tutt'oggi connotazioni negative e suscita terrore.

In realtà, i Tuareg sono mussulmani che cercano conforto professando la loro fede nell'oasi perduta di Gewas, simbolo del desiderio di un mondo perfetto e paradisiaco, un regno ideale di ricchezza e abbondanza, una visione immaginaria in contrasto con la realtà scarna e spietata della vita nel deserto.

Ancora oggi i Tuareg compongono le carovane del sale, le cosiddette Tarhalamt. In autunno partono per impressionanti marce di 16 – 18 ore al giorno diretti verso i pochi pozzi. Si orientano osservando la posizione del sole, perché qui non esistono segnali. Gli abitanti delle oasi aspettano le carovane con impazienza: la loro esistenza dipende dal miglio e dallo zucchero che i Tuareg portano con sé. Li scambiano con i prodotti più importanti delle oasi, sale e datteri. Durante il viaggio di ritorno i cammelli, già provati dalla fatica, devono trasportare 150 – 200 chili di sale. Spesso raggiungono i pascoli con le ultime forze.

Da millenni gli uomini trasportano attraverso il Sahara le loro merci. All'inizio si servivano di buoi, cavalli e carri,

Seit Jahrtausenden befördern Menschen Güter durch die Sahara. Anfangs mit Ochsen, Pferden und Wagen, später mit Kamelen, die den Massentransport von Gold, Elfenbein, Straußenfedern und Sklaven auf der „Straße der Qualen" nach Norden und Metall, Glaswaren sowie Stoffen nach Süden ermöglichten.

Sahara – magischer Ort, von dem Zauber und Faszination ausgehen. Reise durch Zeit und Raum. Ununterbrochen arbeiten Wind und Sand an der Landschaft, formen ihre Architektur im Raum. Raum der Veränderung, wenn ein aufgeheizter Felsbrocken mit lautem Knall zerspringt. Oder wenn sich im Windschatten eines Steins Sandkörner niederlassen und diese winzige Erhebung, an der sich nachrückende Sandkörner stauen, könnte der Beginn einer Düne sein. Sanddünen wirken lebendig, wie die Meeresoberfläche scheinen die Sandwogen in ständiger Bewegung zu sein. Veränderung im Meer ohne Wasser. Zum Raum der Sahara gehört für Uwe George, dem Journalisten und Wüstenexperten, auch die „Stille einer Wüstennacht und die wahrhaft schwindelerregende Tiefe des Sternenhimmels, dessen Bilder in windstillen Nächten klar und leuchtend dem fernen Horizont entsteigen, sodass man meint, die Rotation der Erde zu spüren." Stille, die das pochende Blut in den Adern zum einzig vernehmbaren Geräusch der Nacht werden lässt.

Zeit ist in der Sahara eine Reise in die erdgeschichtliche Vergangenheit. „In der Wüste fühlt man die Zeit verstreichen", schreibt Saint-Exupéry. Trockenere und feuchtere Phasen wechseln sich im Laufe von Jahrmillionen ab. Forscher vermuten, dass es hier vor sieben Millionen Jahren

and wagons, and later by camel, which enabled the mass transport of gold, ivory, ostrich feathers and slaves on the "road of torment" to the north, and metal, glassware and fabrics to the south.

Sahara – a magical place full of enchantment and fascination. A journey through time and space. The wind and sand work continually on the landscape, shaping its architecture in space – a place of change particularly when a heated boulder suddenly shatters with a loud bang. Or when grains of sand collect in the wind shadow of a rock, and this tiny mound could be the beginning of a dune, as the following grains of sand pile up against it. Sand dunes seem to be alive, the waves of sand apparently in continual motion like the surface of the sea. Change in the sea without water. For Uwe George, journalist and desert expert, the Sahara also epitomises the "silence of a desert night and the truly dizzying depth of the starry sky, which on still nights climbs the far horizon in clear and luminescent shapes, so that one can almost sense and feel the rotation of the Earth." A silence which makes the blood pulsing in the veins the only perceivable sound in the dead of the night.

Time in the Sahara is a journey into the Earth's past. "In the desert, you can feel time passing", wrote Saint-Exupéry. Dryer and damper periods alternate over the course of millions of years. Researchers suspect that there was already a desert here 7 million years ago. While Europe lay under a sheet of ice, the Sahara bathed in a Mediterranean climate. Giraffes, buffalos, wildebeests, elephants and ostriches grazed on the forested savannah, providing the artists of 5,000 or 6,000 years ago with the subjects for their rock

tants. Les habitants des oasis attendent avec impatience les caravanes car ils ont besoin du millet et du sucre que les Touareg leur apportent. Ils troquent ces denrées contre les principaux produits de l'oasis : le sel et les dattes. Au retour, les chameaux déjà affaiblis doivent porter jusqu'à 150 à 200 kilogrammes de sel et ils doivent souvent rassembler leurs dernières forces pour rallier les pâturages.
Depuis des millénaires, des marchandises sont transportées à travers le Sahara. Au début avec des bœufs, des chevaux et des charrettes puis, plus tard, avec des chameaux grâce auxquels il est désormais possible d'acheminer massivement de l'or, de l'ivoire, des plumes d'autruche et des esclaves sur la « route du martyre » vers le nord et du métal, de la verrerie et des étoffes vers le sud.
Le Sahara, un lieu magique, enchanteur et fascinant. Un voyage à travers le temps et l'espace. Le vent et le sable modifient sans cesse le paysage, y laissent les traces de leur travail d'érosion. Ils créent ainsi des architectures fantastiques dans un espace qui change constamment d'aspect, chaque fois par exemple qu'un rocher chauffé à blanc éclate à grand bruit ou que des grains de sable qui s'amoncellent à l'abri d'une pierre forment une minuscule éminence qui, à son tour, s'élève et devient, peut-être, le point de départ d'une dune. Les dunes de sable qui paraissent animées comme les vagues à la surface de la mer, sont constamment en mouvement. Un changement perpétuel dans une mer sans eau. Pour Uwe George, journaliste et spécialiste des déserts, le Sahara c'est aussi « le silence d'une nuit dans le désert et la profondeur vraiment vertigineuse du firmament dont les images montent de l'horizon, claires et lumineuses, dans les

menudo entre 150 y 200 kilogramos de sal. A menudo alcanzan con sus últimas fuerzas los pastos.
Desde hace milenios las personas trasladan mercancías por el Sahara. Al principio con bueyes, caballos y carros, más tarde con camellos que hicieron posible la "Ruta de las torturas" a través de la cual se transportaba masivamente oro, marfil, plumas de avestruz y esclavos hacia el norte y metal, mercancías de vidrio así como telas hacia el sur.
El Sahara, un lugar mágico rodeado por un aura de encanto y fascinación. Un viaje a través del tiempo y el espacio. El viento y la arena ejercen eternamente y sin pausa su labor erosiva sobre el paisaje. De esta forma dan lugar a fantásticas arquitecturas en un espacio que constantemente varía su aspecto cada vez que una roca recalentada estalla emitiendo un fuerte ruido. O cada vez que los granos de arena que empiezan a amontonarse al rebufo de una piedra dan lugar a una pequeña elevación que a su vez va creciendo hasta convertirse quizás en el germen de una duna. Esas dunas de arena que parecen vivas y que, al igual que las olas del mar, permanecen en continuo movimiento. Cambio perpetuo en el mar sin agua. Para Uwe George, el periodista y experto en el desierto, al Sahara también le pertenece "la calma de una noche en el desierto y la verdaderamente vertiginosa profundidad del firmamento estrellado cuya imagen asciende clara y luminosa desde el horizonte en las noches sin viento. Contemplando ese espectáculo se tiene la impresión de sentir la rotación de la tierra". Una calma que convierte al latido de nuestro corazón en el único sonido percibible en la noche.

più tardi dei cammelli. I cammelli consentivano di trasportare a nord, sulla „strada dei tormenti", masse d'oro, avorio, penne di struzzo e schiavi. A sud trasportavano metallo, articoli di vetro e tessuto.
Il Sahara è un luogo magico, avvolto da incanto e fascino. Il Sahara è un viaggio attraverso il tempo e lo spazio. Il vento e la sabbia modellano continuamente il paesaggio, foggiando la loro architettura in uno spazio in un continuo mutamento. Lo spazio muta quando un frammento di roccia riscaldato si spacca emettendo un tonfo fragoroso o quando i granelli di sabbia si posano nel versante sottovento di una pietra e dal rilievo microscopico sul quale si accumulano altri granelli potrebbe formarsi a poco a poco una duna. Le dune sembrano vive: le onde di sabbia sembrano in costante movimento, come la superficie del mare. Mutazioni in un mare asciutto. Secondo Uwe George, giornalista ed esperto del deserto, anche il „silenzio della notte nel deserto e la profondità veramente vertiginosa del cielo stellato, le cui immagini, nelle notti senza vento, brillano così chiare e luminose all'orizzonte da far credere di percepire la rotazione terrestre" fanno parte dello spazio del Sahara. Nella quiete della notte l'unico rumore che si percepisce è il sangue che pulsa nelle vene.
Nel Sahara, il tempo diventa un viaggio nel passato della storia terrestre. „Nel deserto si sente il tempo scorrere" scriveva Saint-Exupéry. Nel corso di milioni di anni si sono alternati periodi di siccità a periodi piovosi. Gli scienziati suppongono che qui, sette milioni di anni fa, fosse già esistito un deserto. Quando l'Europa era coperta da una corazza di ghiaccio, nel Sahara regnava un clima mediterra-

bereits einmal eine Wüste gab. Als Europa unter einem Eispanzer lag, herrschte in der Sahara mediterranes Klima. Giraffen, Büffel, Gnus, Strauße und Elefanten weideten in der baumreichen Savanne und dienten Künstlern vor 5000 oder 6000 Jahren als Motive für ihre Felsmalerei. Später kamen Jagdszenen und grazile Frauengestalten hinzu, genauso wie Gravuren von Rindern und Pferden, die geschickte Hände in den Fels ritzten. Galerien der Steinzeitkunst. Museen der Erdgeschichte. Ein Klimawandel sorgt noch vor der heutigen Zeitrechnung für den Niedergang dieser Kulturen. Die Sahara wird zur größten Wüste der Erde.

Sahara heißt sie nicht von Anbeginn. Die Römer nennen sie Terra Deserta – unbewohntes, verlassenes Land. Im Mittelalter ist sie die „Große Wüste", erst im 19. Jahrhundert bekommt sie ihren heutigen Namen: Sahara – Meer ohne Wasser.

Hier herrschen Schein und Realität, Traum und Wirklichkeit. Luftspiegelungen, die das Reale bis zur Unkenntlichkeit verzerren. Saint-Exupéry, der nach einer Bruchlandung tagelang ohne Wasser, den Tod vor Augen, durch die Sahara irrte: „Die Hitze stieg, und mit ihr begannen die Luftspiegelungen. Zunächst waren sie noch ganz harmlos. Große Seen bildeten sich und verschwanden, wenn wir uns ihnen näherten. (...) An der Grenze des Himmels führte uns das Spiel des Lichts seine Spiegelungen vor. Die waren jetzt ernsthafter, nahmen die Gestalt von Festungen an, von Minaretten. (...) Jenseits der Luftspiegelungen ist die Gegend vielleicht reich an wirklichen Städten, an Wasser an Wiesen. (...) Wie lange würden wir es aushalten?" Häufig wird Reisenden die wellenbewegte Oberfläche eines tiefblauen Sees

paintings. Later came hunting scenes and graceful female figures, together with engravings of cattle and horses, carved into the rock by skilful hands. Galleries of Stone Age art. Museums of the Earth's history. Climatic change long before the modern counting of the years brought about the disappearance of these cultures. The Sahara became the greatest desert on Earth.

It was not called the Sahara from the very beginning. The Romans called it Terra Deserta – the deserted land. In the Middle Ages, it was known as the "great desert", only acquiring its current name in the 19th Century: Sahara – the sea without water.

Appearance and reality, dreams and truth prevail here. Mirages, which distort reality beyond recognition. Saint-Exupéry, who after a forced landing wandered through the Sahara for days on end without water, staring death in the face, wrote: "The heat rose, and with it began the mirages. At first they were quite harmless. Great lakes took shape and disappeared again when we approached them. (...) At the border of the sky, the play of light presented its reflections. These were now more serious, taking the form of fortresses, of minarets. (...) Beyond the mirages there are perhaps many real cities, water and meadows. (...) How long would we be able to hold out?" Travellers are frequently buoyed up by the wave-topped surface of a deep blue sea. They will never reach its shores however, since the sea is nothing but the reflection of the sky on layers of air shimmering with heat close to the ground, whose surface acts like a mirror. The Fata Morgana. The Arabs call it Bacher el-Alfrid, the water of Satan. For those dying of

nuits sans vent. Face à ce spectacle, on a l'impression de sentir la terre tourner». Un silence dans lequel on ne perçoit la nuit que le sang qui palpite dans nos veines.

Le temps dans le Sahara est aussi un voyage dans le passé de notre planète. «Dans le désert, on sent l'écoulement du temps», a écrit Saint-Exupéry. Les phases de sècheresse et de pluies alternent ici depuis des millions d'années. Les chercheurs supposent qu'un désert a déjà existé ici il y a de cela sept millions d'années. Tandis que l'Europe était ensevelie sous une carapace de glace, il régnait un climat méditerranéen dans le Sahara. Des girafes, des buffles, des gnous, des autruches et des éléphants paissaient entre les nombreux arbres de la savane et ont inspiré les peintures rupestres exécutées par des artistes il y a 5000 ou 6000 ans. Plus tard, des scènes de chasse et des figures graciles de femmes sont venues s'y ajouter tout comme des gravures représentant des bœufs et des chevaux probablement réalisées par des mains adroites dans le rocher. D'authentiques galeries d'art de l'âge de pierre. Des musées de l'histoire de la terre. Mais avant que ne débute notre ère, un changement climatique entraîne la disparition de ces cultures et fait du Sahara le plus grand désert de la planète.

Le Sahara n'a pas toujours porté ce nom. Les Romains l'appelaient «Terra Deserta» – terre inhabitée et abandonnée. Au Moyen Age, on parle simplement du «Grand Désert» et ce n'est qu'au 19ème qu'on lui donne son nom actuel : le Sahara – la mer sans eau.

Il est très difficile ici de discerner entre les apparences et la vérité, entre le rêve et la réalité. Les mirages déforment les objets réels jusqu'à les rendre méconnaissables. Saint-Exu-

El tiempo en el Sahara también es un viaje al pasado de nuestro planeta. "En el desierto se siente como va transcurriendo el tiempo", escribía Saint-Exupéry. En el transcurso de los millones de años se fueron sucediendo fases de sequía y humedad. Los investigadores creen que aquí ya hubo un desierto hace siete millones de años. En la época en la que Europa estaba cubierta por una capa de hielo, en el Sahara reinaba un clima mediterráneo. Jirafas, búfalos, ñus, avestruces y elefantes pastaban entre los copiosos árboles de las sabanas y sirvieron de inspiración para las pinturas rupestres de artistas que vivían aquí hace entre 5000 y 6000 años. Más tarde los artistas aumentaron su repertorio con escenas de caza y gráciles figuras femeninas así como con gravados que representan vacas y caballos y que sin duda fueron realizados por manos maestras. Auténticas galerías del arte de la Edad de Piedra. Museos de la historia de la Tierra. Pero antes del comienzo de nuestra era un cambio climático dio lugar a la decadencia de esas culturas y convirtió al Sahara en el mayor desierto de la Tierra.

Al principio no se llamaba Sahara. Los romanos lo llamaron "Terra Deserta", haciendo así referencia a su despoblamiento. En la Edad Media se lo denominaba simplemente "El Gran Desierto". Es a principios del siglo XIX cuando adquirió su actual nombre: Sahara, el mar sin agua.

Aquí es muy difícil discernir entre las apariencias y la realidad, entre el sueño y la vigilia. Aquí abundan los espejismos que deforman los objetos reales hasta convertirlos en irreconocibles. Saint-Exupéry, que tras un aterrizaje forzoso se vio obligado a vagar sin agua durante días por el Sahara y que durante aquella experiencia vio la muerte muy cerca,

neo. Giraffe, bufali, gnu, struzzi ed elefanti pascevano nella savana cosparsa di alberi e offrivano agli artisti di 5.000 o 6.000 anni fa il tema per la loro pittura rupestre. Più tardi si aggiunsero scene di caccia e gracili figure femminili, incisioni di bovini e cavalli, scalfite nella roccia da mani abili: erano le gallerie d'arte dell'Età della pietra, sono i musei della storia della terra. Un cambiamento climatico, ben prima dell'epoca odierna, causò l'estinzione di queste culture. Il Sahara divenne il più grande deserto della terra.

Il Sahara non si è sempre chiamato così. I romani lo definivano Terra Deserta, ovvero disabitata, abbandonata. Nel Medioevo divenne „il grande deserto". Solo nel XIX secolo ricevette il suo nome attuale: Sahara, mare senz'acqua.

Nel Sahara, illusione e realtà, sogno e verità si confondono. Le allucinazioni deformano la realtà fino a renderla irriconoscibile. Saint-Exupéry che, in seguito ad un atterraggio di fortuna, vagò nel deserto senz'acqua per giorni interi, vide la morte in faccia: „Il caldo aumentò e con il caldo iniziarono i miraggi. All'inizio erano innocui. Si formavano grandi laghi che scomparivano non appena ci avvicinavamo. (...) Al confine con il cielo, la luce ci presentava la sua immagine riflessa. I miraggi, poi, divennero più inquietanti, formavano fortezze, minareti. (...) Forse, al di là dei miraggi, la regione è ricca di vere città, acqua, prati. (...) Quanto potremo resistere?" Spesso i viaggiatori credono di scorgere la superficie ondulata di un profondo lago blu, di cui non raggiungono mai la riva perché il lago non è nulla più che l'immagine del cielo blu, riflessa sugli strati d'aria calda vicini al terreno: la loro superficie agisce come uno specchio. Fata Morgana. Gli Arabi la chiamano

vorgegaukelt. Nie werden sie sein Ufer erreichen, denn der See ist nichts anderes, als die Abbildung des Himmelblaus auf bodennahen, hitzewabernden Luftschichten, deren Oberfläche wie ein Spiegel wirkt. Fata Morgana. Die Araber nennen sie Bacher el-Alfrid, Wasser des Satans. Für Durstende, Verdurstende ein teuflisches Spektakel an der Pforte des Todes. Selbst Wasservögel, Enten und Pelikane fallen auf das gefährliche Verwirrspiel herein und lassen sich in die trockene, todbringende Wüste locken.

Expeditionen und Karawanen leiden nicht nur unter dem Wasser des Satans, sondern auch unter Sandstürmen. Der deutsche Forscher Heinrich Barth, der fünf Jahre lang durch die Sahara reiste, hatte um 1850 genauso mit ihnen zu kämpfen, wie mehr als hundert Jahre später der englische Journalist Richard Trench: „Auf einmal frischte der Wind auf, blies in kurzen und heftigen Böen. Mit dem Wind erhob sich der Wüstensand. Er warf sich mir gegen die Beine, wirbelte um meinen Körper und prickelte auf meinen bloßen Armen. Damit nicht genug, packte er mich beim Hals, biss in mein Gesicht, verkrustete meine Kehle, verstopfte meine Nasenlöcher und nahm mir die Sicht. Ich fühlte mich verloren und fürchtete zu ersticken." Bis dahin sah Trench die Wüste nüchtern als ein Gebiet mit einer Niederschlagsmenge von weniger als 250 Millimetern, danach bewahrheitete sich auch bei ihm das alte arabische Sprichwort: „Wer in die Wüste geht, wird nicht der bleiben, der er vorher war."

Die Landschaft gebiert Demut. Der Landschaft gebührt Demut. Wenn die grellen Strahlen der höher steigenden Sonne das morgendliche Idyll der Sanddünen entzaubern.

thirst a devilish spectacle at the gates of death. Even waterfowl, ducks and pelicans are sometimes taken in by this dangerous deception, and are lured to their death in the desert.

Expeditions and caravans suffer not only from the water of Satan, but also sandstorms. The German researcher Heinrich Barth, who travelled for five years through the Sahara, had to struggle against these around 1850 just as much as the English journalist Richard Trench over a century later: "Suddenly the wind got up, blowing in short and powerful gusts. Along with the wind arose the desert sand. It threw itself against my legs, whirled around my body and prickled against my bare arms. Not satisfied with that, it grabbed me by the neck, bit into my face, encrusted my throat, blocked my nostrils and blinded me. I felt completely lost and was afraid of suffocating." Until then, Trench had thought of the desert simply as an area with a rainfall of less than 250 mm, although he soon came to learn the truth of the old Arabic saying: "Whoever goes into the desert will not remain he who he was before."

The landscape breeds humility. The landscape demands humility. When the blazing rays of the rising sun burn away the morning idyll of the sand dunes. When new, harmonious order is created from the sand. When the almost uninhabited landscape of rock and sand appears to be boundless. When a small oasis becomes a life-giving spring, an island in the sea of sand. When the well becomes the umbilicus of the world. When the forces of the weather create new formations. Then the overpowering feeling is one of humility. Old caravan-drivers say that Allah has

péry qui a erré sans eau à travers le désert pendant des jours, face à la mort, après un atterrissage forcé a écrit : « La chaleur monte, et, avec elle, naissent les mirages. Mais ce ne sont encore que des mirages élémentaires. De grands lacs se forment, et s'évanouissent quand nous avançons. (…) Mais, à l'horizon, des jeux de lumière composent des mirages déjà plus troublants. Forteresses et minarets, masses géométriques à lignes verticales. (…) Au-delà des mirages, l'horizon est peut-être riche de cités véritables, de canaux d'eau douce et de prairies. (...) Combien de temps résisterons-nous ? » Souvent, les mirages trompent les voyageurs qui croient alors voir un lac d'un bleu profond à la surface duquel les vagues ondulent sans jamais atteindre la rive, car ce lac n'est rien d'autre que le reflet du bleu du ciel sur les couches d'air surchauffées proches du sol dont la surface agit comme un miroir. Un mirage. Les Arabes parlent de « Bacher el-Alfrid », eau de Satan. Pour ceux qui ont soif et sont sur le point de mourir, un spectacle diabolique aux portes de la mort. Même les oiseaux aquatiques, les canards et les pélicans tombent dans ce piège dangereux et se laissent attirer dans ce désert aride et mortel.

Les expéditions et les caravanes sont exposées non seulement à ces visions imaginaires mais aussi aux tempêtes de sable. Heinrich Barth, chercheur allemand qui a passé cinq ans de sa vie à parcourir le Sahara, s'est vu également obligé de lutter contre elles vers 1850 tout comme, plus d'un siècle après, le journaliste anglais, Richard Trench : « Tout à coup, un vent frais se lève, soufflant en de brèves et violentes rafales. Avec le vent, le sable du désert se soulève également, me battant les jambes, s'enroulant autour

decía: "Con el aumento del calor empezaron los espejismos. Al principio parecían inofensivos. Grandes lagos aparecían y desaparecían en la nada cuando nos acercábamos. (...) Hasta en los confines del cielo nos presentaba la luz sus reflejos. Se trataba ahora de espejismos mucho más complejos que tomaban la forma de fortalezas y minaretes. (...) Quizás más allá de los espejismos la región es realmente rica en ciudades reales, en agua y en praderas. (...) ¿Cuánto tiempo podríamos soportarlo?". A menudo los espejismos engañan a los viajeros dándole la impresión de la agitada superficie de un lago muy azul. Pero nunca llegarán a alcanzar su orilla, pues el lago no es otra cosa que el reflejo del azul del cielo sobre las recalentadas capas de aire cercanas al suelo, cuya superficie actúa como un espejo. Fata Morgana. Los árabes llaman a este fenómeno "Bacher el-Alfrid", las aguas de Satán. Para los sedientos y aquellos que ya están casi a punto de morir de sed se trata de un diabólico espectáculo a las puertas de la muerte. Incluso aves acuáticas, como patos y pelícanos, caen en la peligrosa trampa y se dejan atraer al seco y mortal desierto.

Pero las expediciones y las caravanas no sólo tienen que sufrir la visión de las aguas de Satán, sino también las tormentas de arena. El investigador alemán Heinrich Barth, que viajó durante cinco años a través del Sahara, se vio obligado a luchar contra las tormentas en torno a 1850, al igual que unos cien años más tarde el periodista inglés Richard Trench: "De repente el viento se levantaba y refrescaba, soplaba con cortas y fuertes ráfagas. Con el viento se levantaba la arena del desierto que fustigaba mis piernas, se arremolinaba en torno a mi cuerpo y me provocaba picores en

Bacher el-Alfrid, l'acqua di Satana, per gli assetati la danza macabra che si materializza davanti ai loro occhi poco prima della morte. Persino gli uccelli acquatici, le anitre e i pellicani cedono a questo gioco sconcertante e pericoloso e si lasciano attirare nel deserto arido, fatale.

Le spedizioni e le carovane sono possibili vittime non solo dell'acqua di Satana, ma anche delle tempeste di sabbia. Vi si imbatté attorno al 1850 lo scienziato tedesco Heinrich Barth, che viaggiò per cinque anni attraverso il Sahara, così come cento anni più tardi il giornalista inglese Richard Trench: „Improvvisamente il vento rinfrescò l'aria, le sue folate divennero brevi e violente. Con il vento si sollevò la sabbia del deserto. Si scagliava contro le mie gambe, girava vorticosamente attorno al mio corpo e mi pizzicava le braccia nude. Come se non bastasse, mi afferrò il collo, mi morse il viso, mi incrostò la gola, mi intasò le narici e mi oscurò la vista. Mi sentii perso e temetti di soffocare." Fino a quel momento Trench aveva visto nel deserto solo una regione caratterizzata da una quantità di precipitazioni inferiore a 250 millimetri. Poi, si avverò anche per lui il vecchio proverbio arabo: „Chi va nel deserto, non vi torna mai uguale a prima."

Il paesaggio incute umiltà. Al paesaggio spetta umiltà. Gli si deve rispetto quando i raggi abbaglianti del sole levante disperdono l'idillio mattutino delle dune di sabbia. Quando, con la sabbia, si formano nuovi ordini armonici. Quando il paesaggio di roccia e sabbia, quasi desertico, sembra essere sconfinato. Quando una piccola oasi diventa fonte di vita, un'isola in un mare di sabbia. Quando un pozzo si trasforma nell'ombelico del mondo. Quando l'azione degli

Wenn aus Sand neue, harmonische Ordnungen entstehen. Wenn die fast menschenleere Landschaft aus Fels und Sand grenzenlos erscheint. Wenn eine kleine Oase zum lebensspendenden Quell, zur Insel im Sandmeer wird. Wenn der Brunnen zum Nabel der Welt wird. Wenn die Kräfte der Verwitterung neue Formationen kreieren. Dann ist Demut angebracht. Alte Karawanenführer sagen, dass Allah aus der Sahara alles Überflüssige entfernt habe, damit die Menschen das wahre Wesen der Dinge erkennen.
Und T.E. Lawrence, der Lawrence von Arabien, fügt hinzu: „Auf die Denker, die in den Städten aufwuchsen, übte der Ruf der Wüste schon immer eine unwiderstehliche Anziehungskraft aus. Ich glaube nicht, dass sie in ihr Gott finden werden. Vielmehr werden sie inmitten der Einsamkeit jenen Wert mit Deutlichkeit vernehmen, der in ihnen wohnt: leben." Leben im Meer ohne Wasser.

removed everything superfluous from the Sahara, so that people may experience the true essence of existence.
And T. E. Lawrence, Lawrence of Arabia, added: "The call of the desert has always exerted an irresistible attraction on thinkers who have grown up in towns. I do not believe that they will find God here. In the midst of this loneliness, they will rather perceive clearly that value which exists within them: life." Life in the sea without water.

de mon corps et brûlant mes bras nus. Mais il ne s'arrête pas là, il me prend au cou, me mord le visage, s'incruste dans ma gorge, me bouche les narines du nez et m'empêche de voir. J'ai l'impression d'être perdu et j'ai peur de m'étouffer. » Jusque-là, Trench avait considéré le désert avec objectivité, tout simplement comme une région où il tombe moins de 250 millimètres d'eau par an, mais cette expérience l'a changé, comme le dit un vieux proverbe arabe : « Quiconque entre dans le désert ne sera plus le même qu'avant ».

Ce paysage invite à l'humilité. Ce paysage mérite qu'on y rentre avec humilité. Lorsque les rayons aveuglants du soleil qui monte de plus en plus haut dans le ciel rompent le charme de l'idylle matinale des dunes de sable. Quand le sable crée de nouvelles formes harmonieuses. Quand ce paysage presque inhabité de roches et de sable donne l'impression de s'étendre jusqu'à l'infini. Quand une petite oasis devient une source de vie, une île dans cette mer de sable. Quand chaque puits semble devenir le centre du monde. Quand les forces de l'érosion façonnent de nouvelles formes. Alors, face à tous ces phénomènes, la seule réaction appropriée est l'humilité. Les vieux conducteurs de caravanes disent qu'Allah a éliminé du désert tout ce qui était superflu afin que les êtres humains reconnaissent l'essence véritable des choses. Et T.E. Lawrence, le fameux Lawrence d'Arabie, ajoute : « L'appel du désert pour les penseurs de la ville a toujours été irrésistible. Je ne crois pas qu'ils y trouvent Dieu, mais qu'ils entendent plus distinctement dans la solitude le verbe vivant qu'ils apportent avec eux. » Une vie dans une mer sans eau.

los brazos. Pero esto no era todo, a continuación se adueñaba de mi cuello, me mordía la cara, se incrustaba en mi garganta, me taponaba los agujeros de la nariz y me impedía ver. Me sentía perdido y temía asfixiarme". Hasta aquel momento Trench había contemplado al desierto con objetividad, simplemente como una zona con una cantidad media de precipitaciones de menos de 250 milímetros al año. Después se hizo también realidad para él aquel viejo proverbio árabe: "Quien se adentra en el desierto no volverá a ser quien era".

Este paisaje invita a la humildad. Este paisaje merece que uno se adentre en él con humildad. Cuando los deslumbrantes rayos del sol saliente rompen el encanto del idilio matutino de las dunas de arena. Cuando la arena produce nuevas y harmónicas formas. Cuando este casi completamente despoblado paisaje de rocas y arena nos da la impresión de extenderse hasta el infinito. Cuando un pequeño oasis aparece surtiendo vida como una isla en el mar de arena. Cuando cada manantial parece convertirse en el centro del mundo. Cuando las fuerzas de la erosión crean nuevas formas. Ante todos esos fenómenos la única reacción apropiada es la humildad. Los viejos guías de caravanas dicen que Alá eliminó del Sahara todo lo superfluo para que los humanos comprendieran la verdadera esencia de las cosas.

T.E. Lawrence, el famoso Lawrence de Arabia, añadió: "Para los pensadores que crecieron en las ciudades la llamada del desierto siempre ejerció un irresistible atractivo. No creo que en él encuentren a dios. Más bien en medio de toda esa soledad hallarán con toda claridad ese valor que en ellos mismos reside: la vida". La vida en el mar sin agua.

agenti atmosferici crea nuove formazioni. Allora l'umiltà diventa d'obbligo. I vecchi carovanieri sostengono che Allah abbia eliminato dal Sahara il superfluo affinché l'uomo possa riconoscere la vera essenza delle cose.

T.E. Lawrence, o Lawrence d'Arabia, aggiunge: „Il richiamo del deserto ha sempre esercitato un'attrazione irresistibile sui pensatori cresciuti in città. Non credo che vi troveranno Dio. Credo, piuttosto, che nella solitudine possano percepire con chiarezza il grande valore che dimora in loro: la vita." La vita, nel mare asciutto.

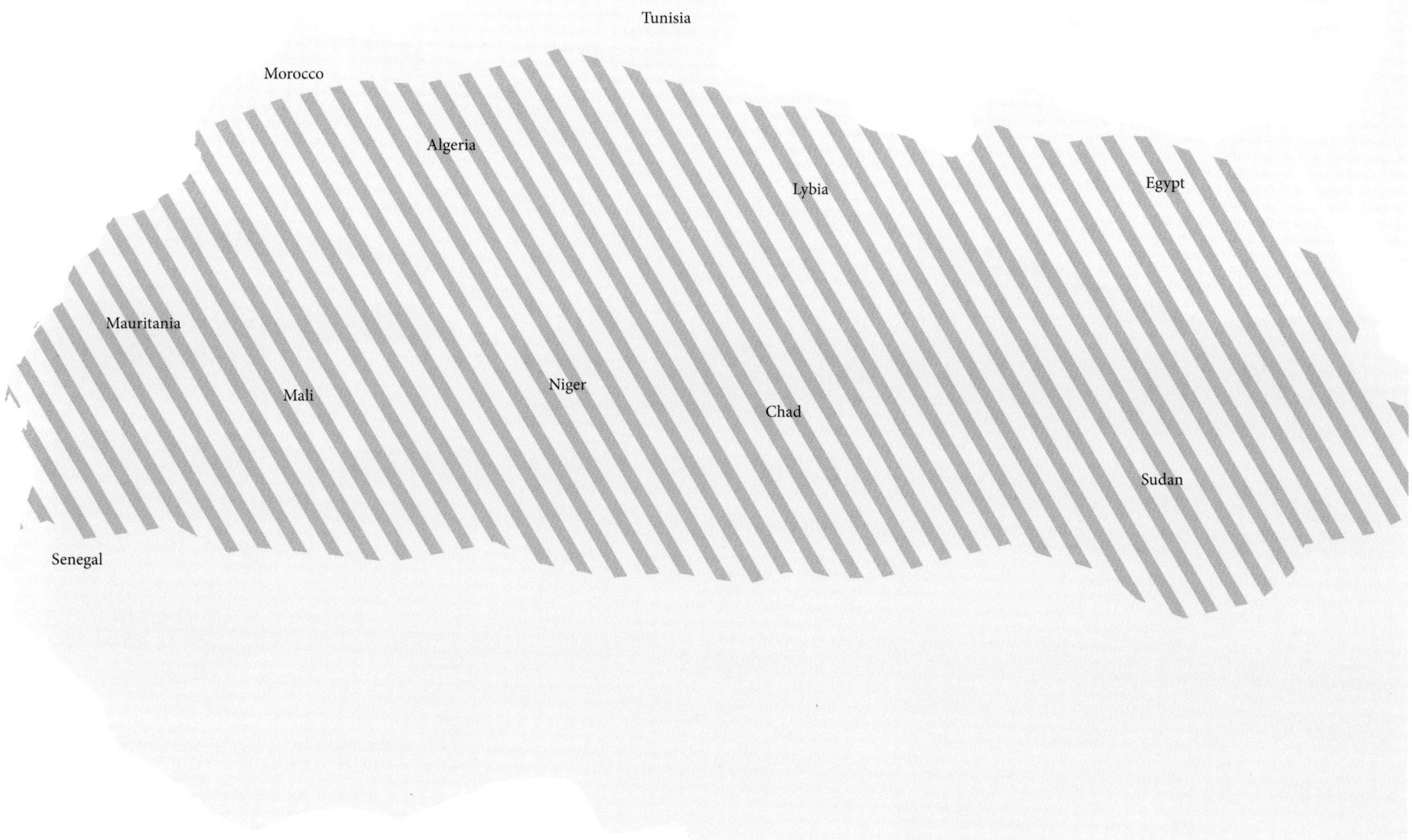
Tunisia
Morocco
Algeria
Lybia
Egypt
Mauritania
Mali
Niger
Chad
Sudan
Senegal

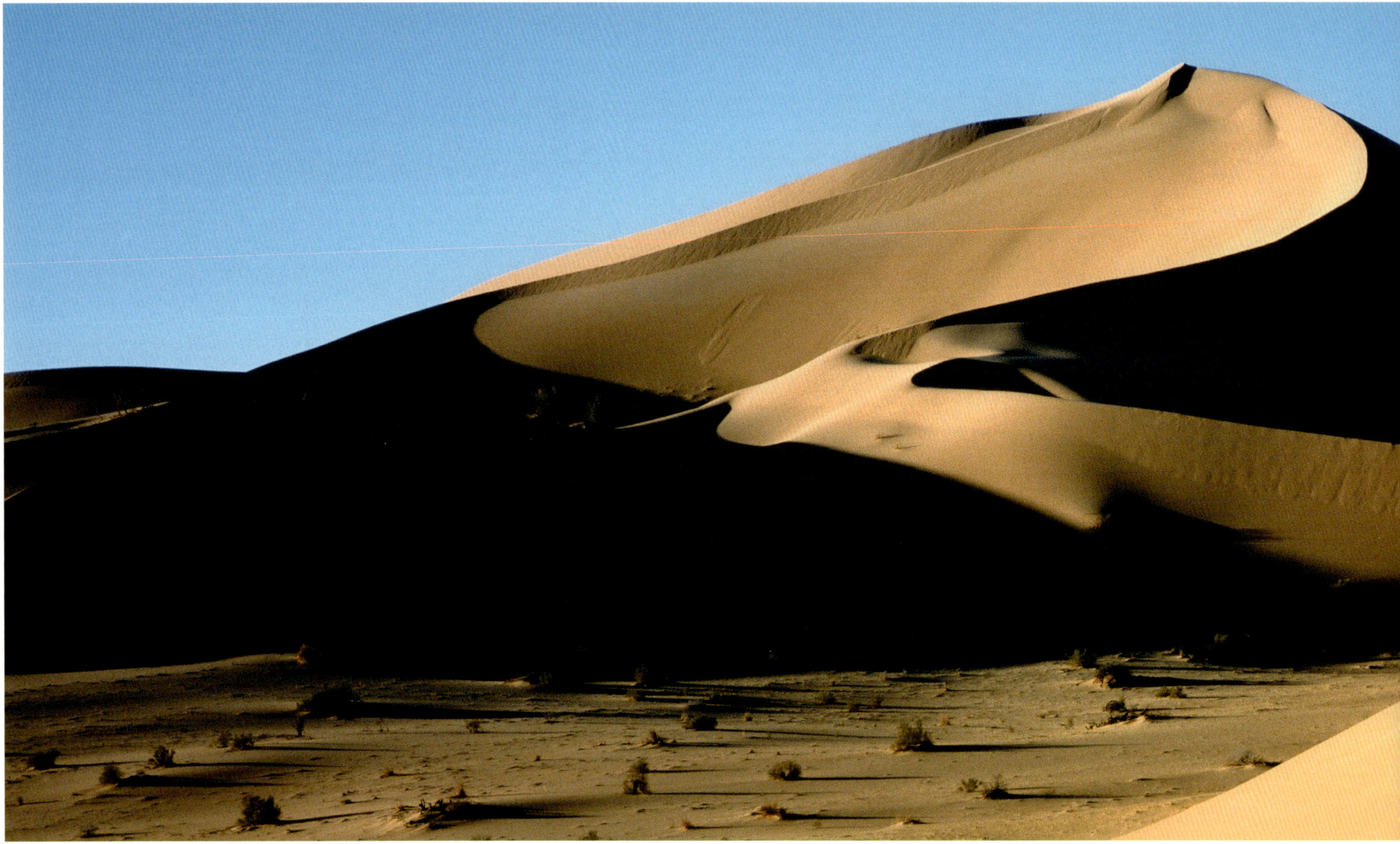

1 Grand Erg Oriental, Algeria

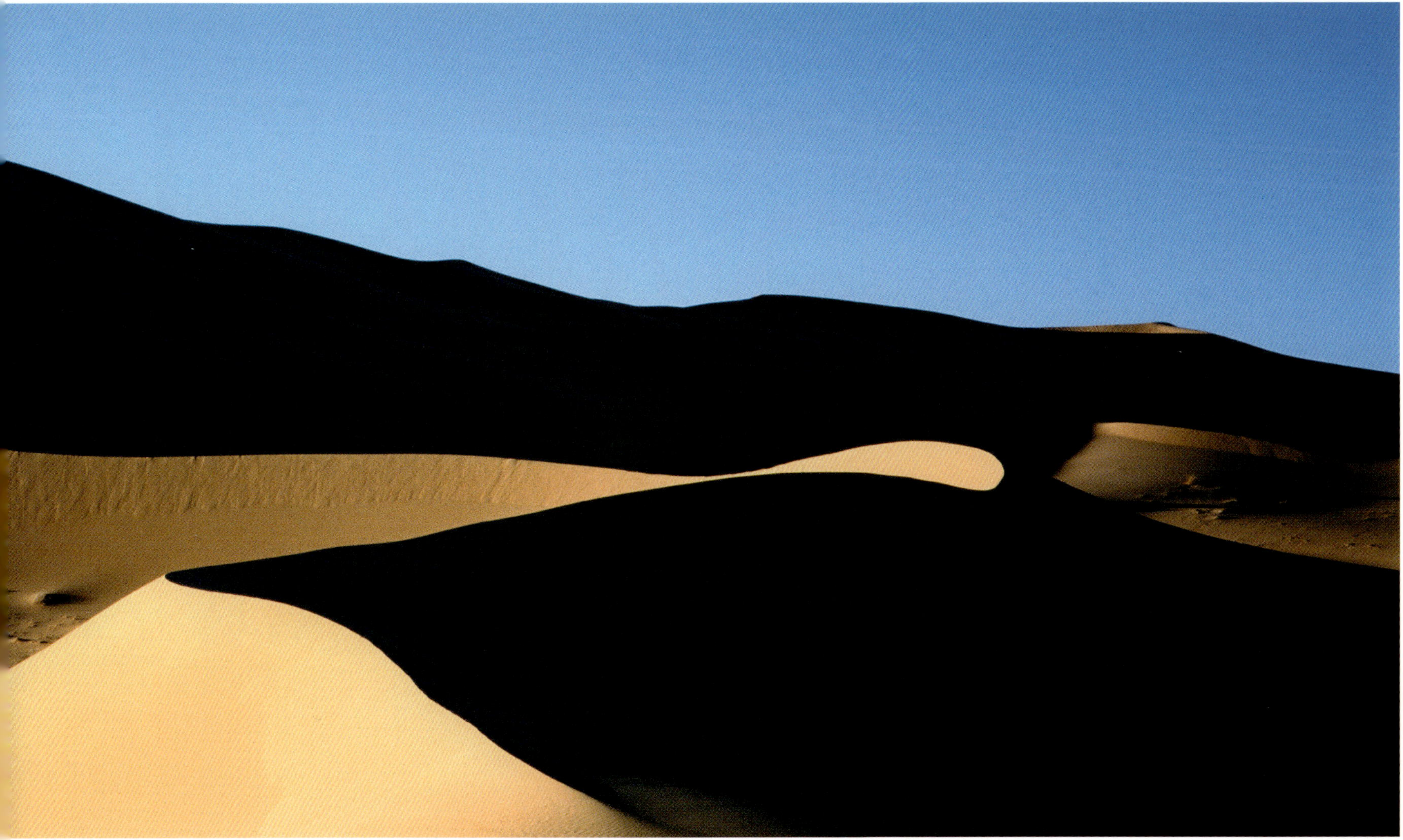

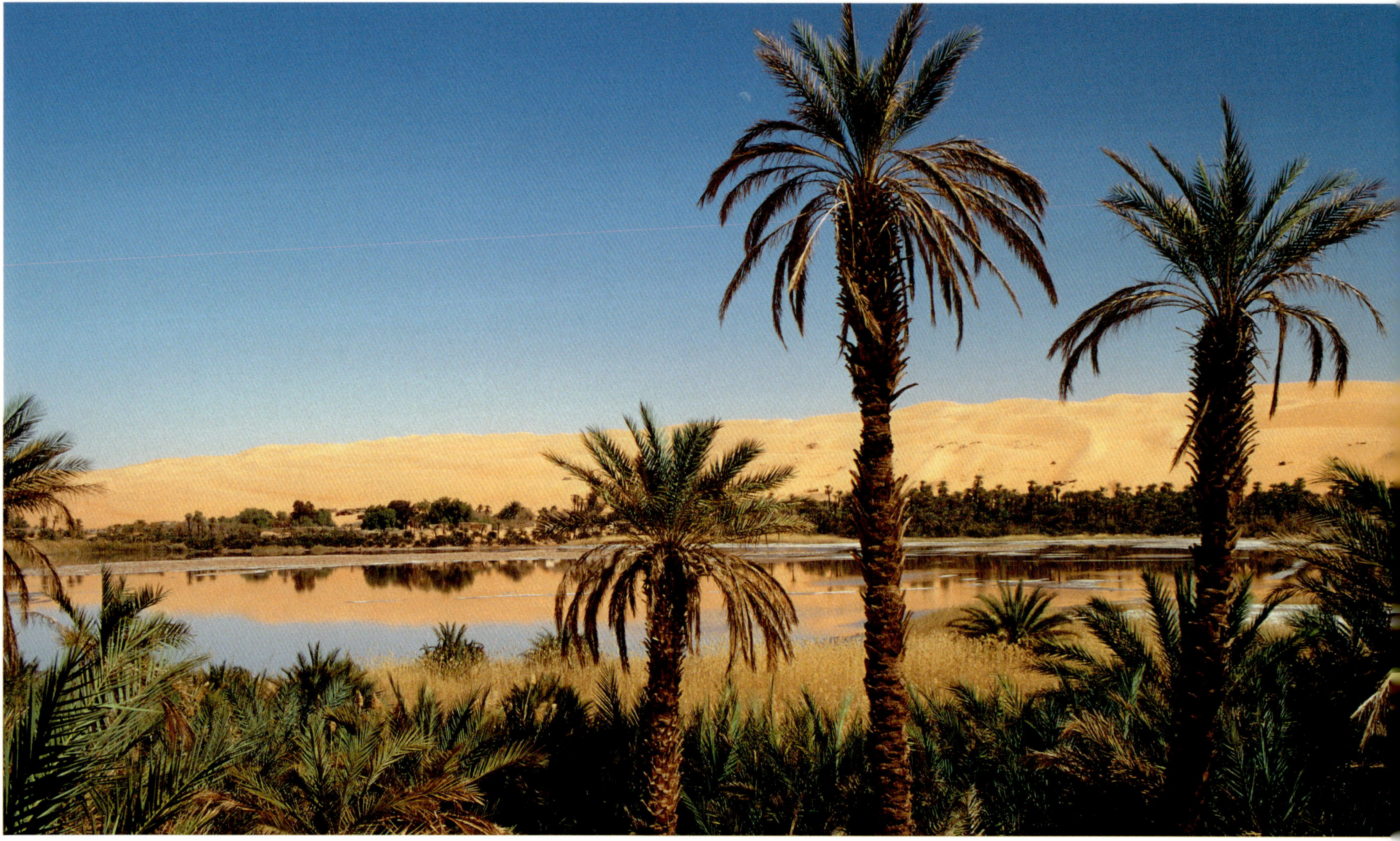

2 Lake Mandara, Libya

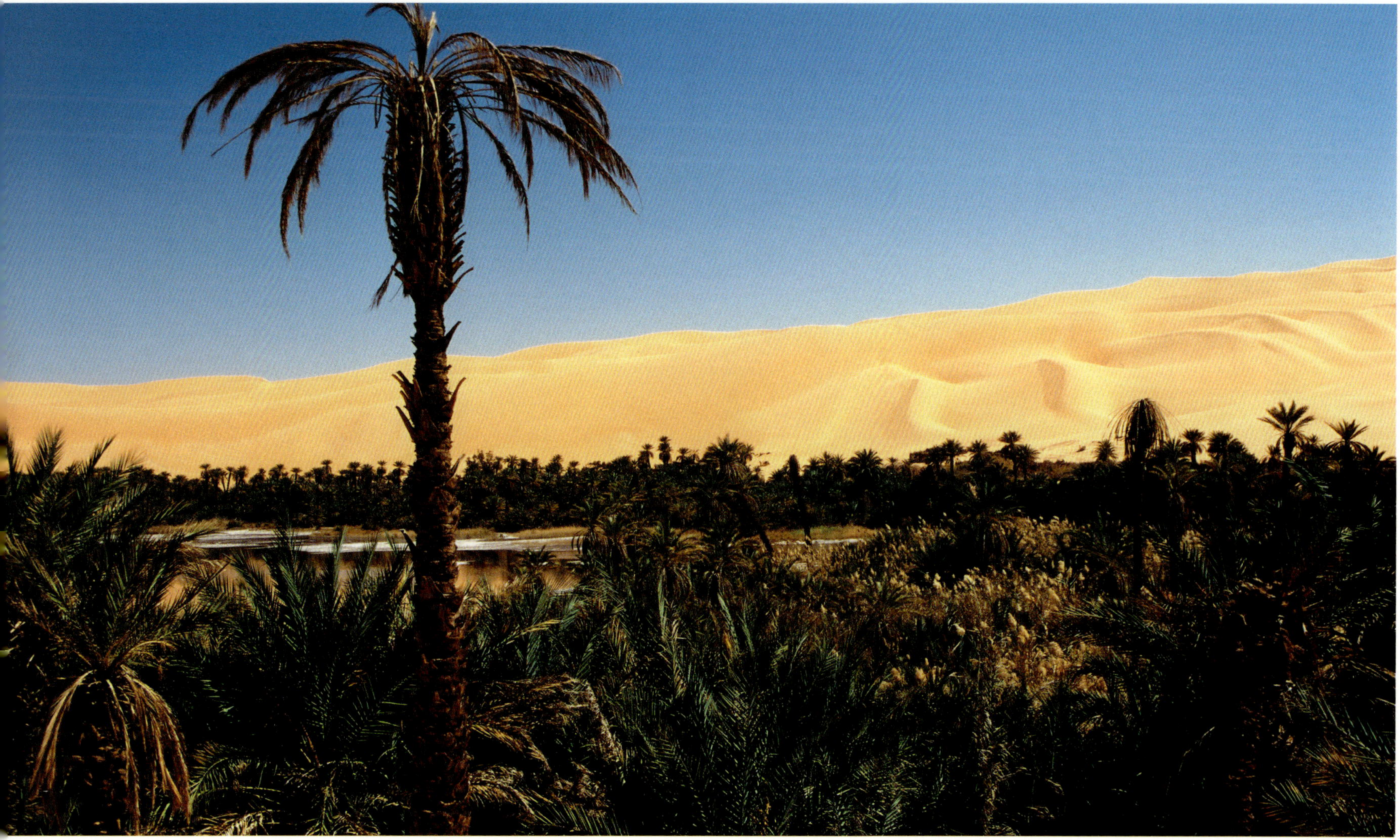

► 3 Near Gassi Touil, Algeria

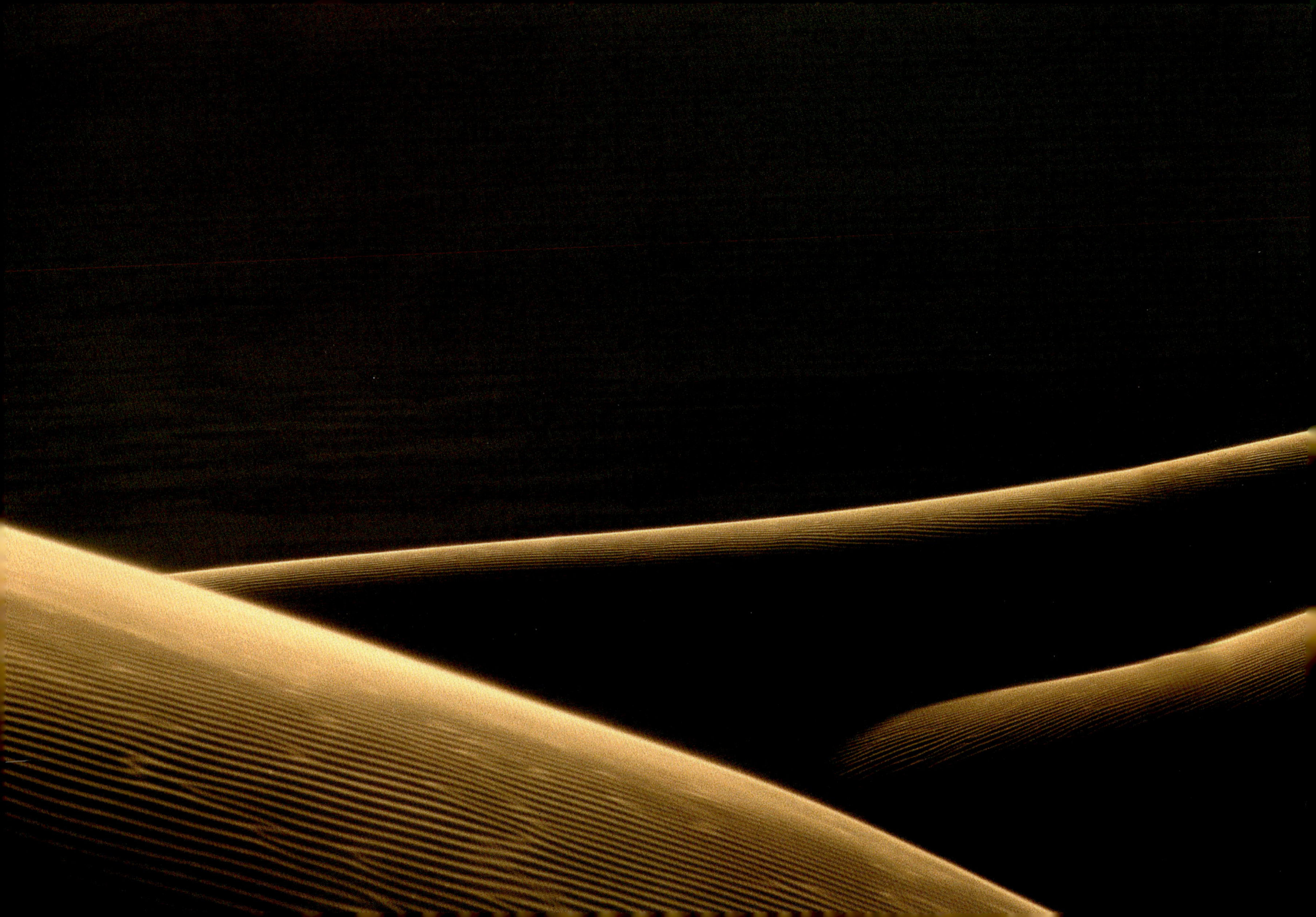

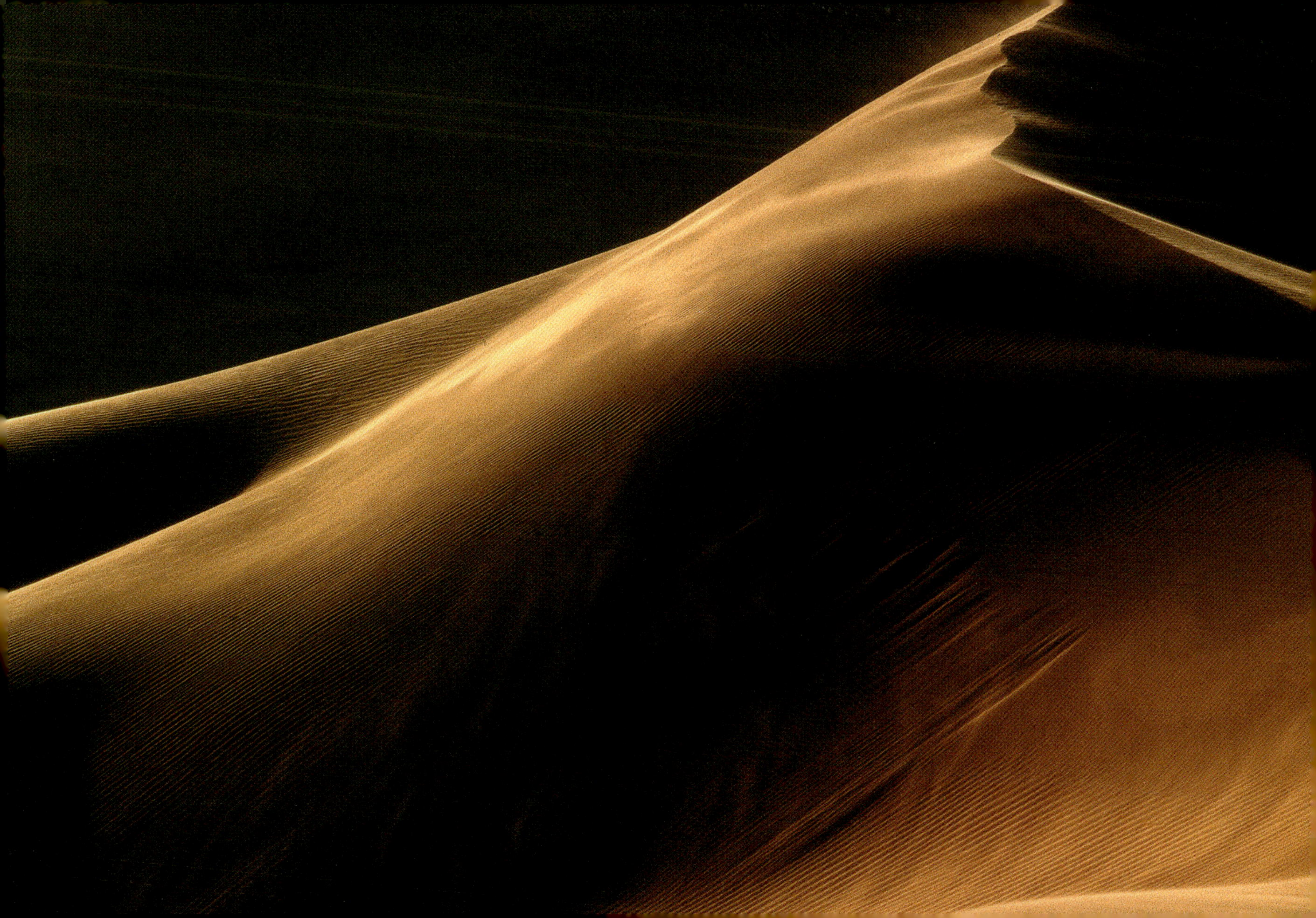

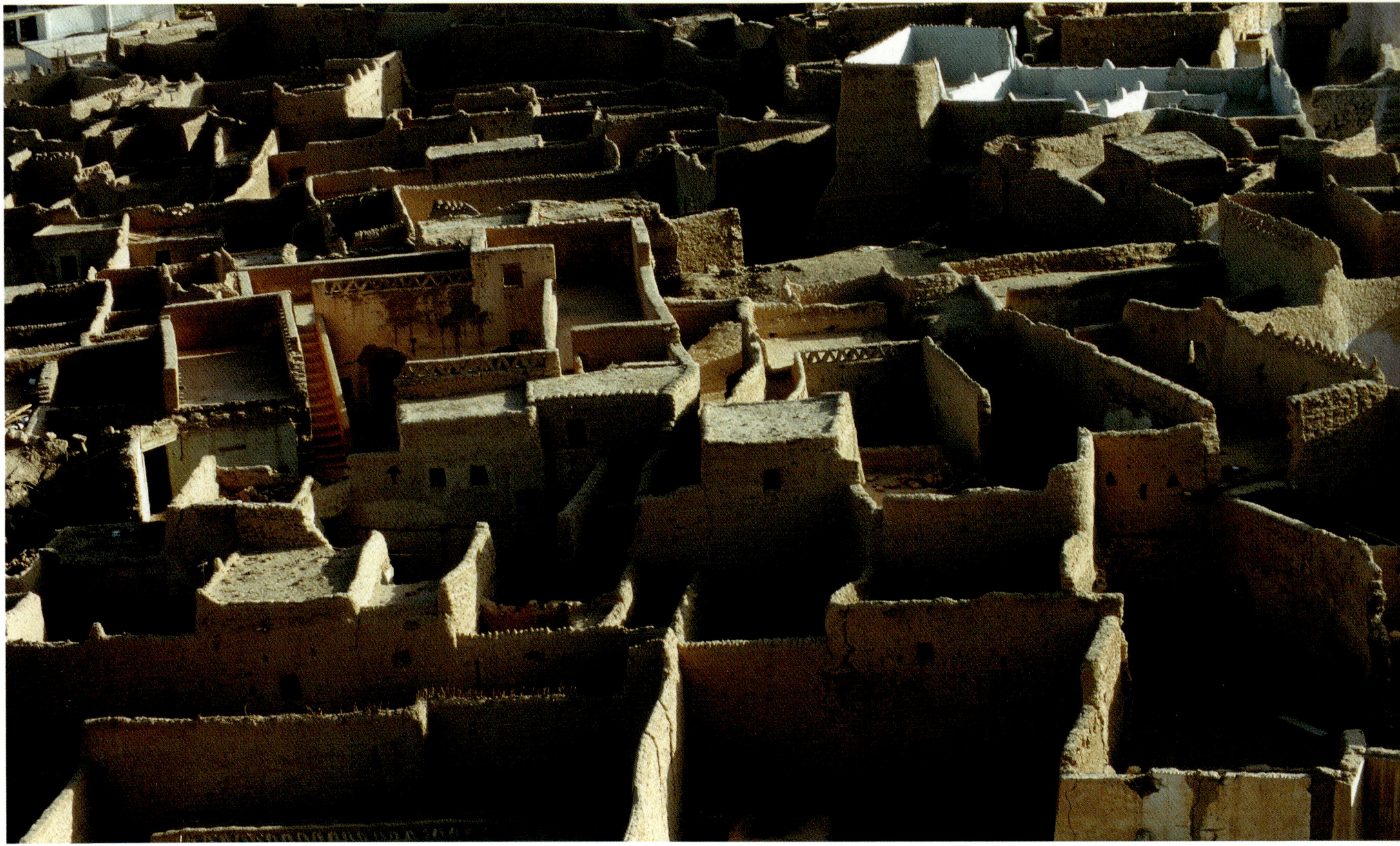

4 Ghat, Libya

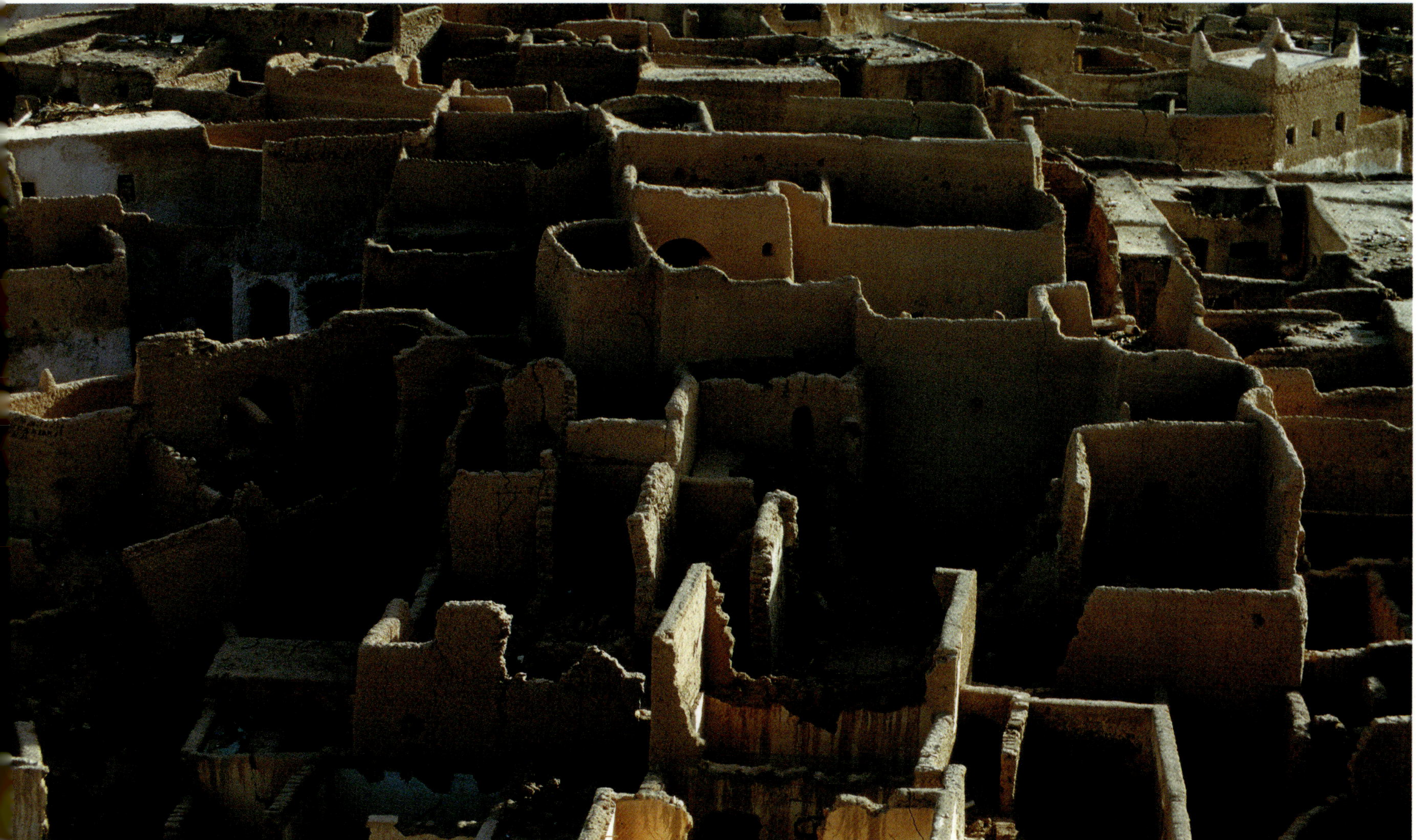

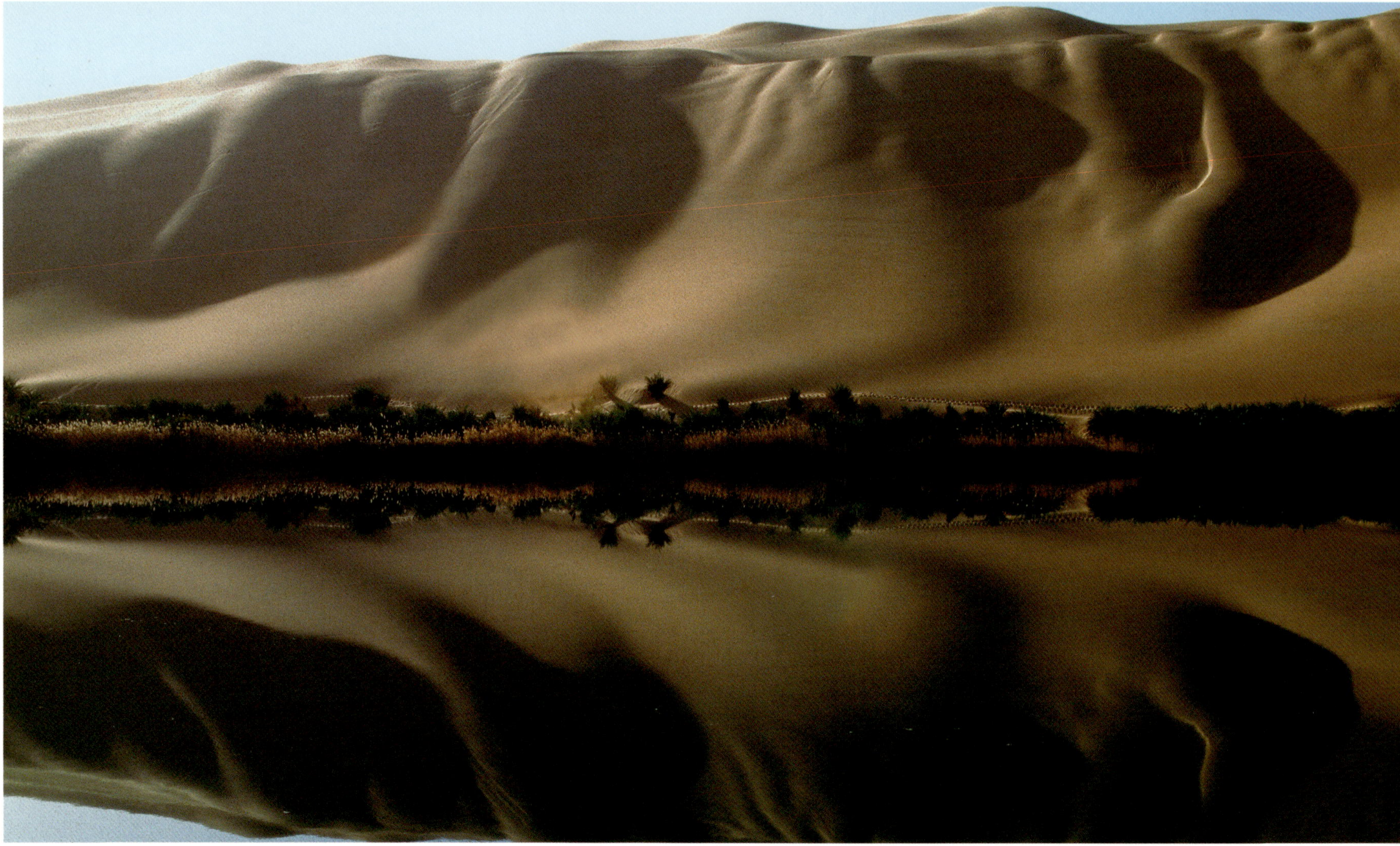

5 Lake Gabroon, Erg Ubari, Libya

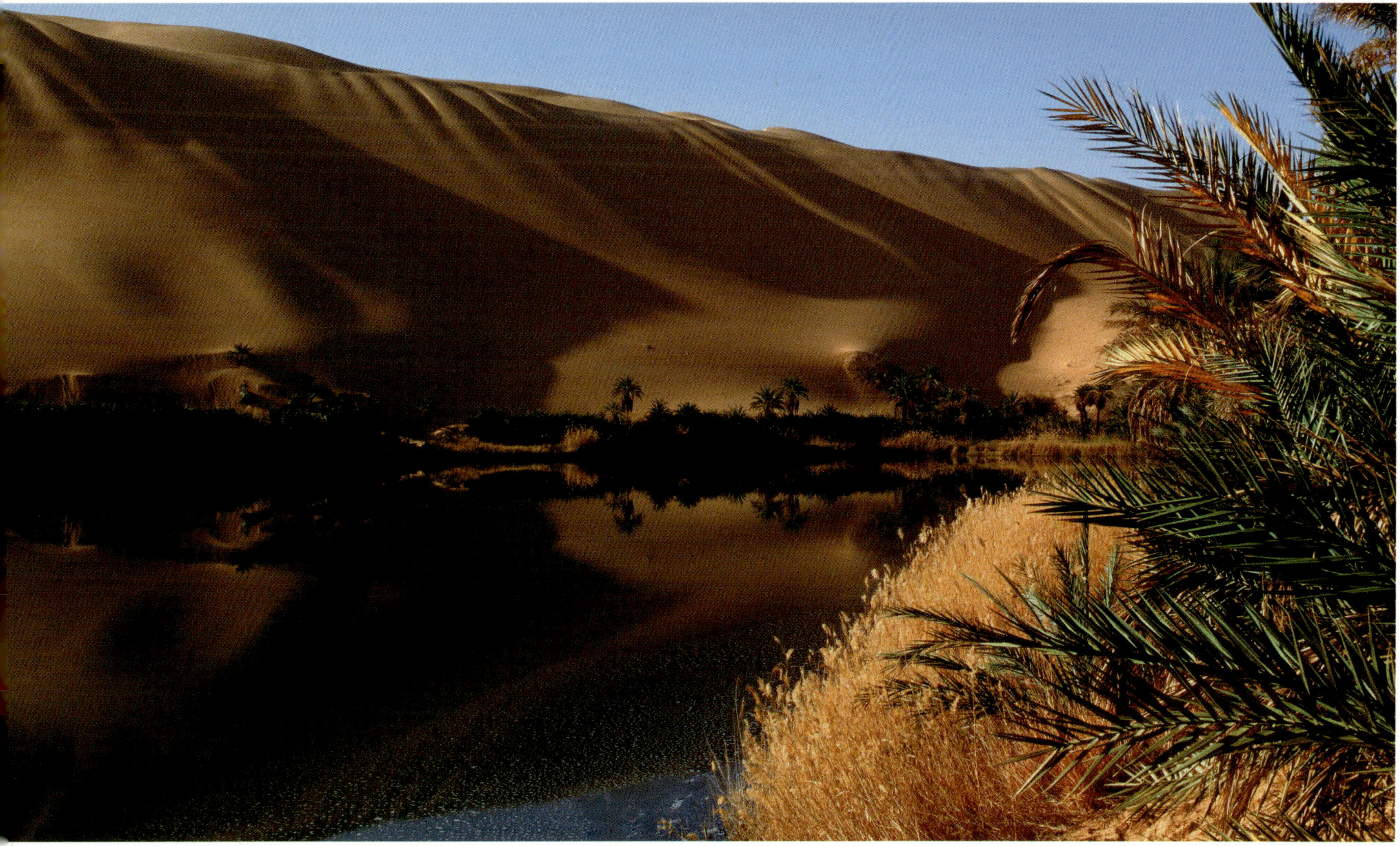

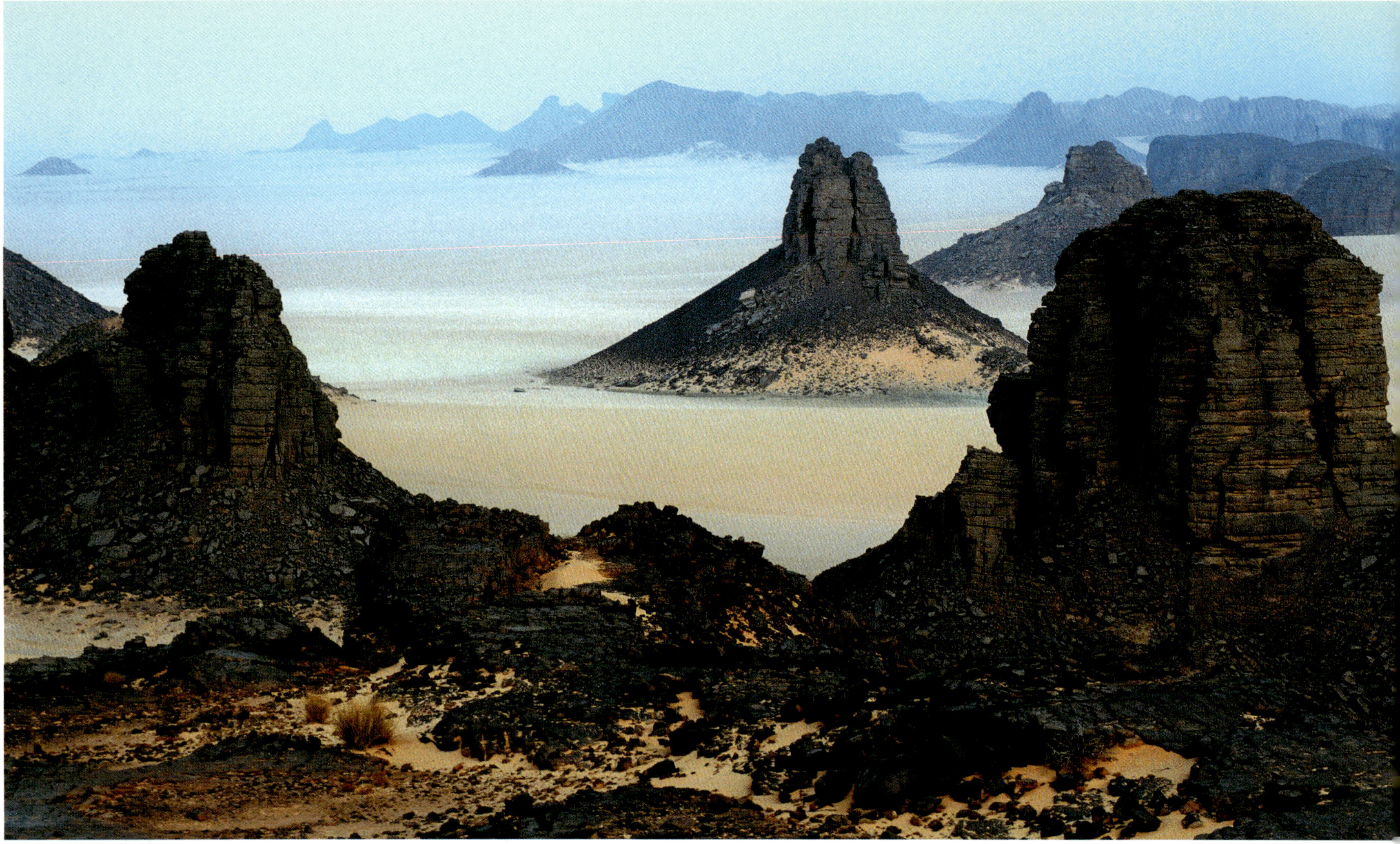

6 Tassili n' Ajjer, Algeria

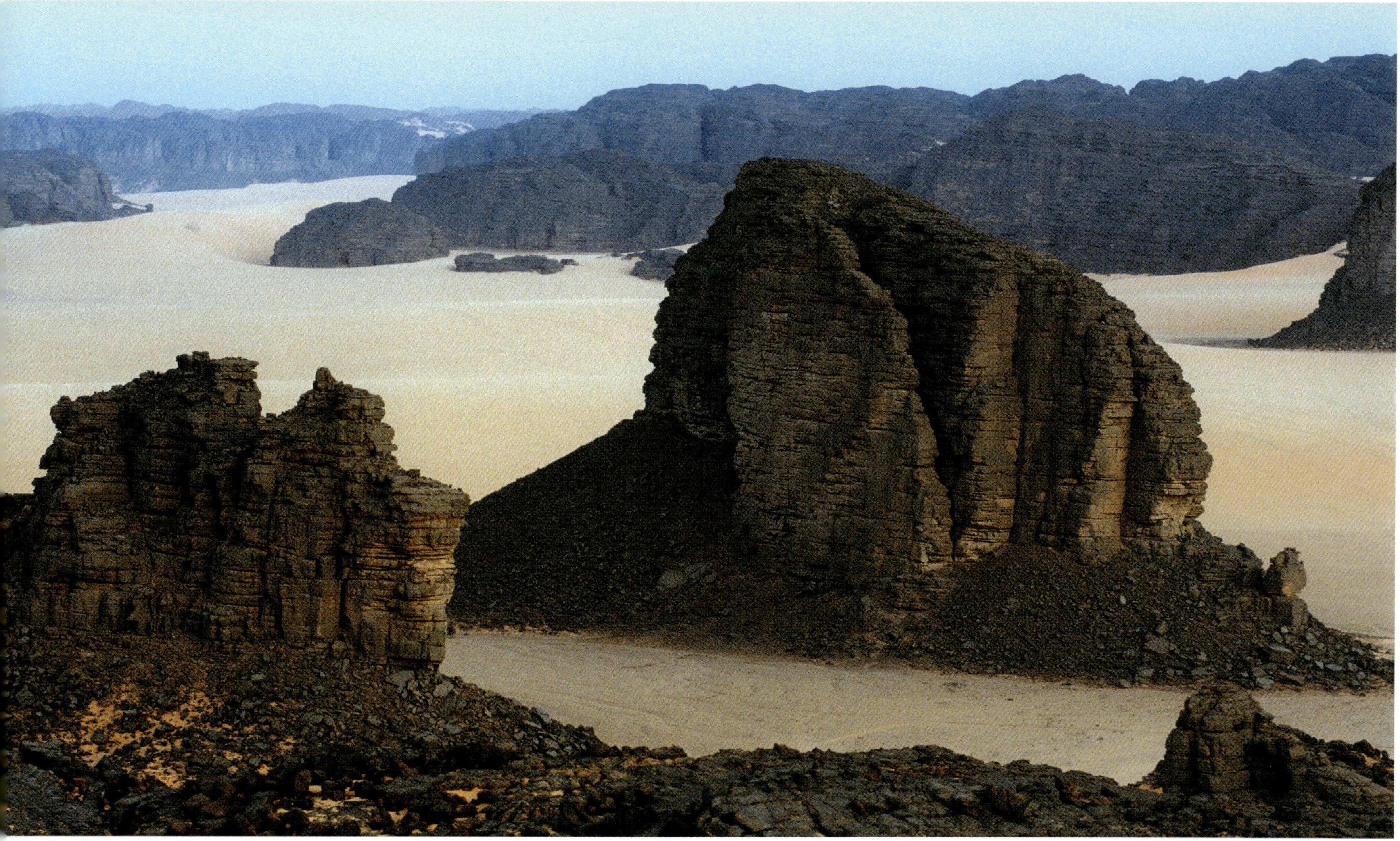

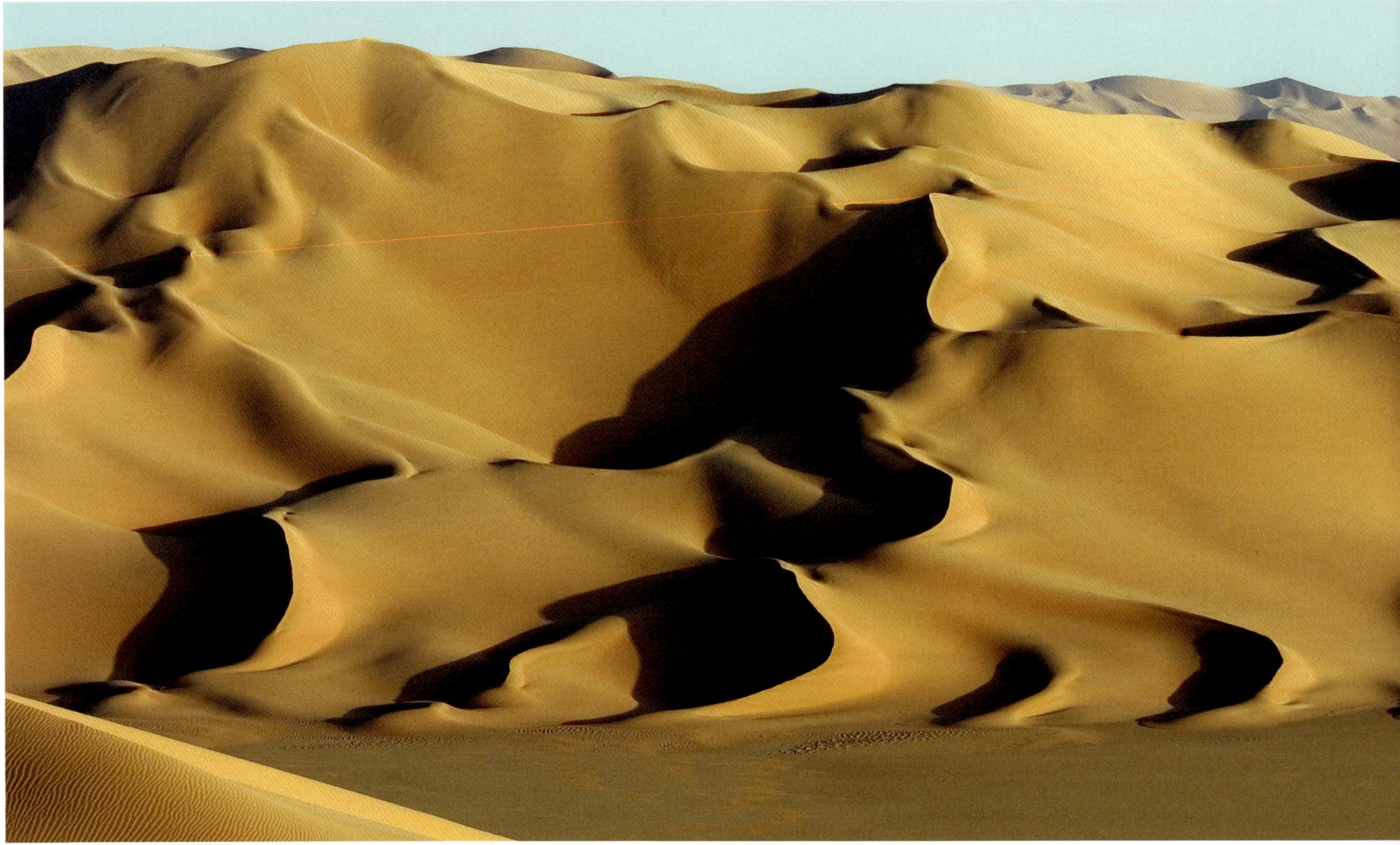

7 Idhan Murzuk, Libya

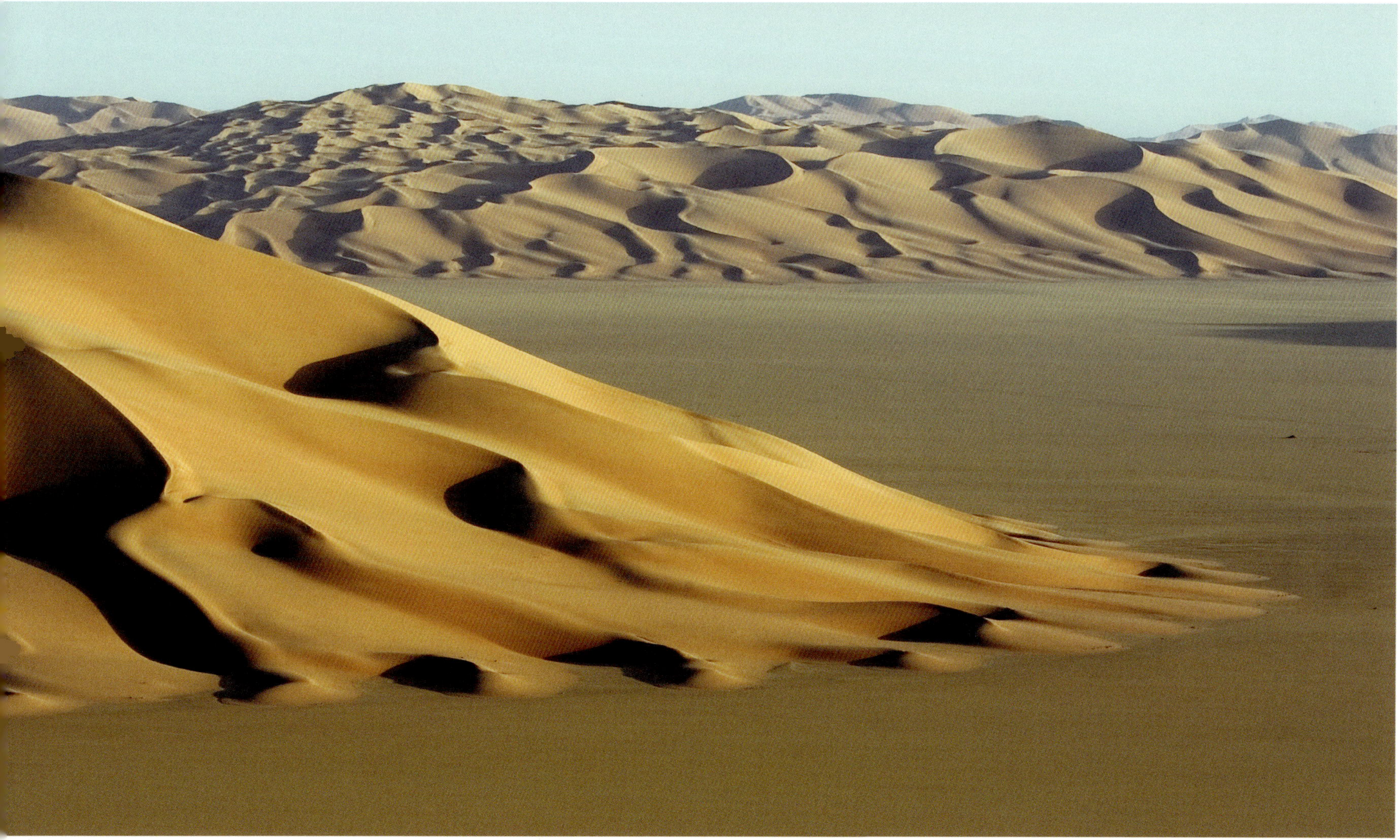

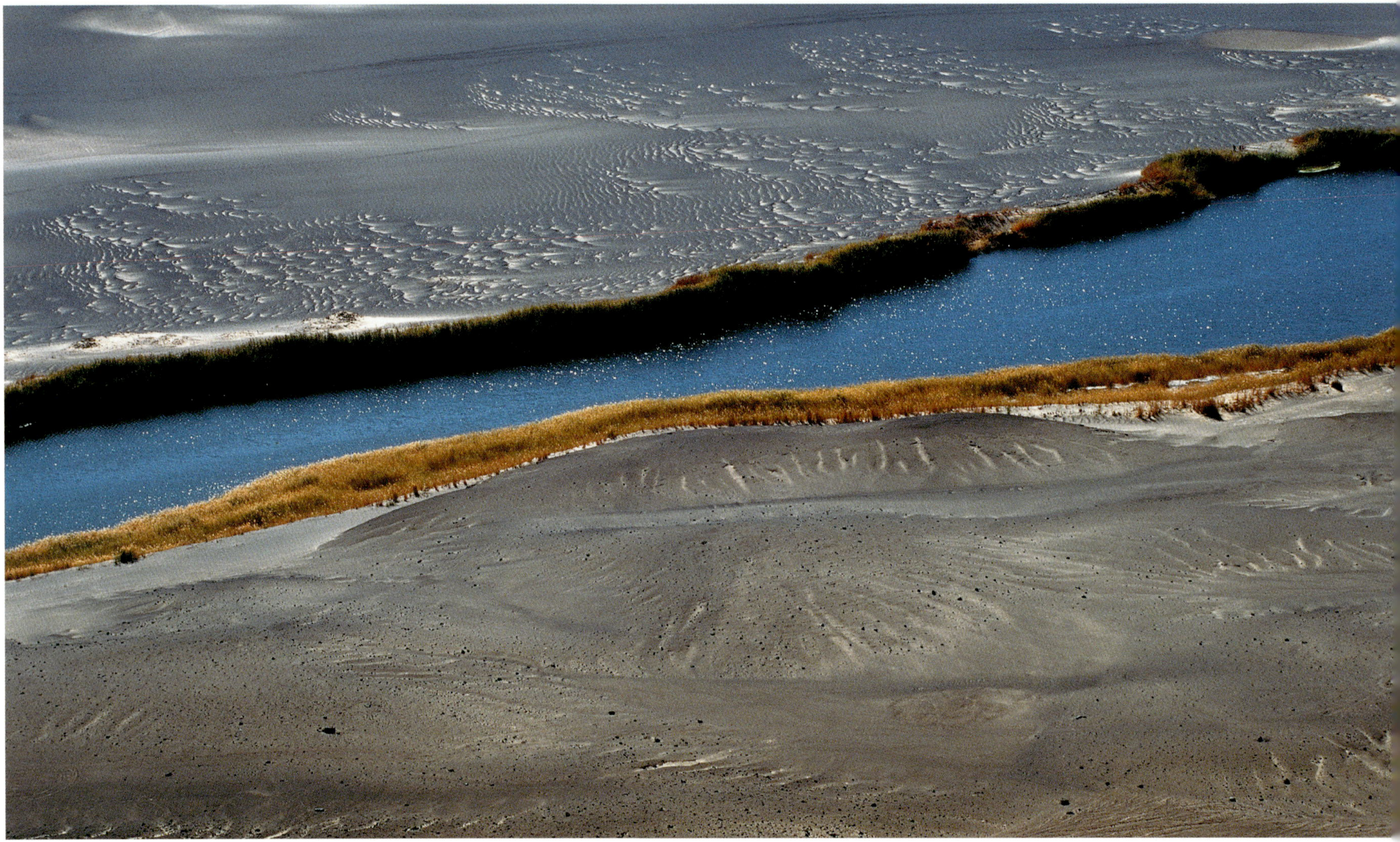

8 Wau an Namus, Red Lake, Libya

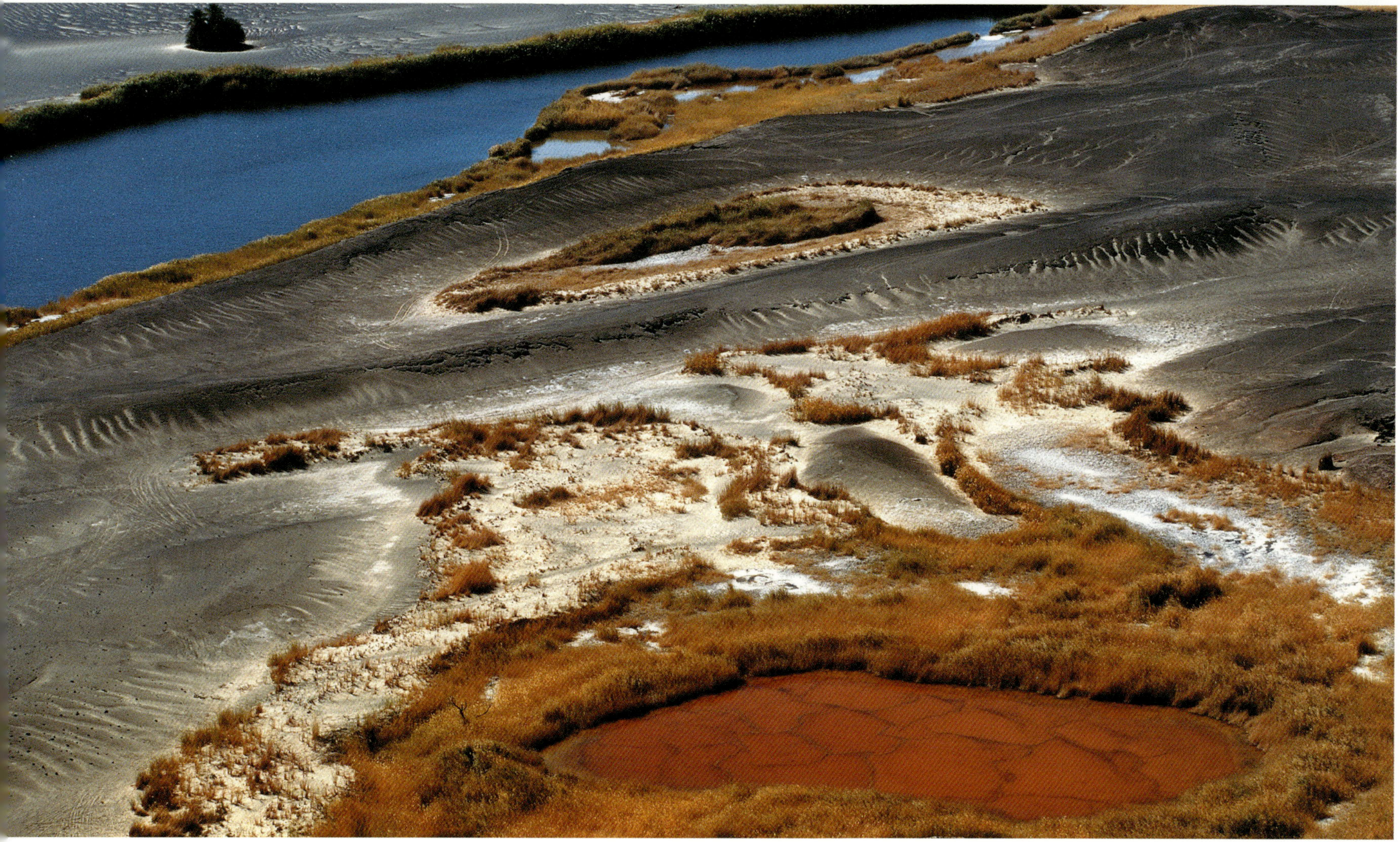

► 9 White Desert, Egypt

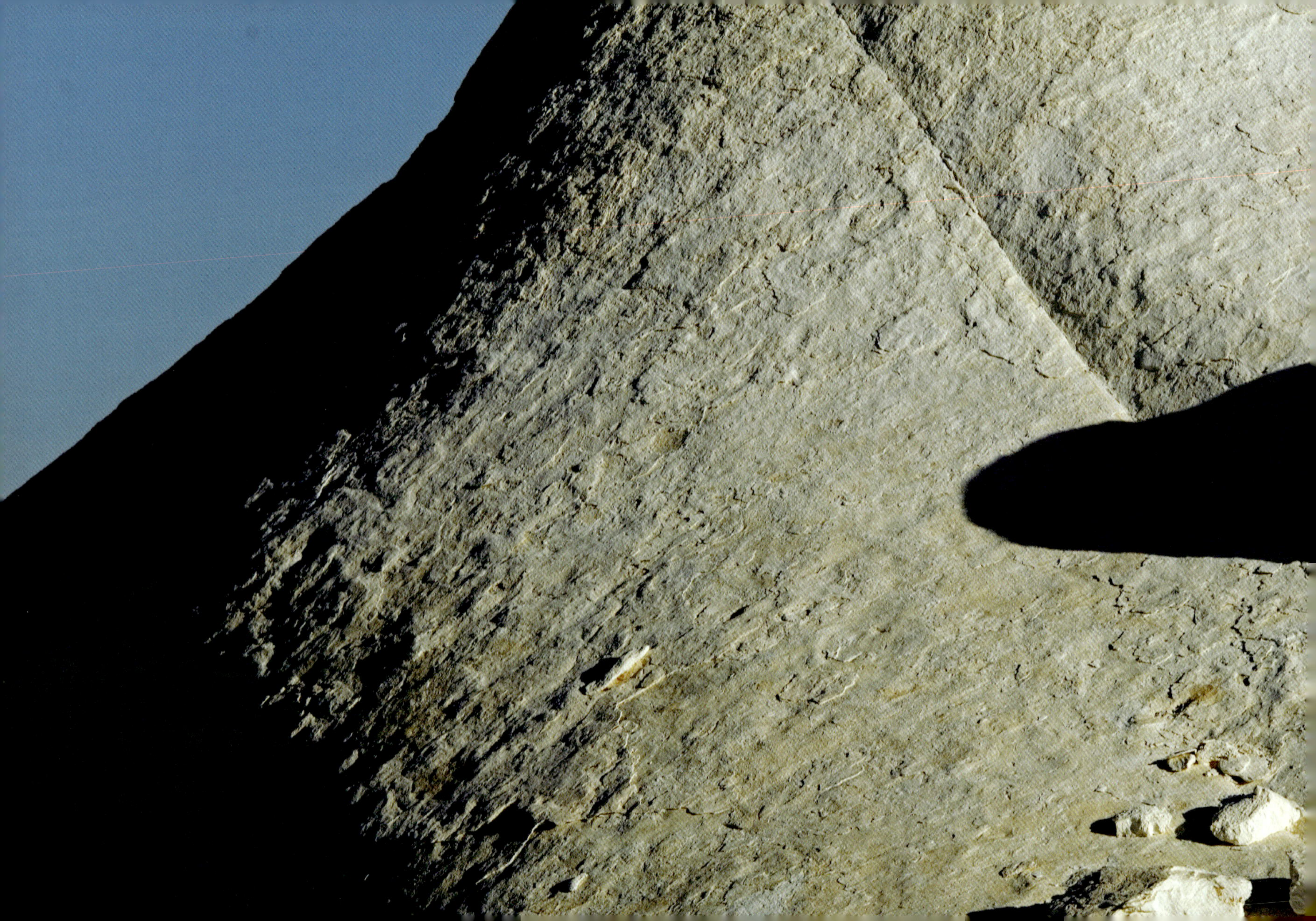

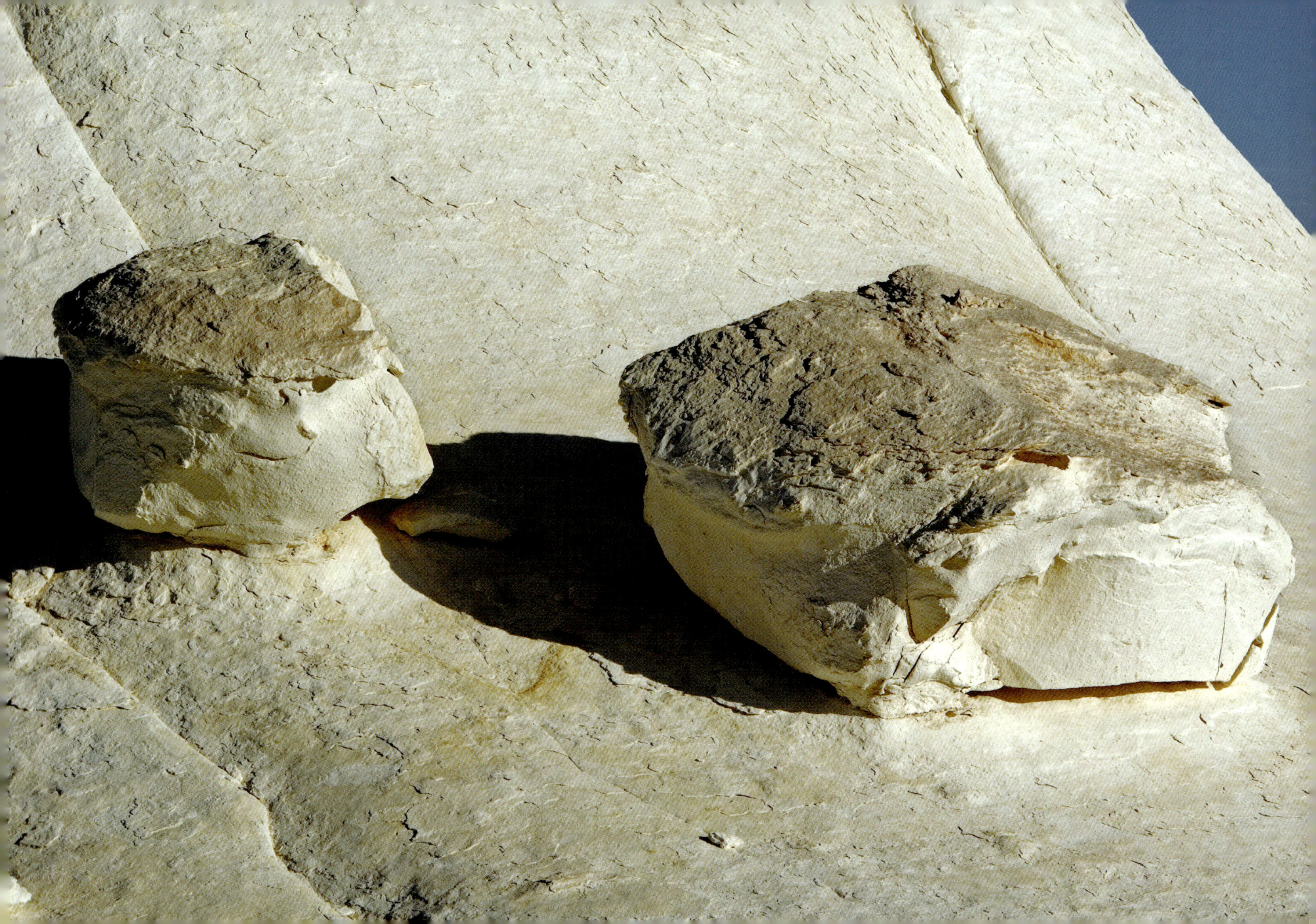

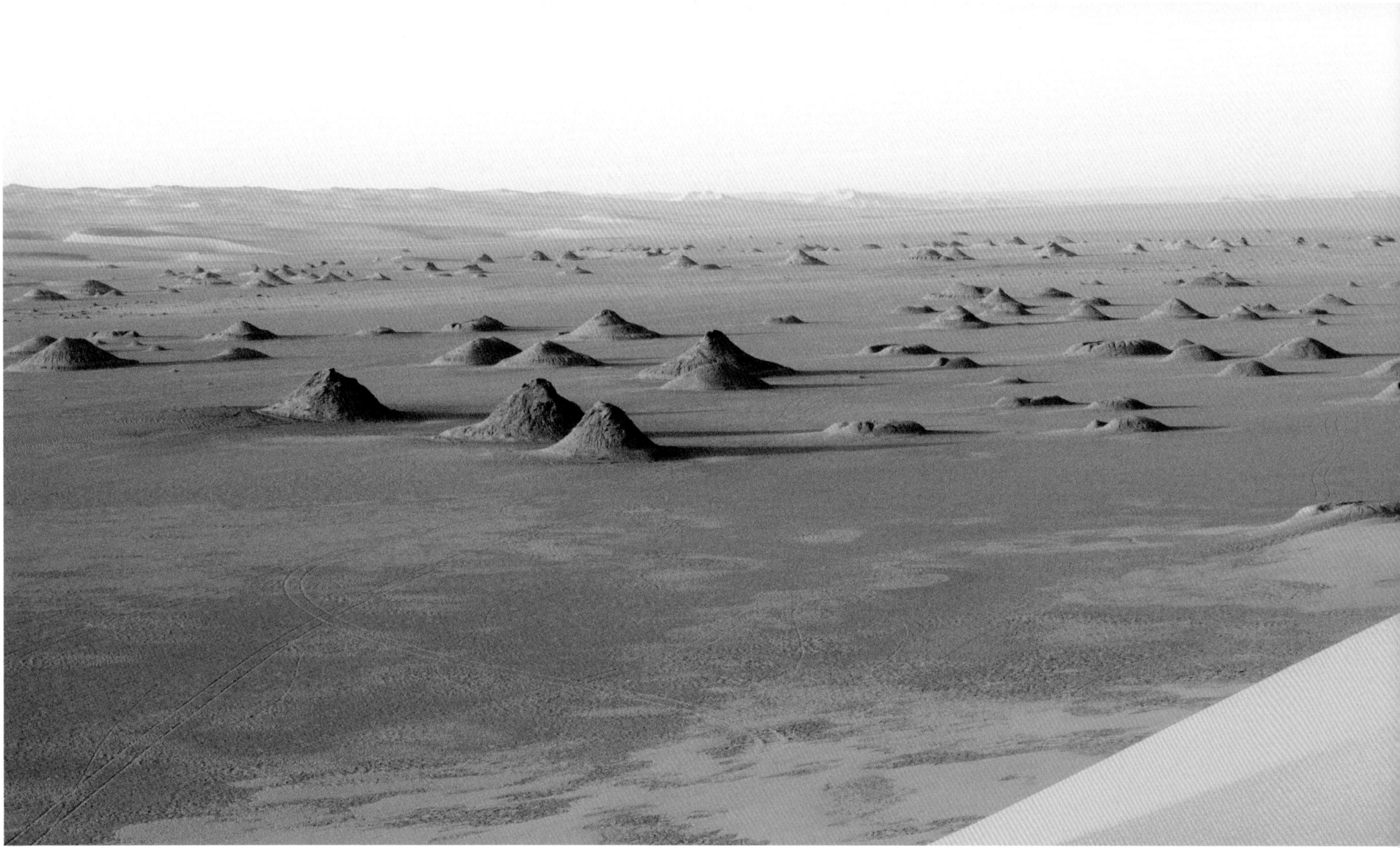

10 Plain with former Tamarisk hills, Erg Ubari, Libya

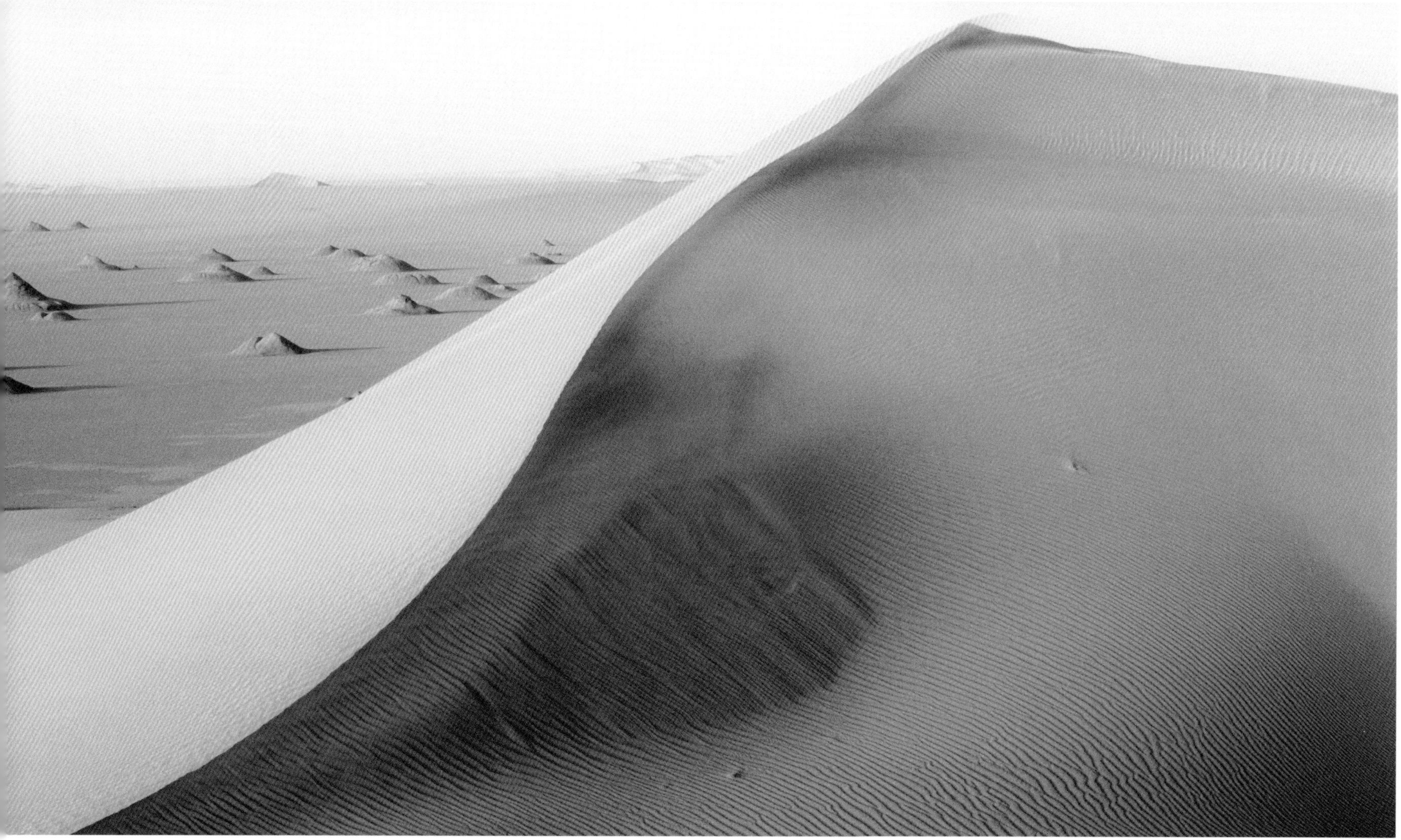

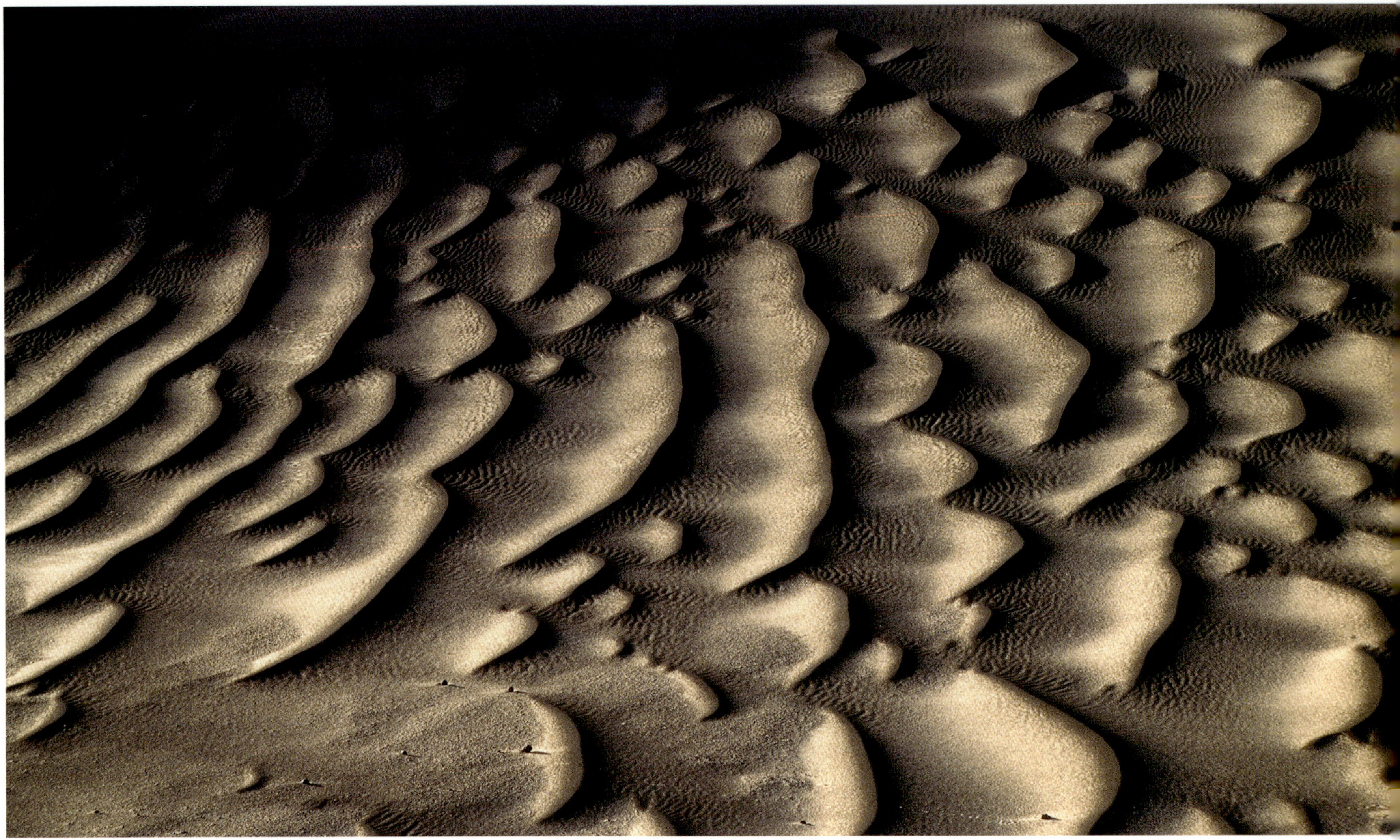

11 Sand waves, Wau an Namus, Libya

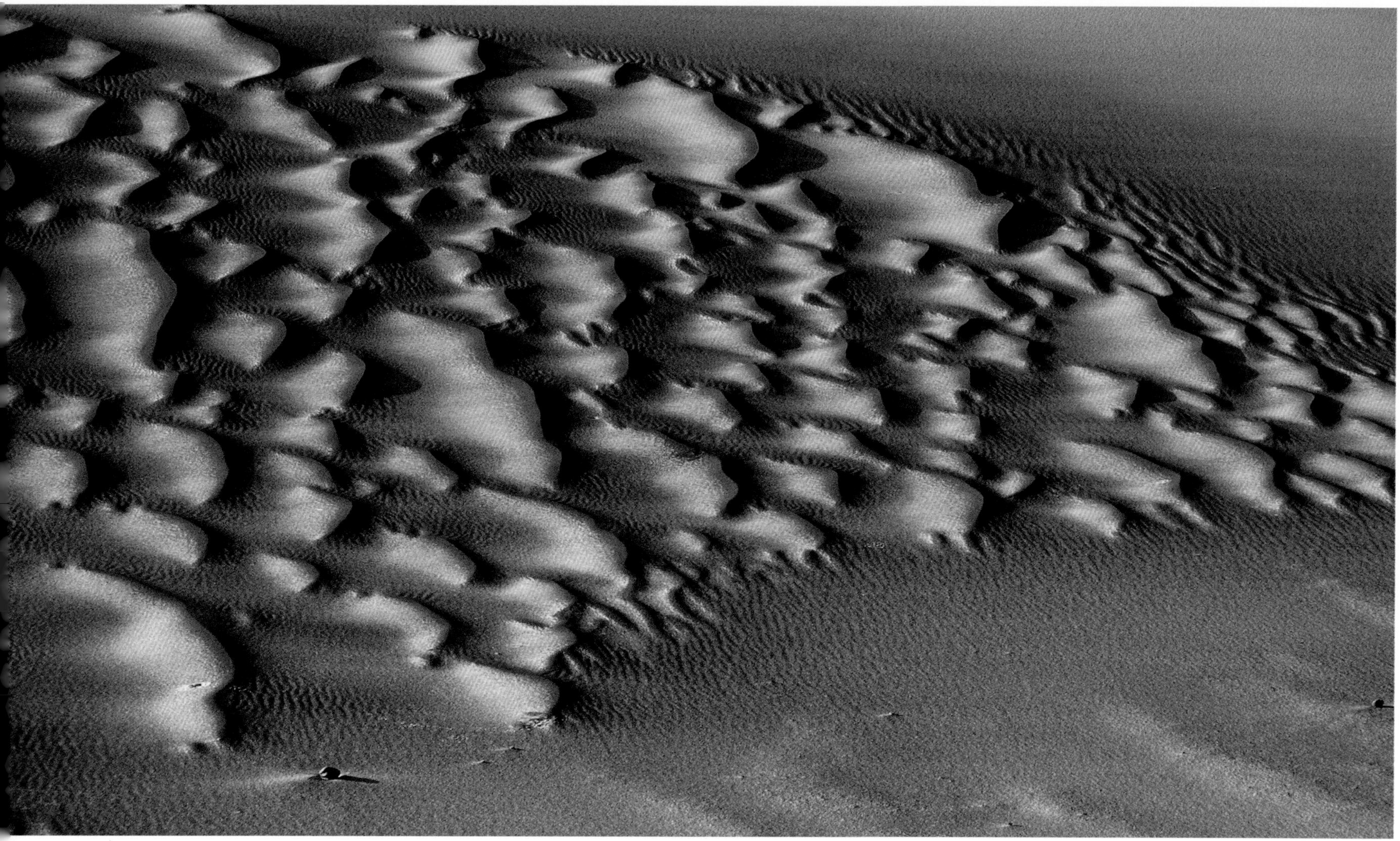

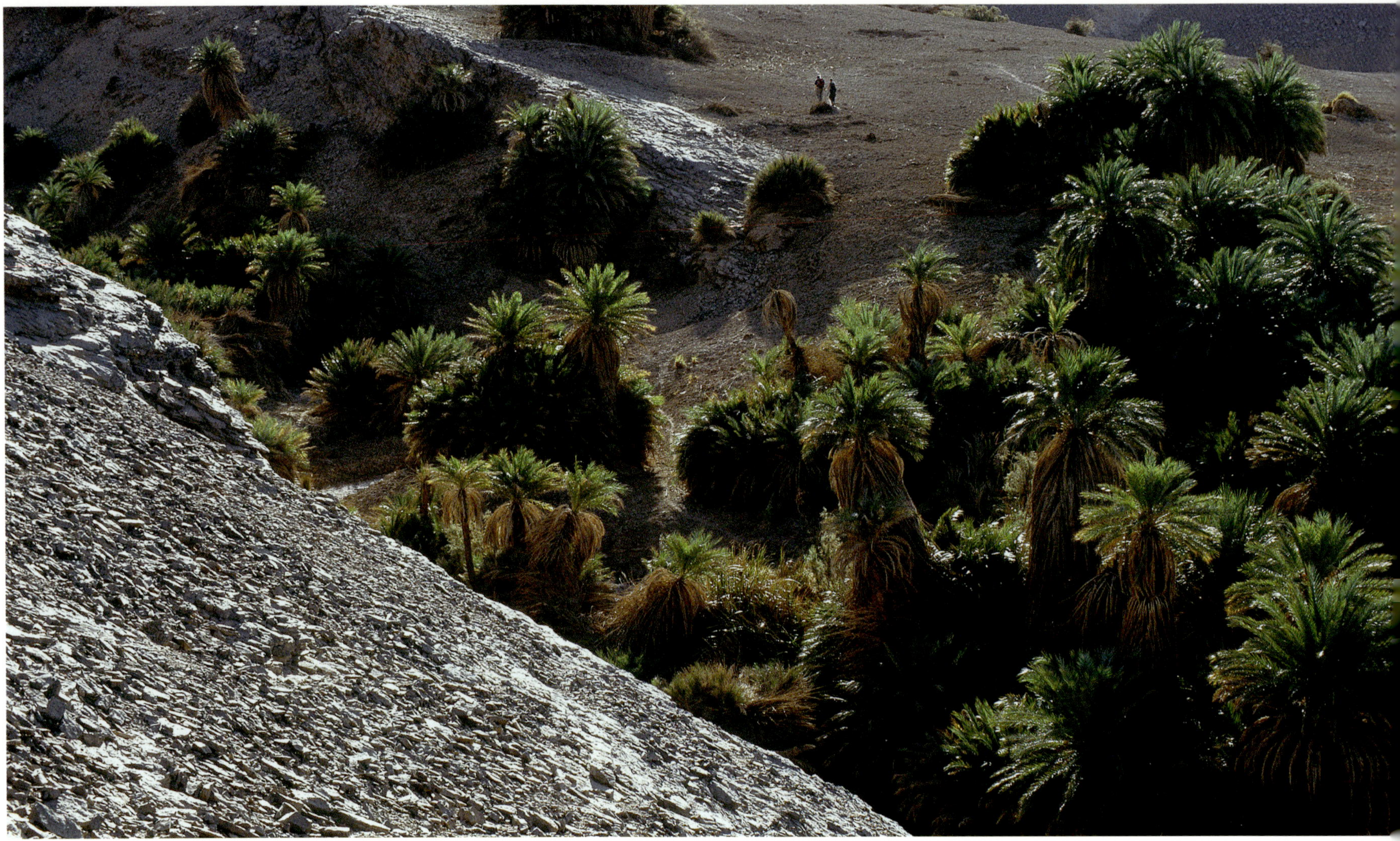

12 Palm valley west of Amguid, Algeria

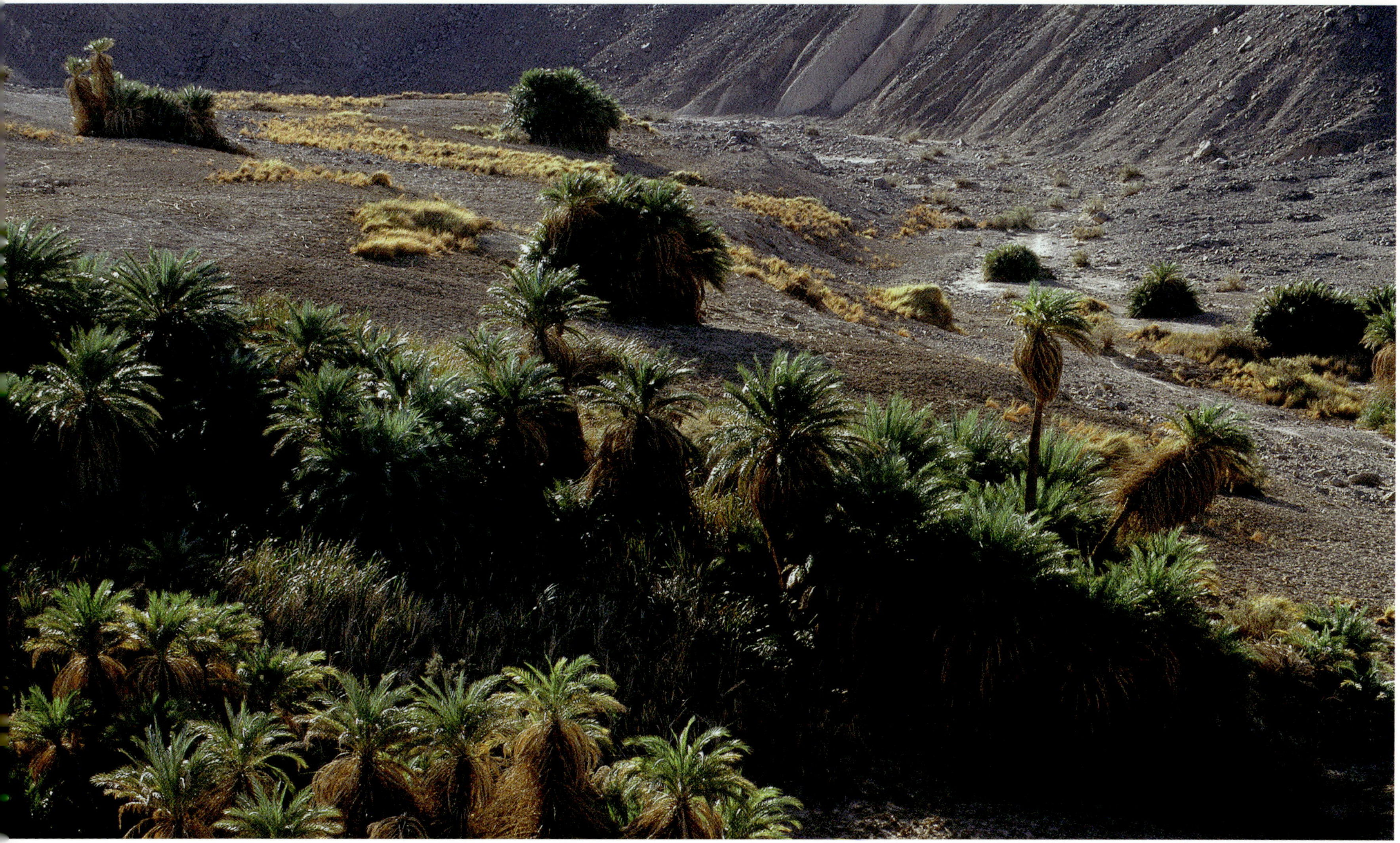

13 Targi, Akakus, Libya

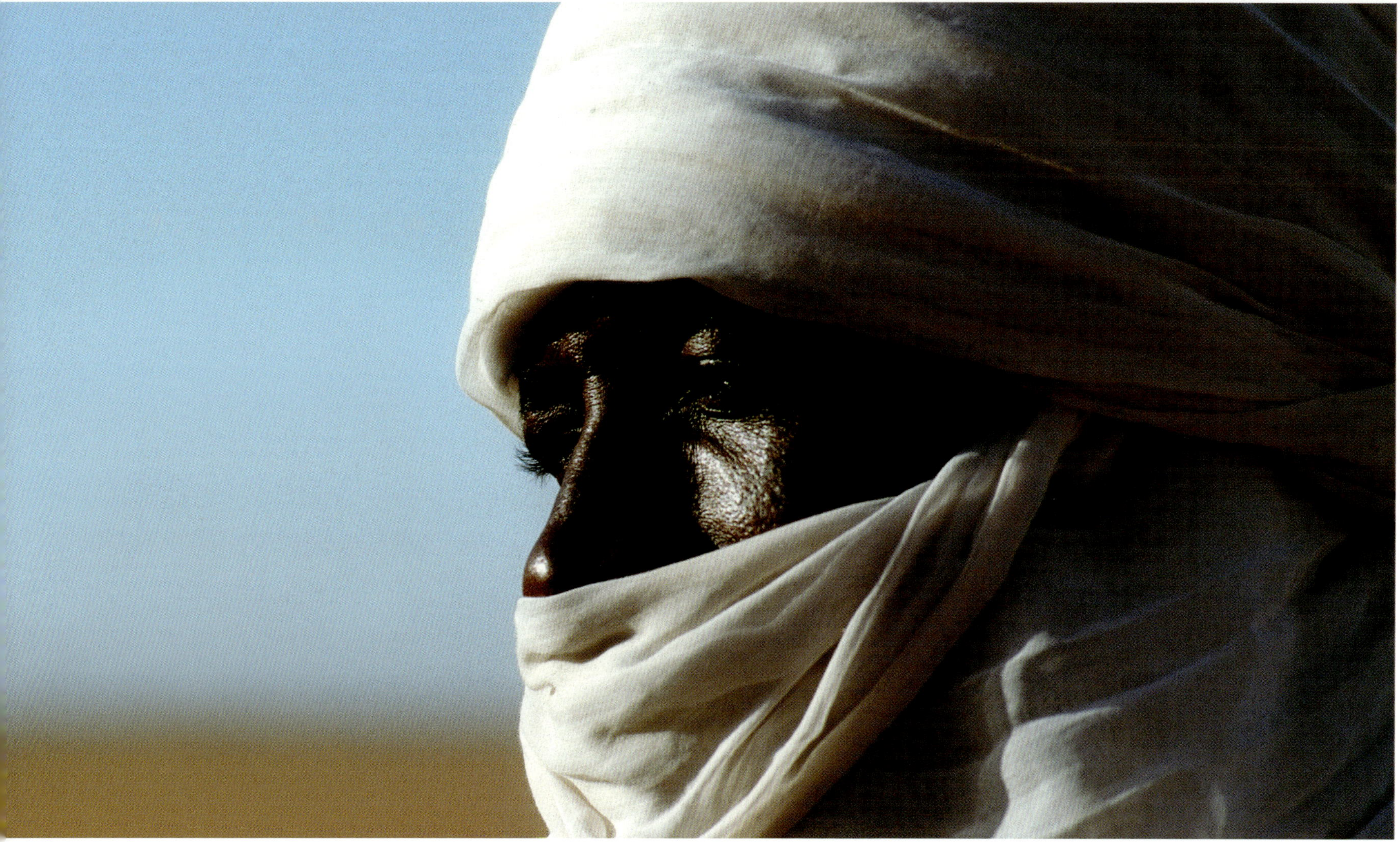

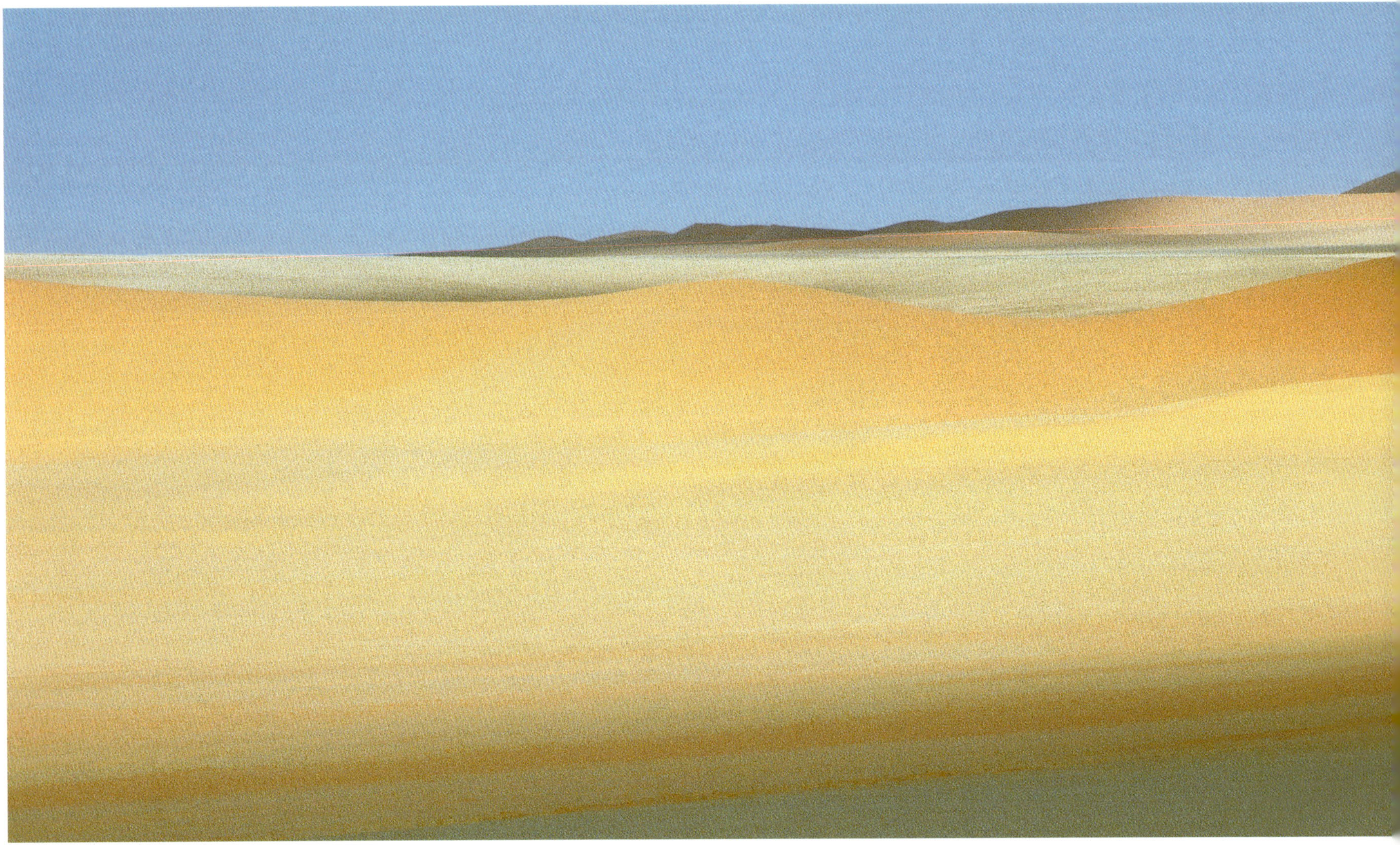

14 Erg Murzuk, Libya

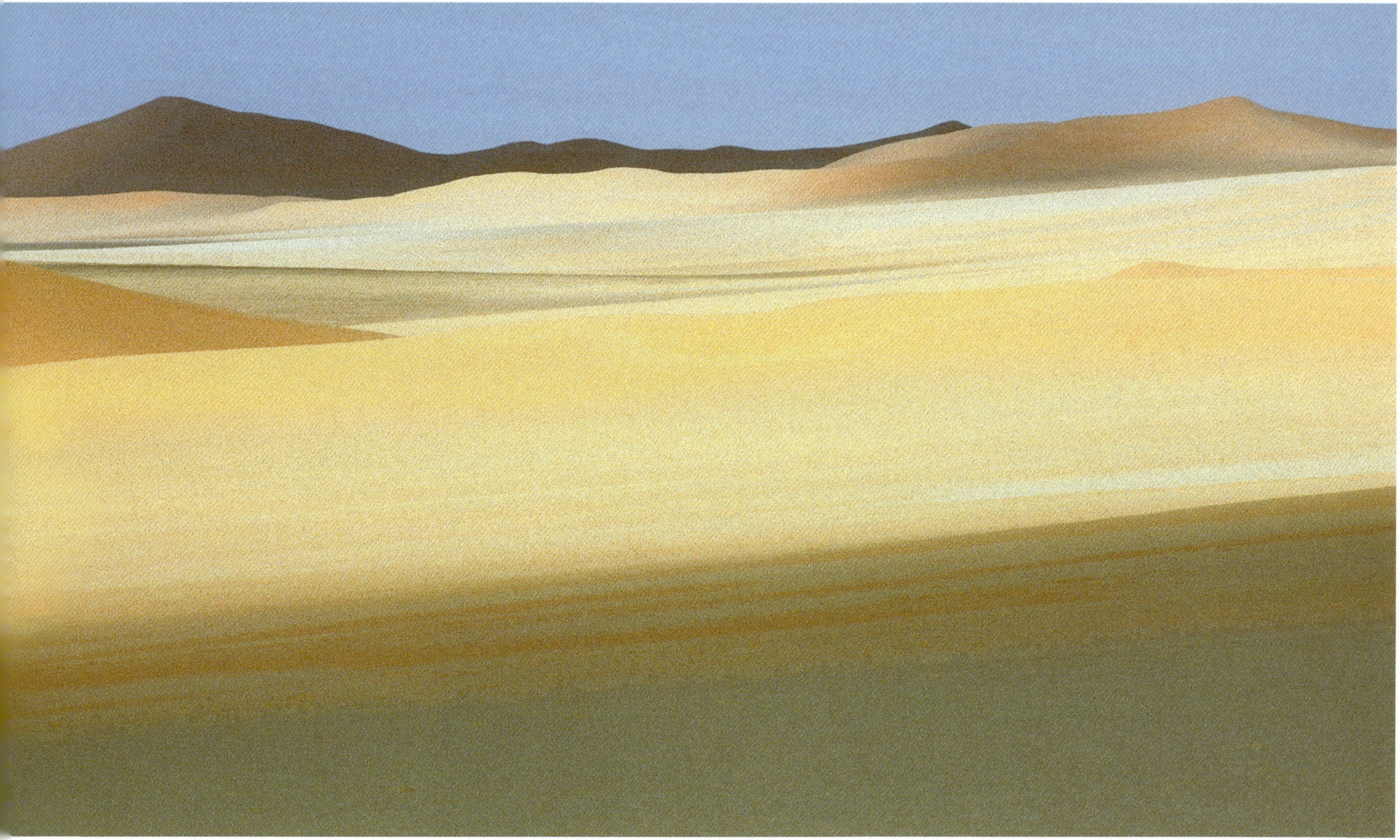

► **15** White Desert, Egypt

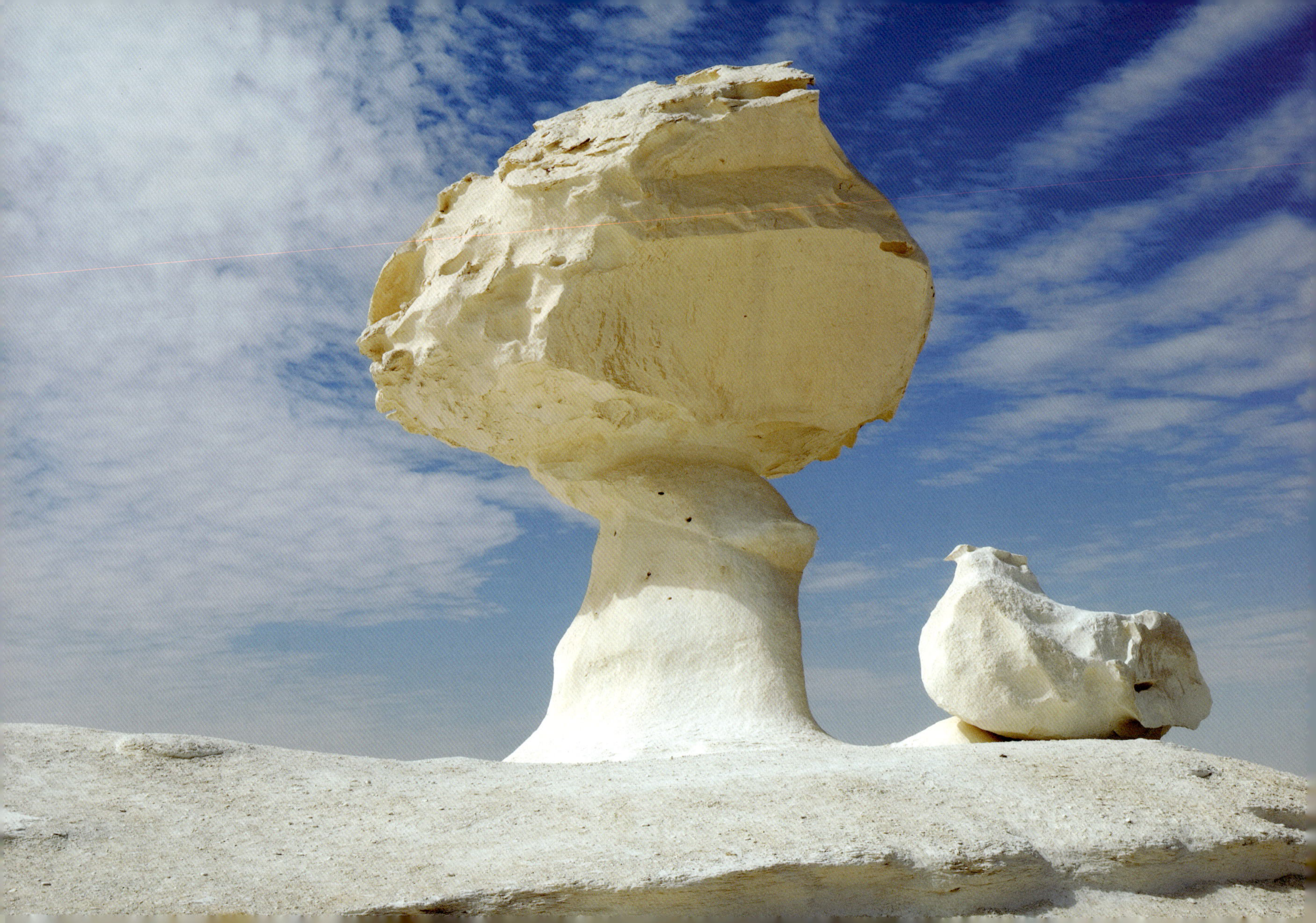

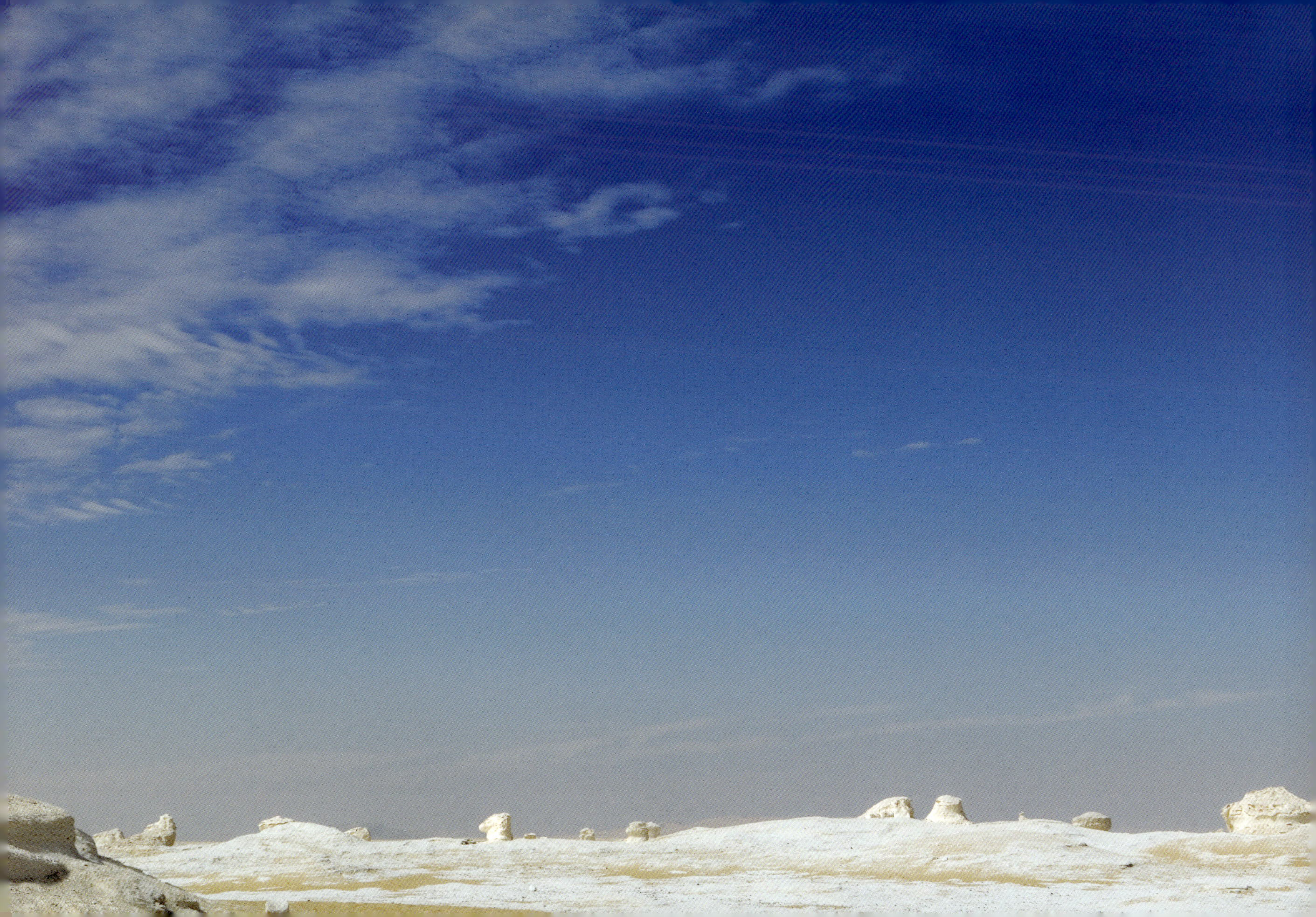

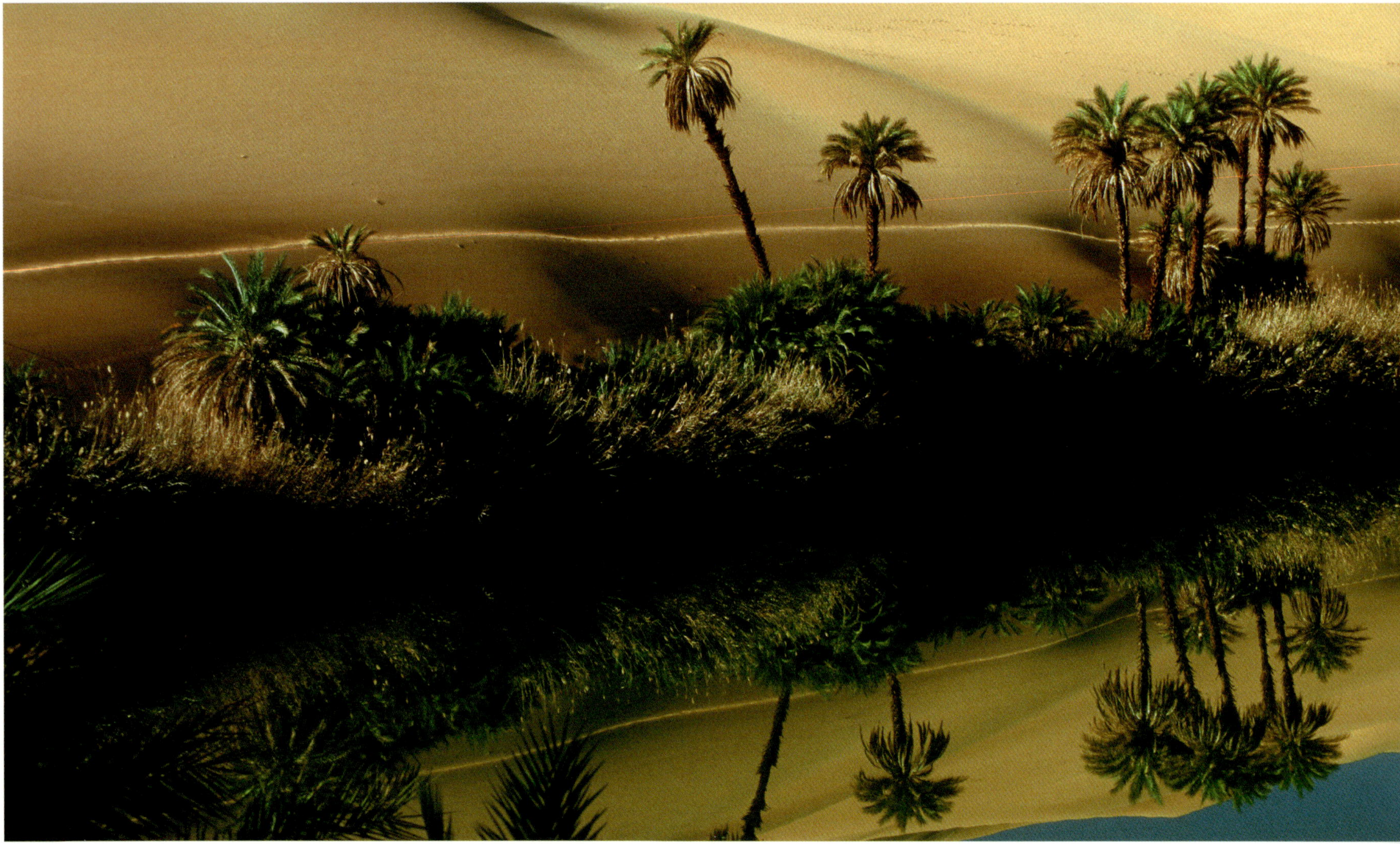

16 Um el Ma, Libya

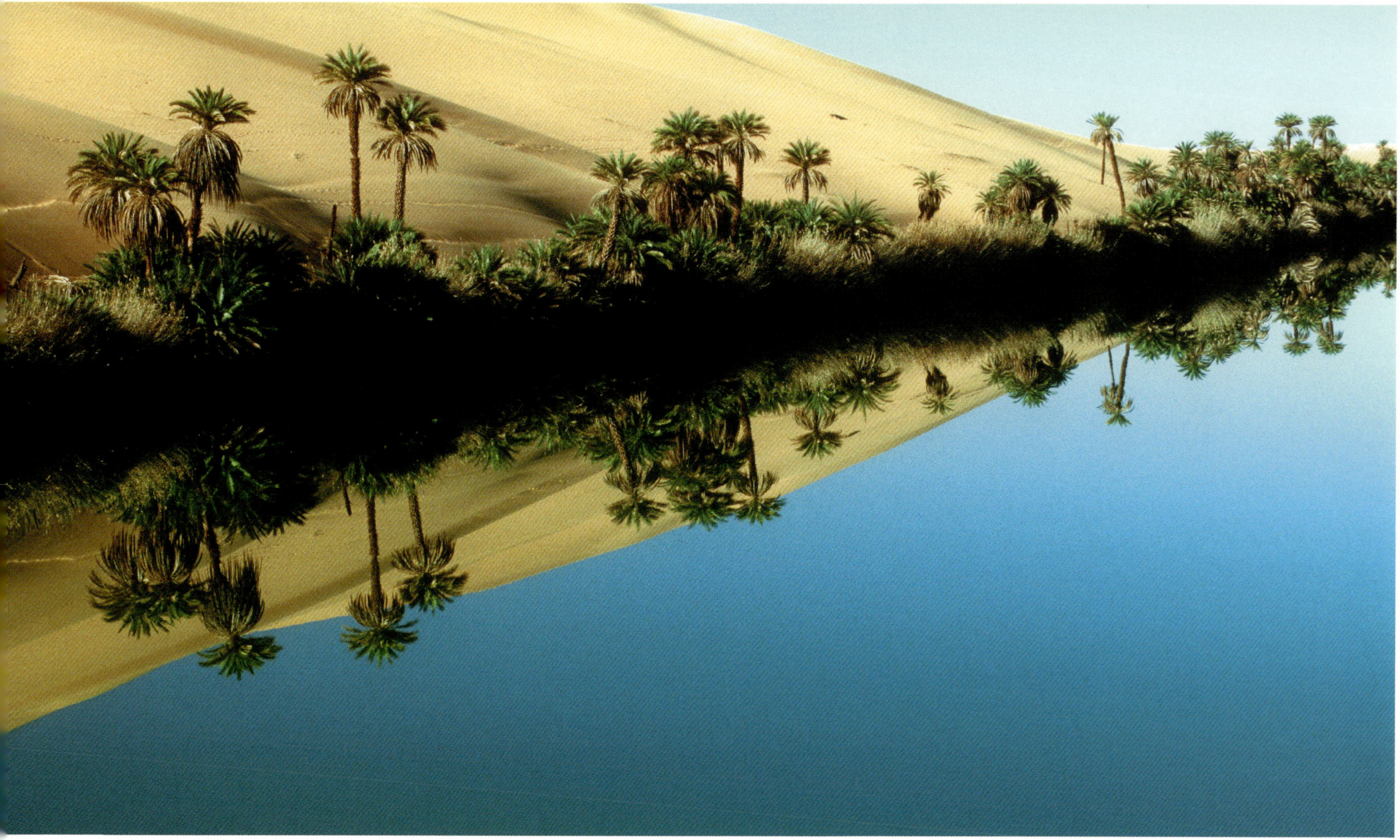

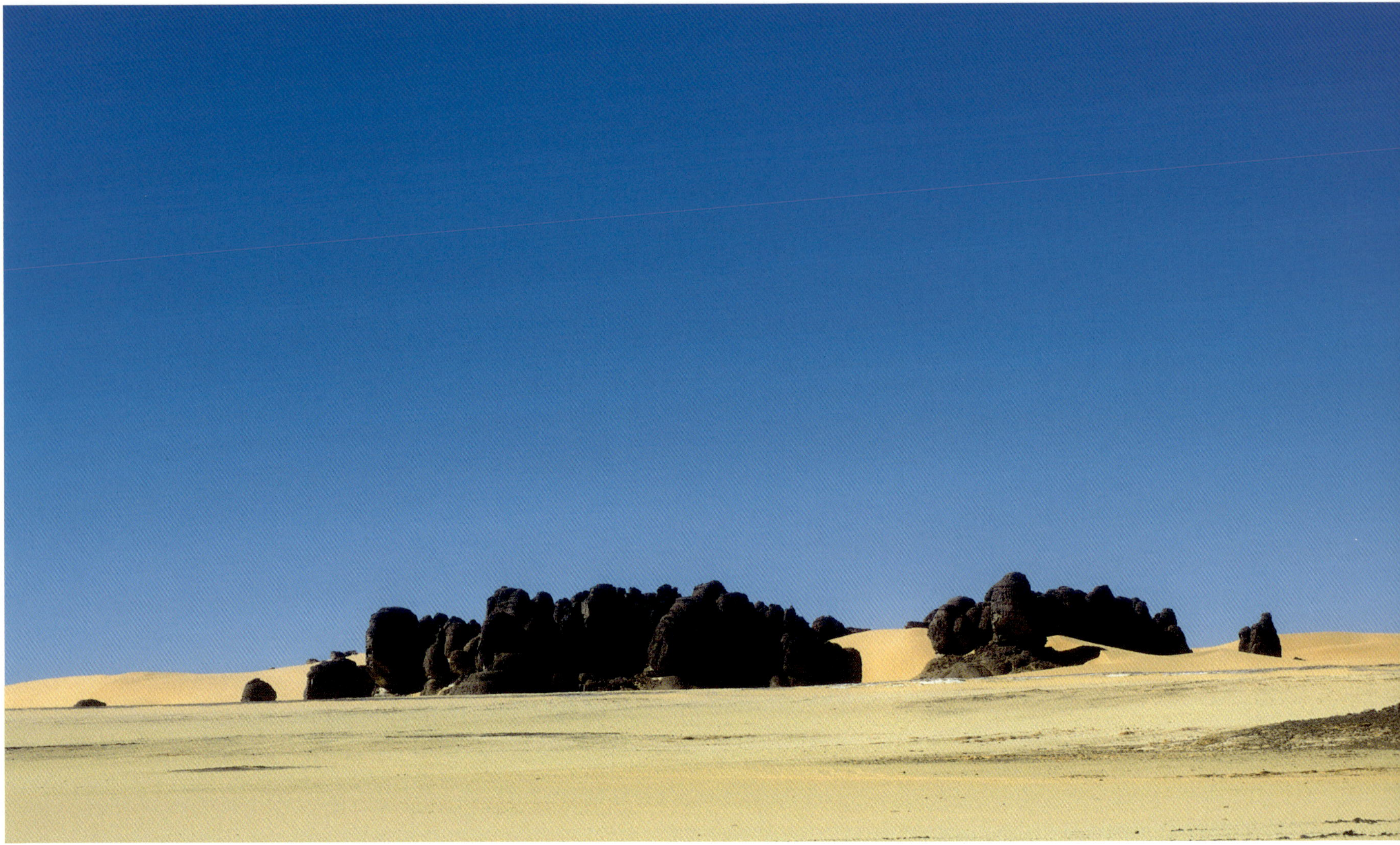

17 Rock formation on the way to Jabal al Awaynat, Libya

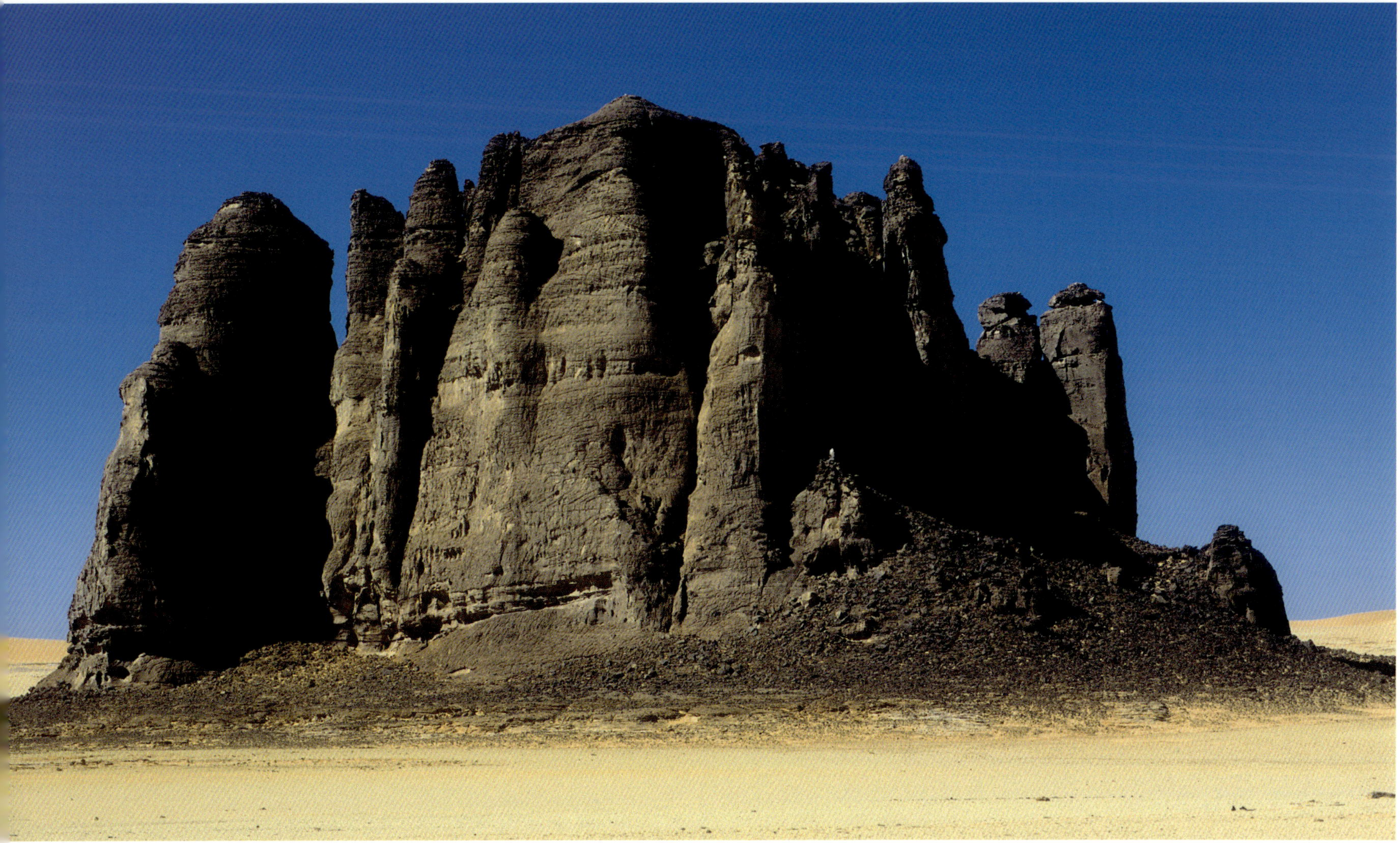

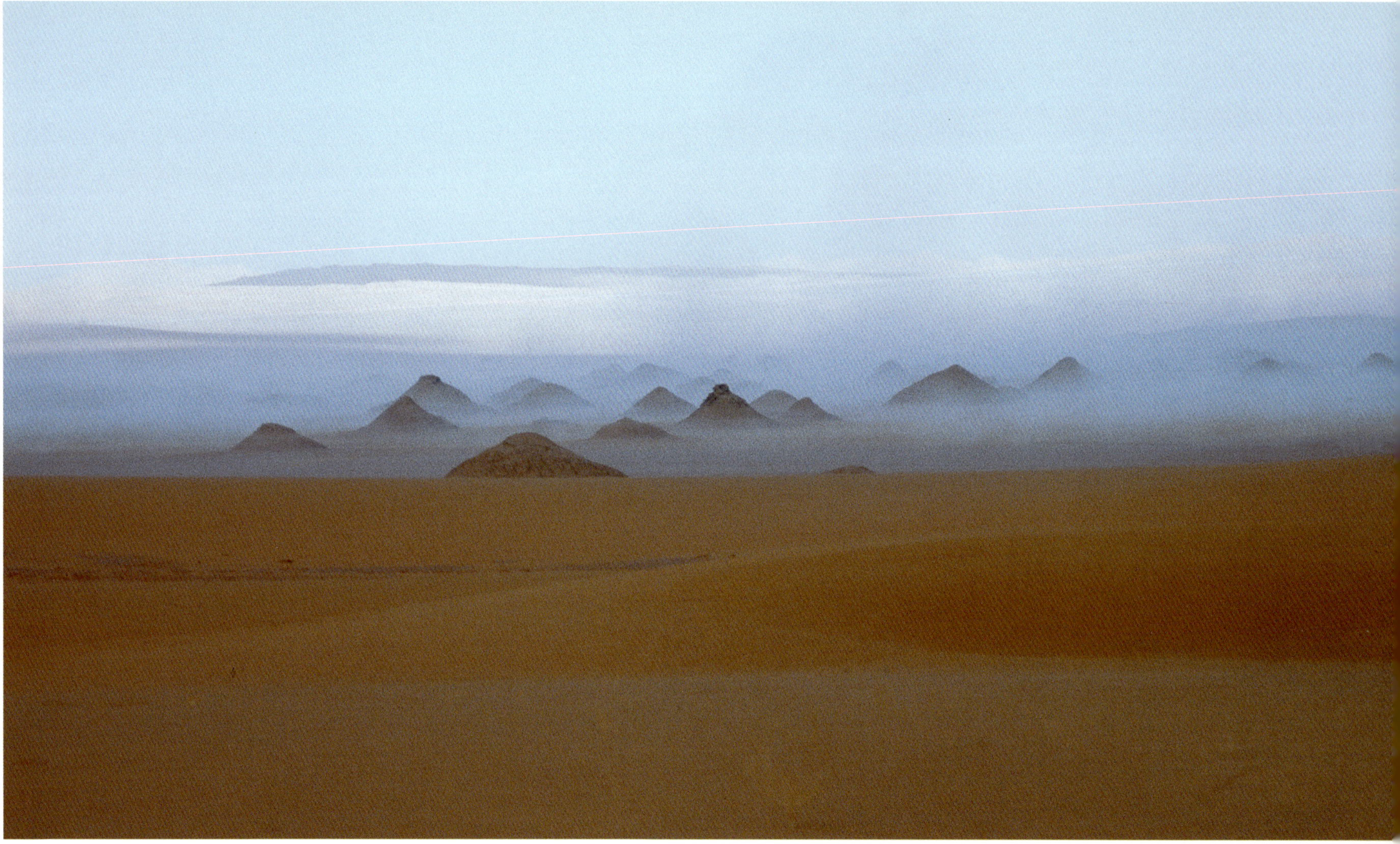

18 Sandstorm at Libyan-Agerian border

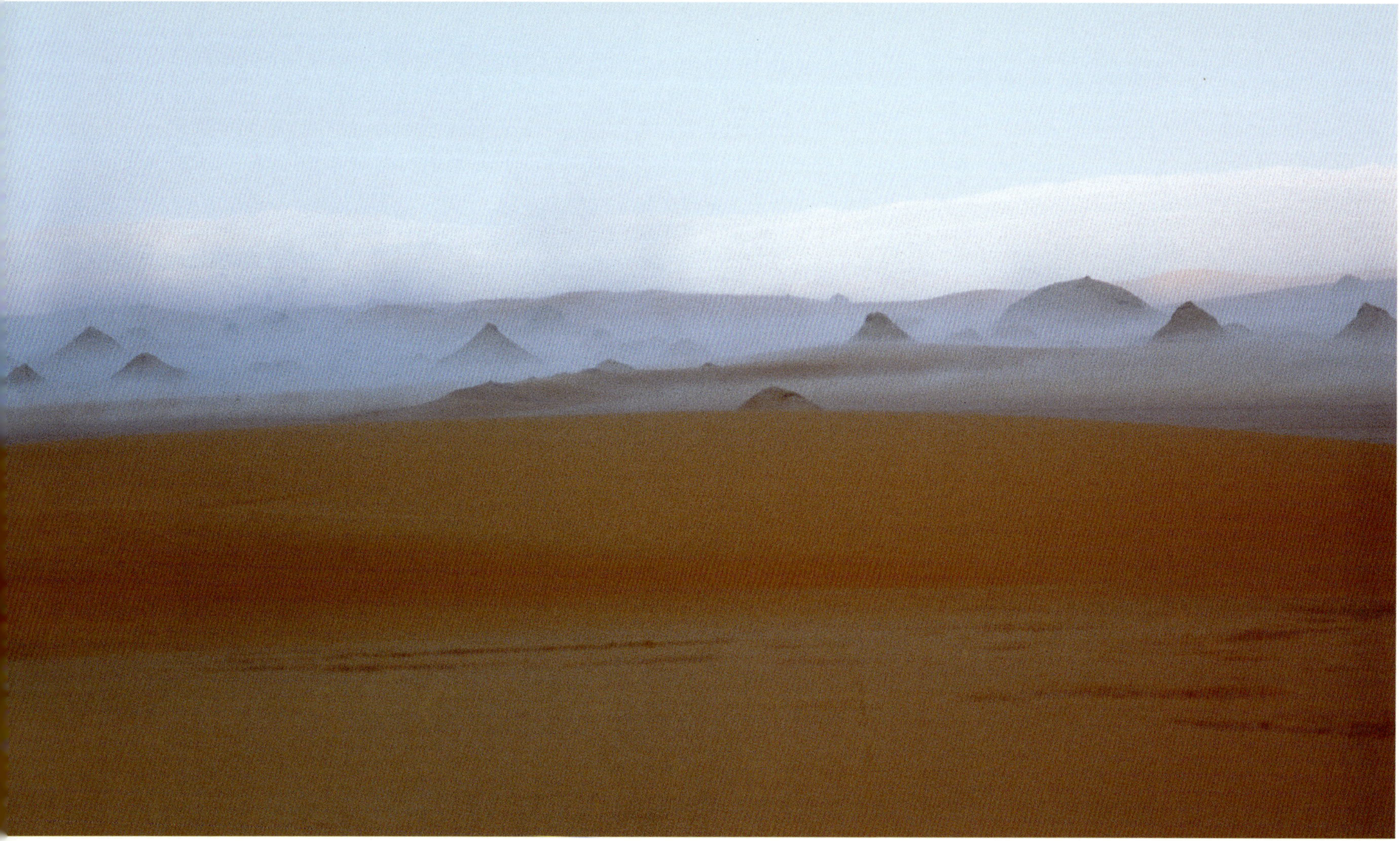

► **19** Wau an Namus, Libya

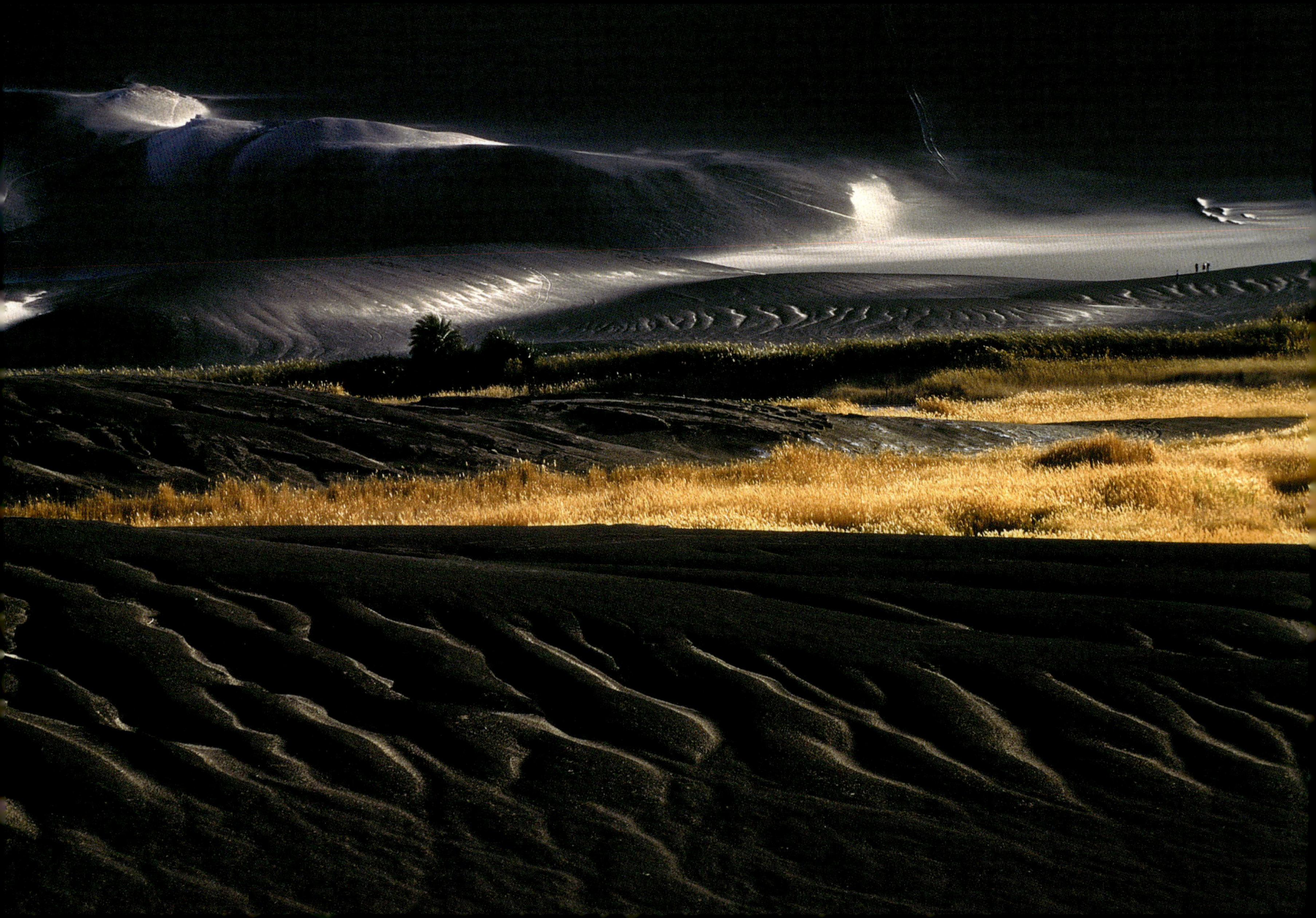

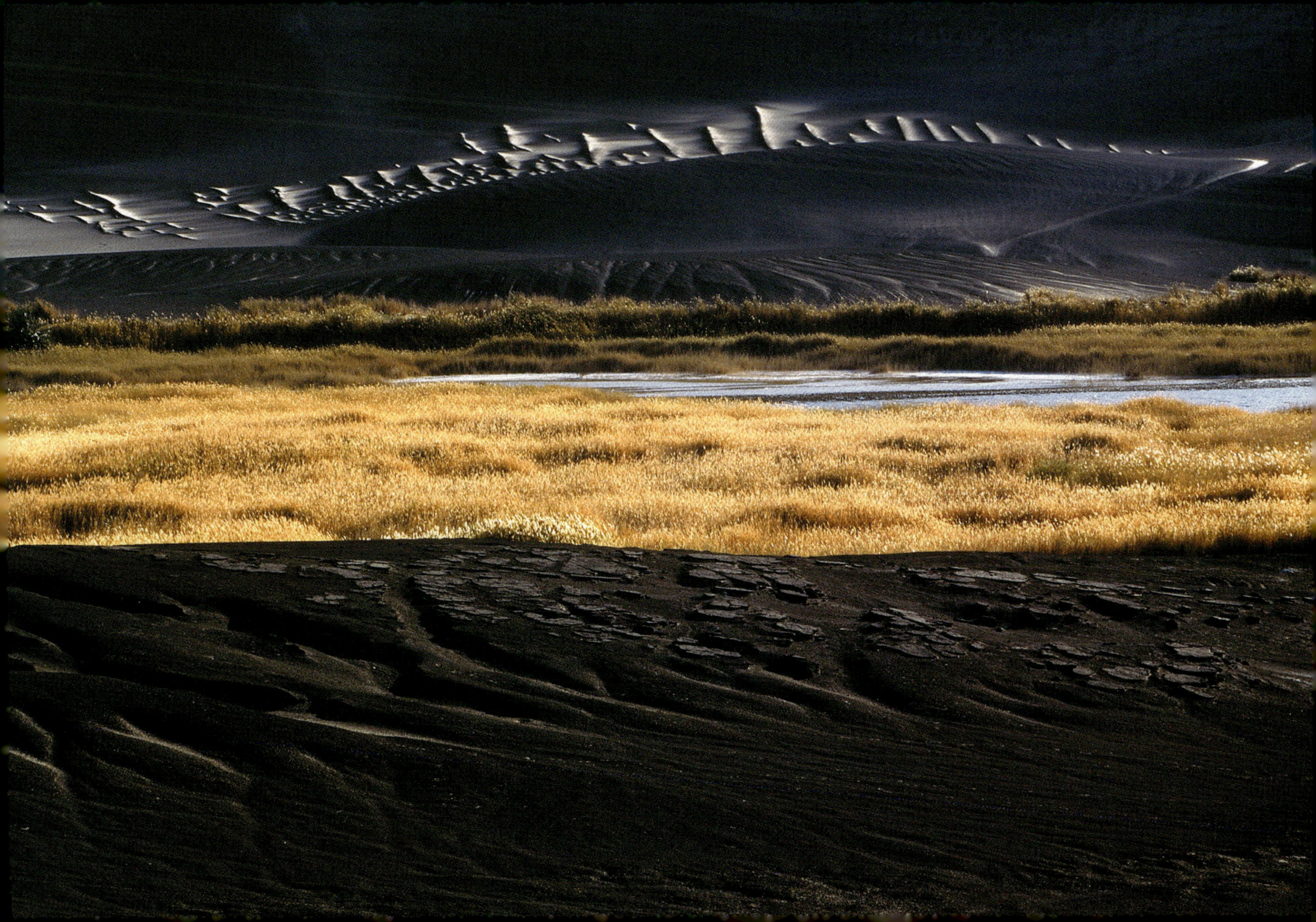

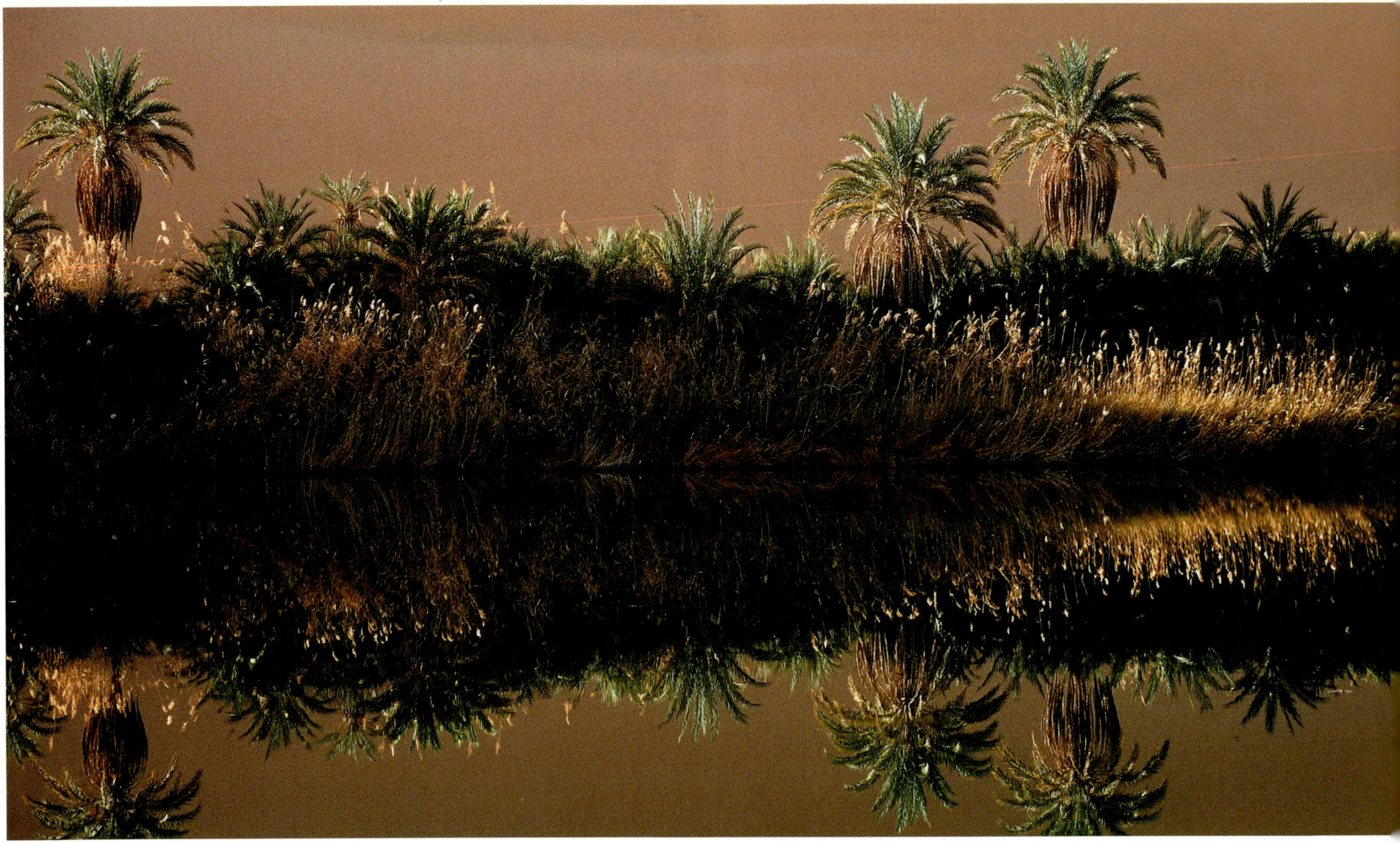

20 Lake Gabroon, Erg Ubari, Libya

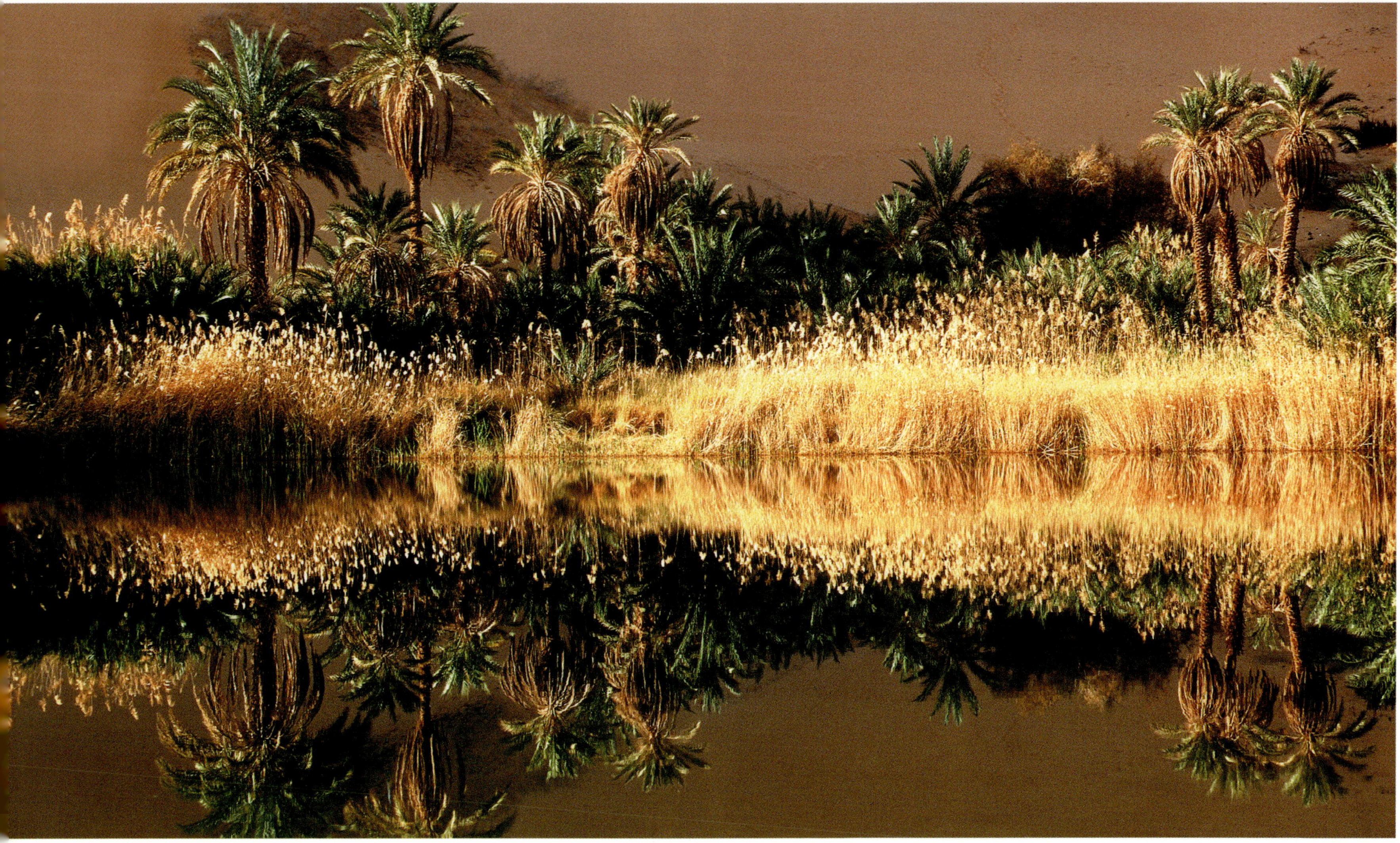

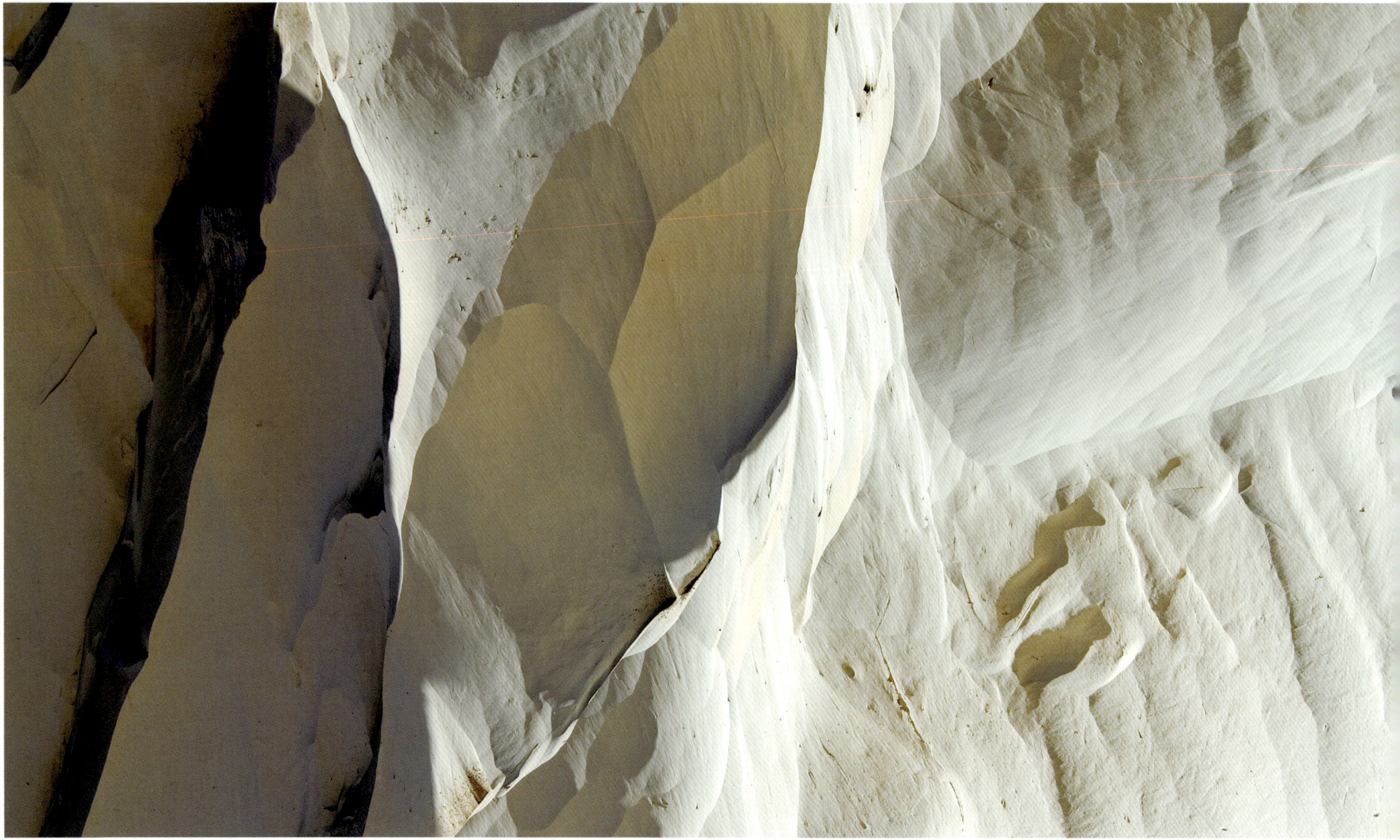

21 White Desert, Egypt

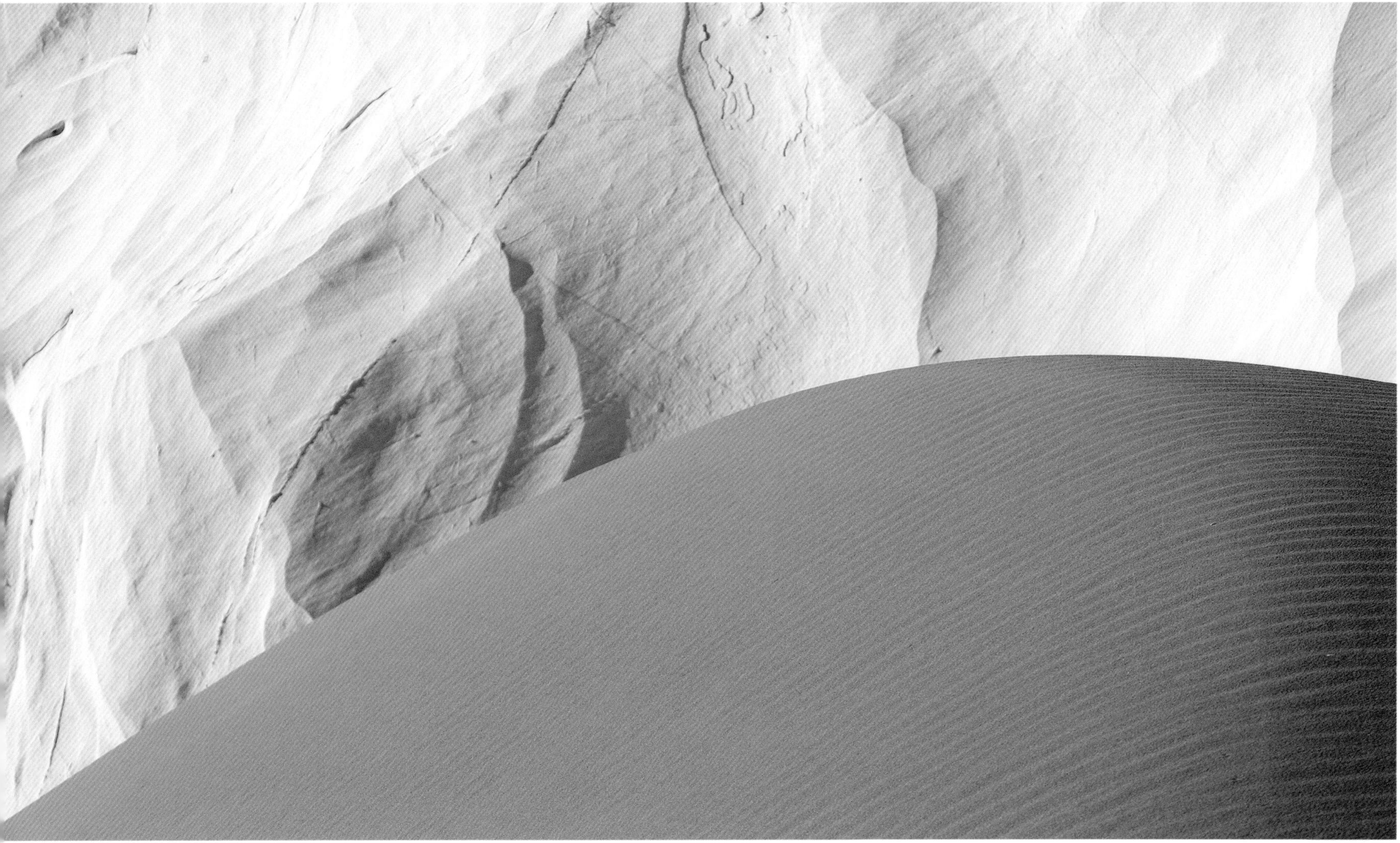

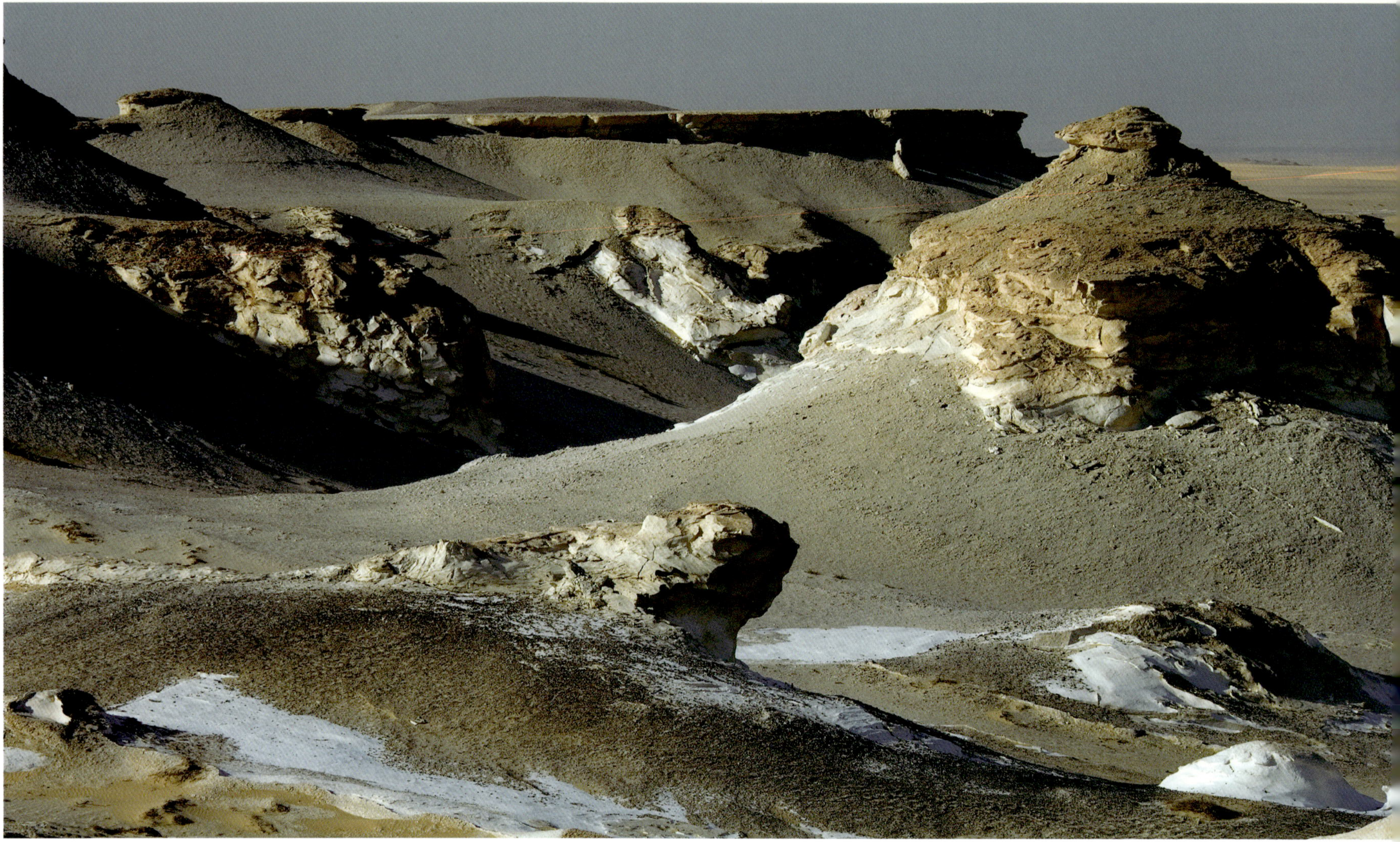

22 White Desert, Egypt

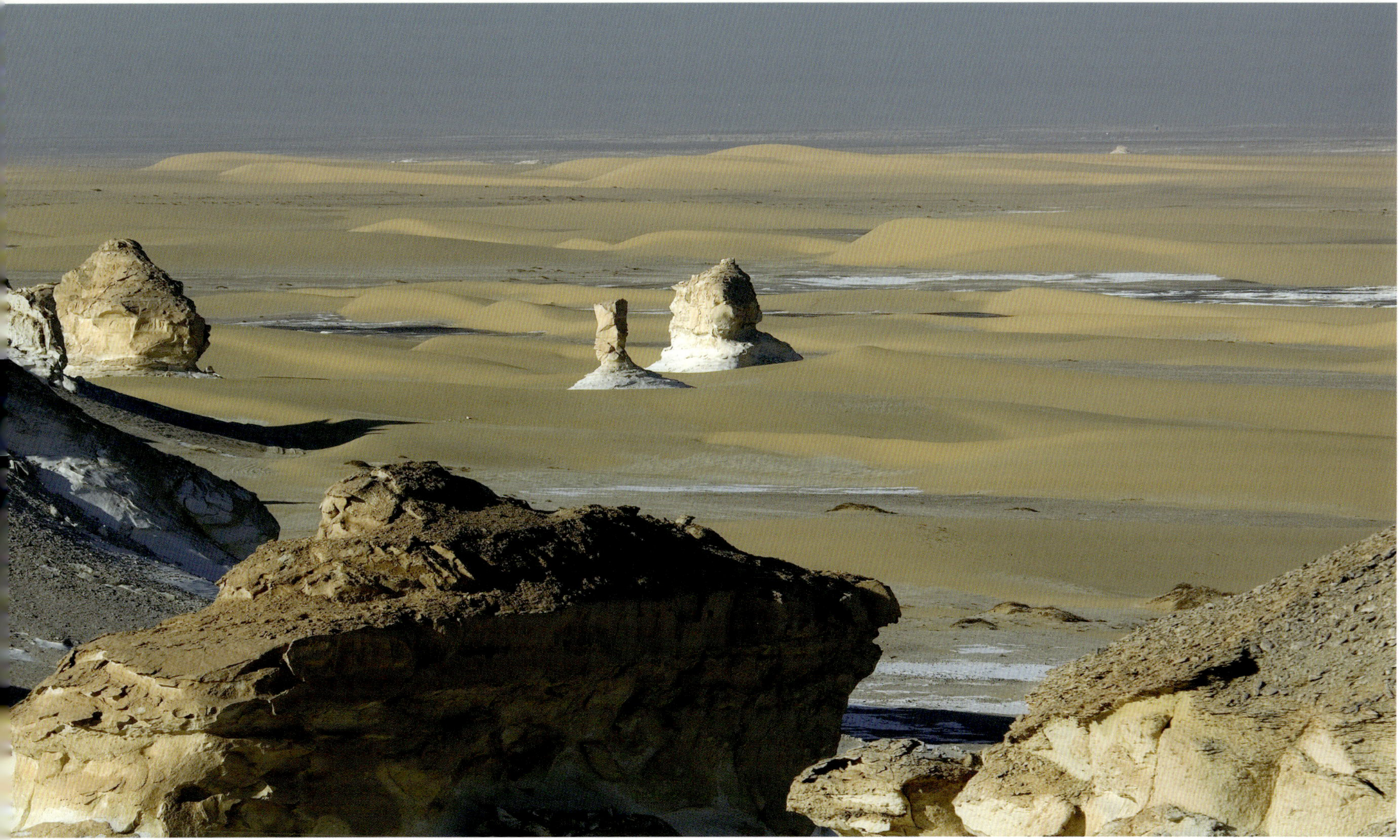

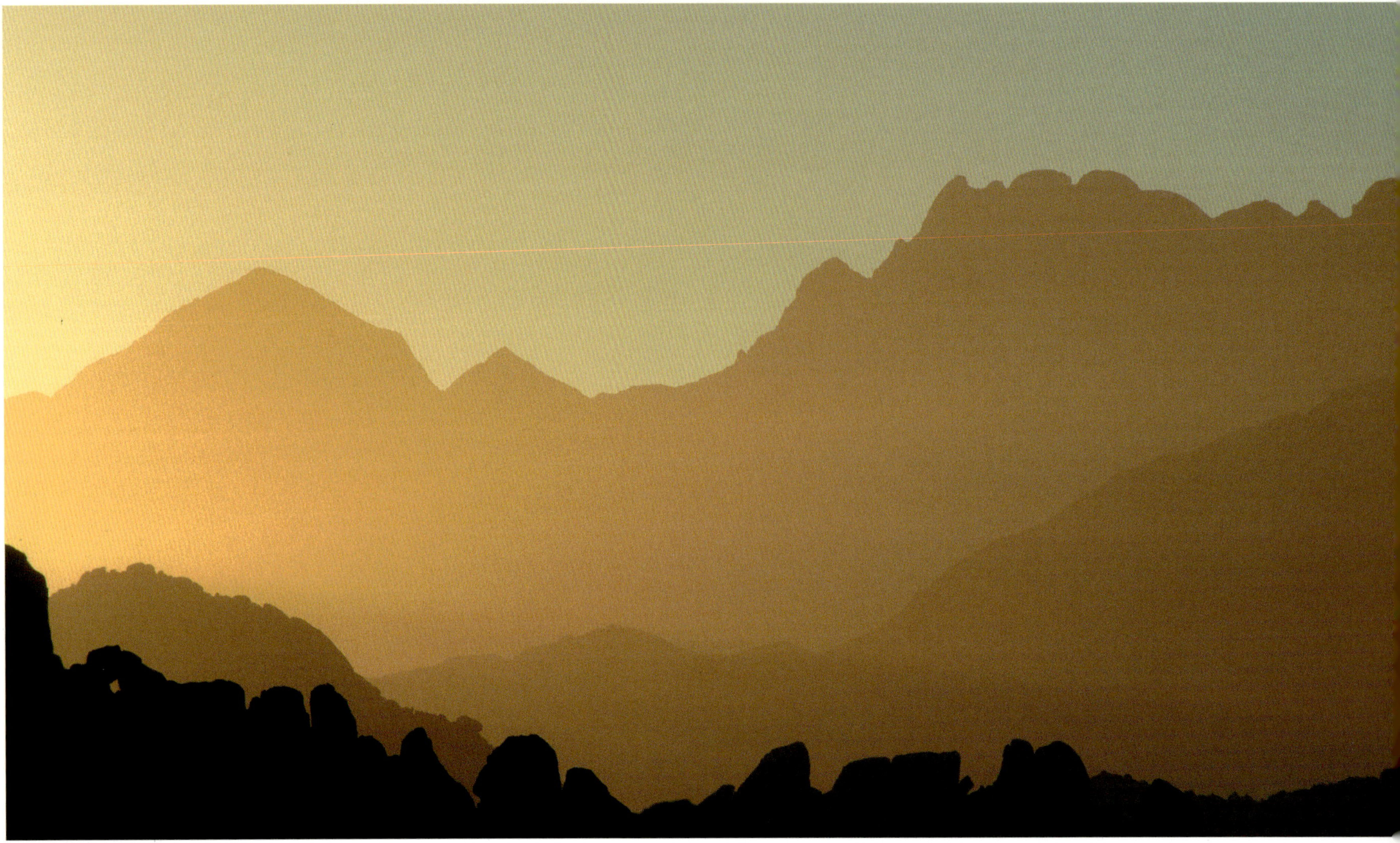

23 Jabal al Awaynat, Libya

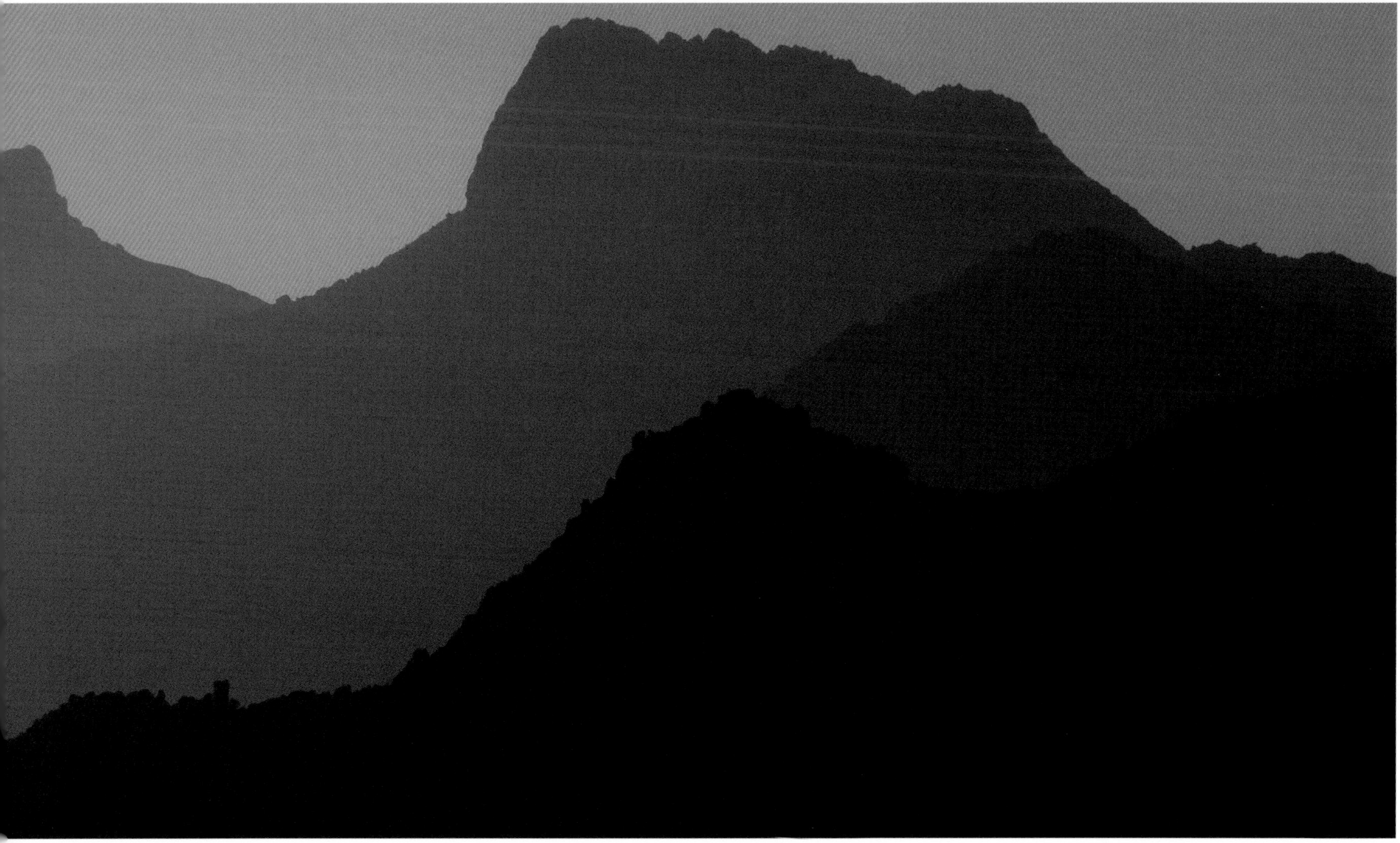

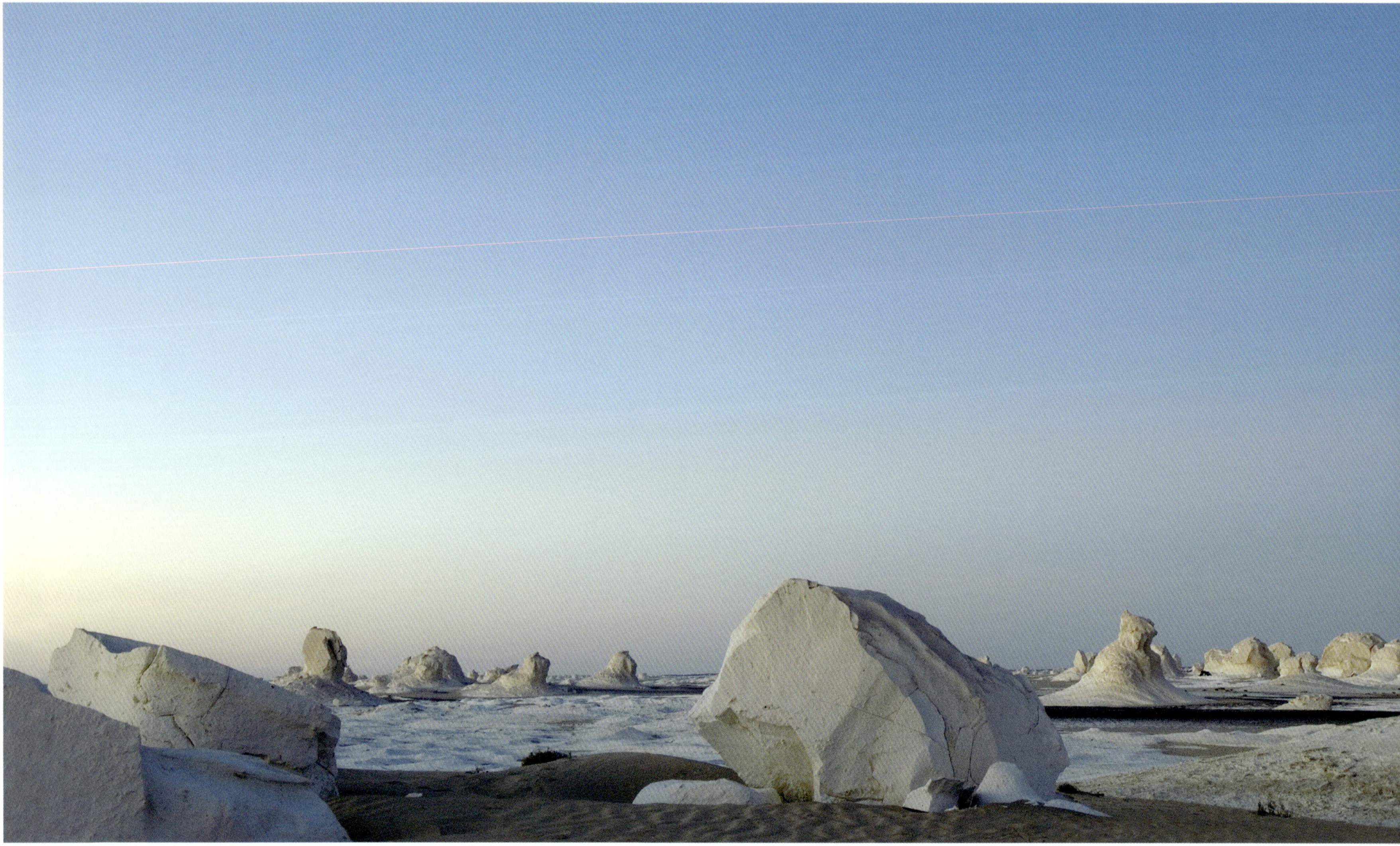

24 White Desert, Egypt

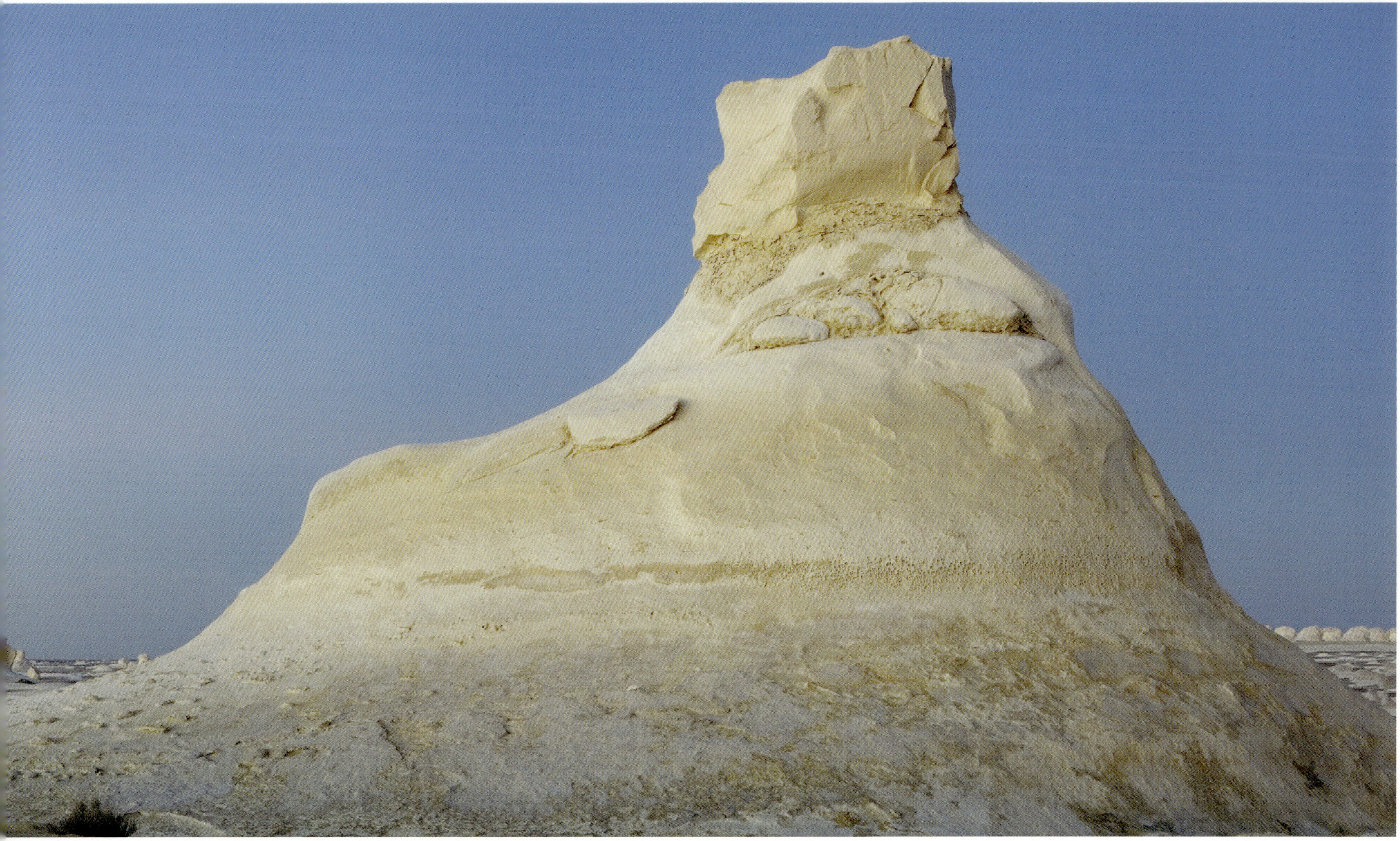

► 25 Erg Ubari, Libya

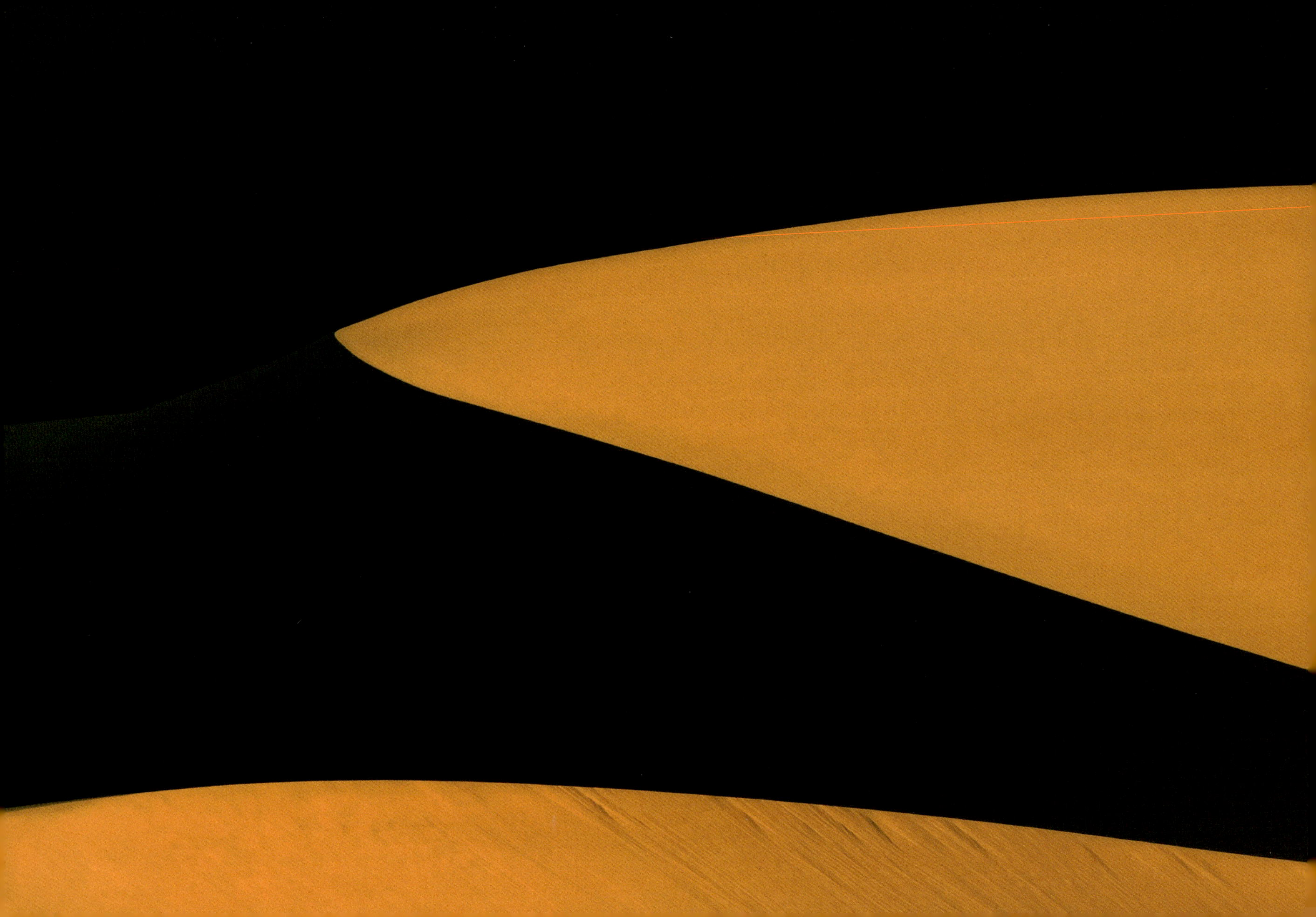

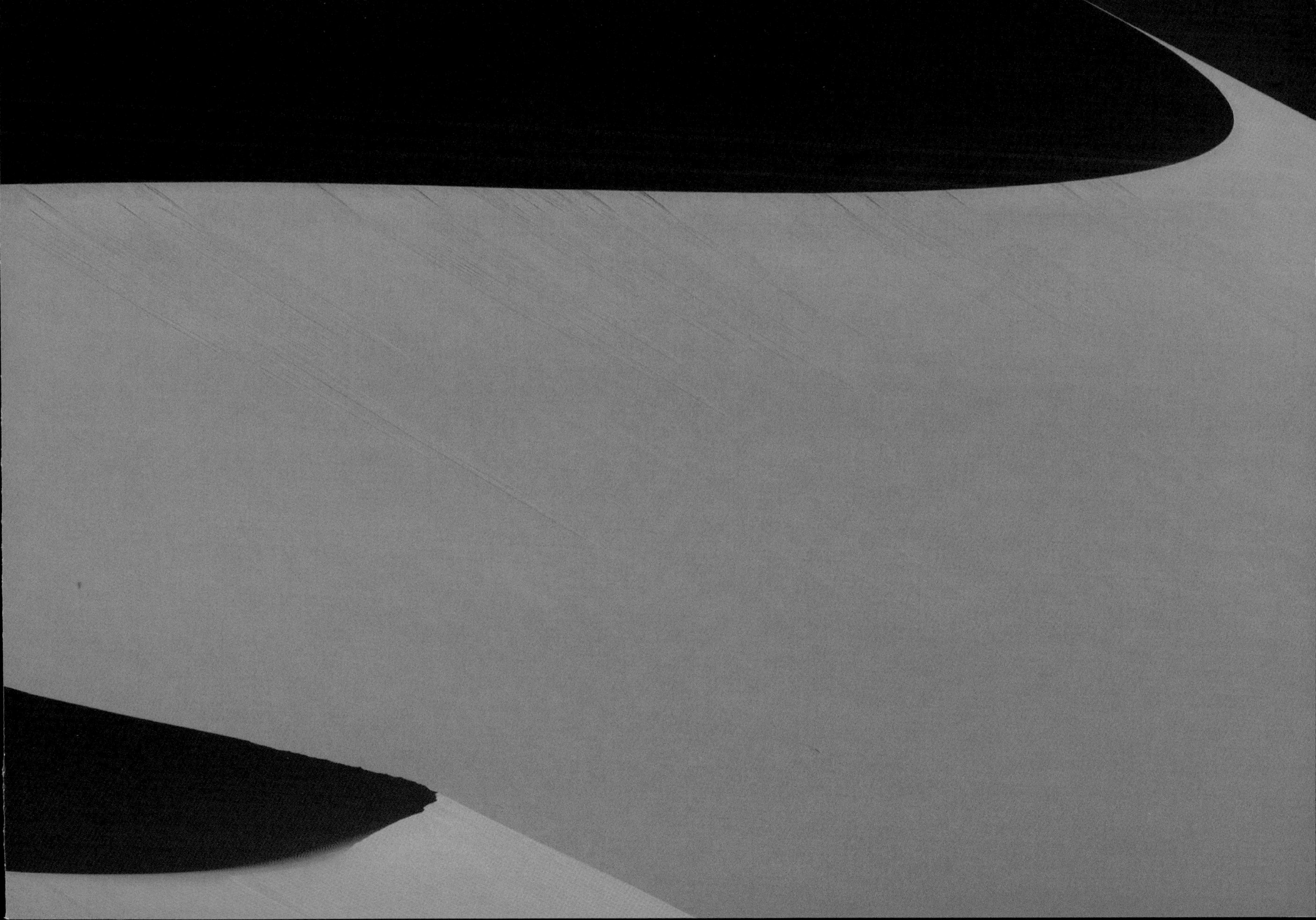

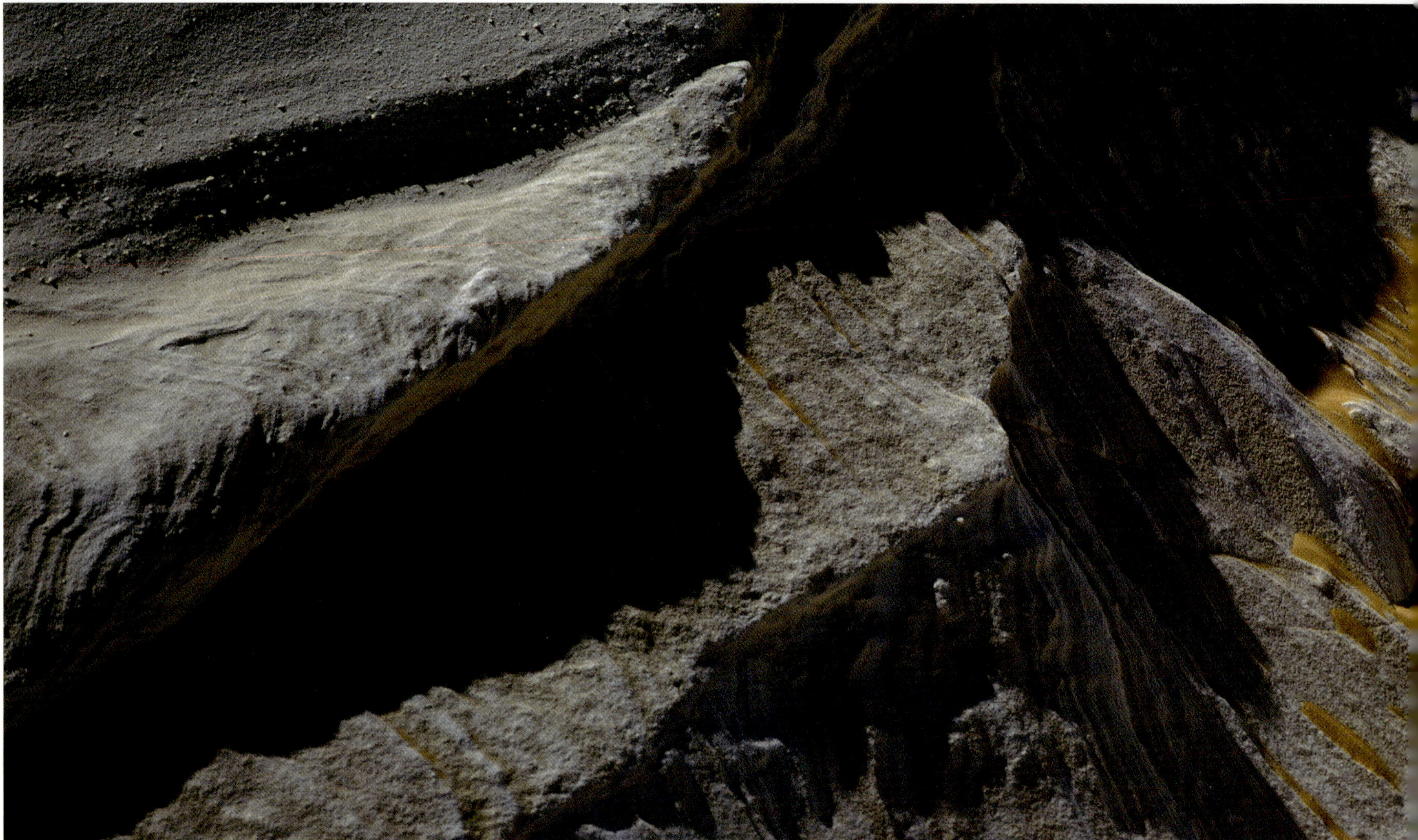

26 Rock formation, Al Awaynat, Libya

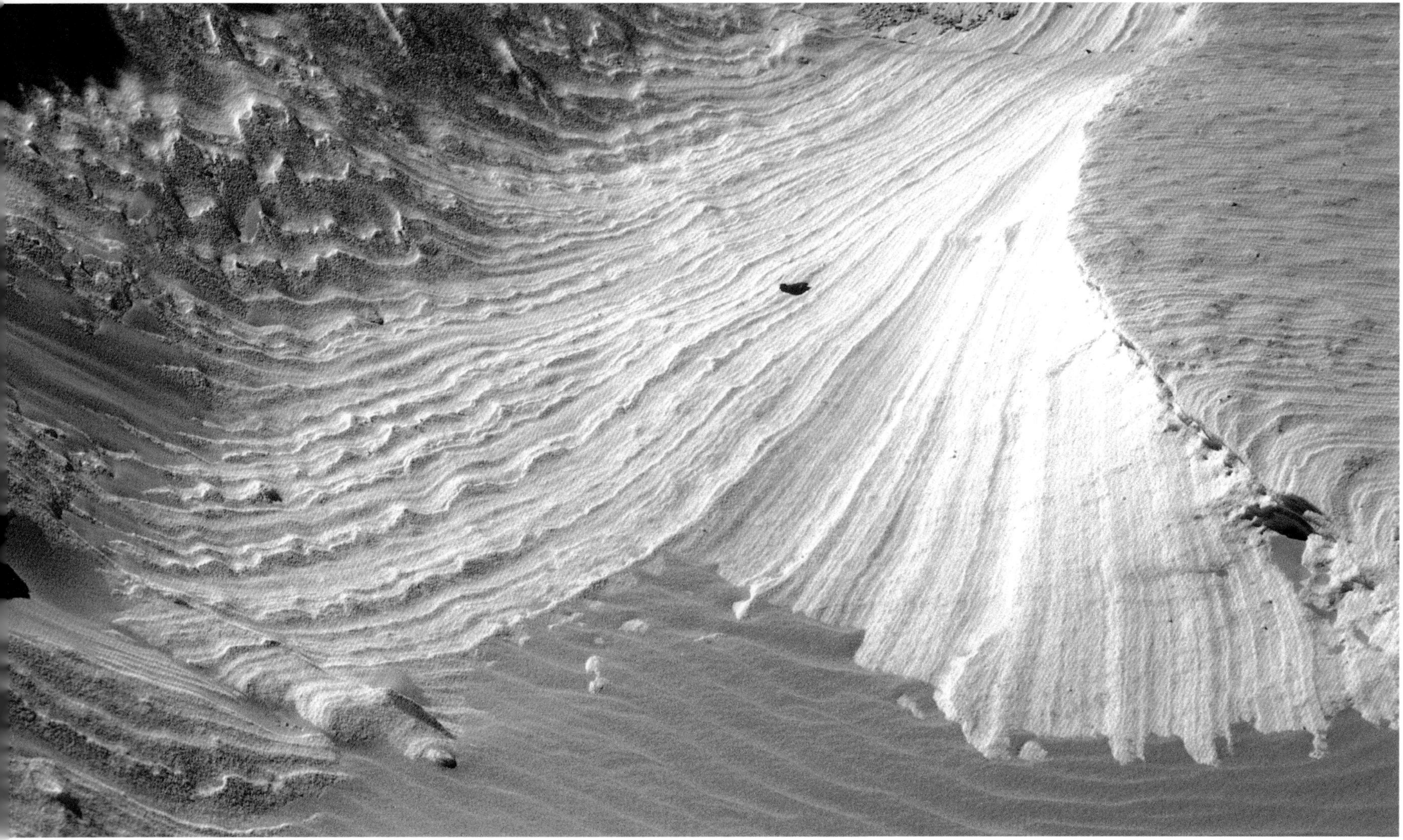

► **27** Rock formations in Oued Tagrira, Algeria

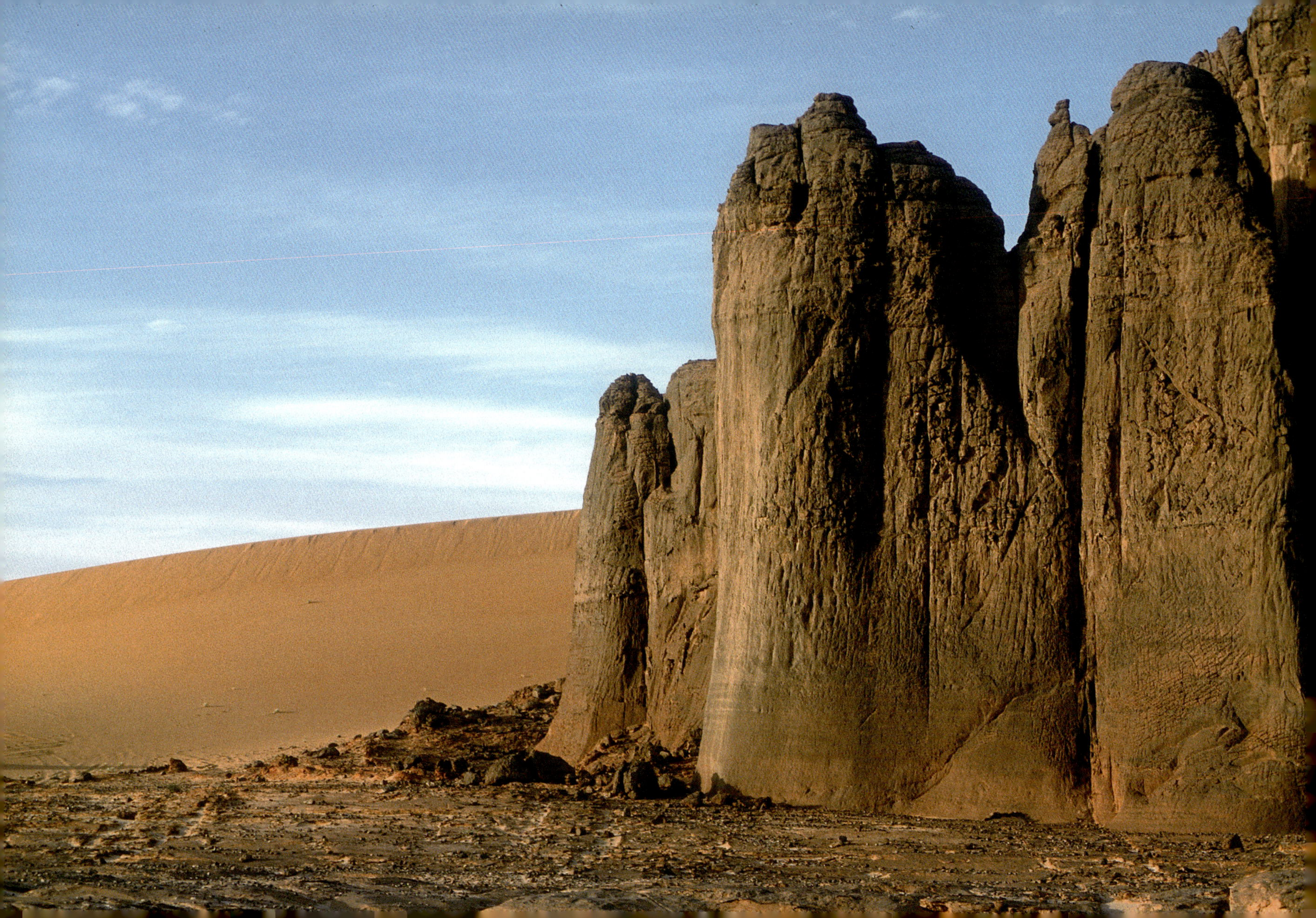

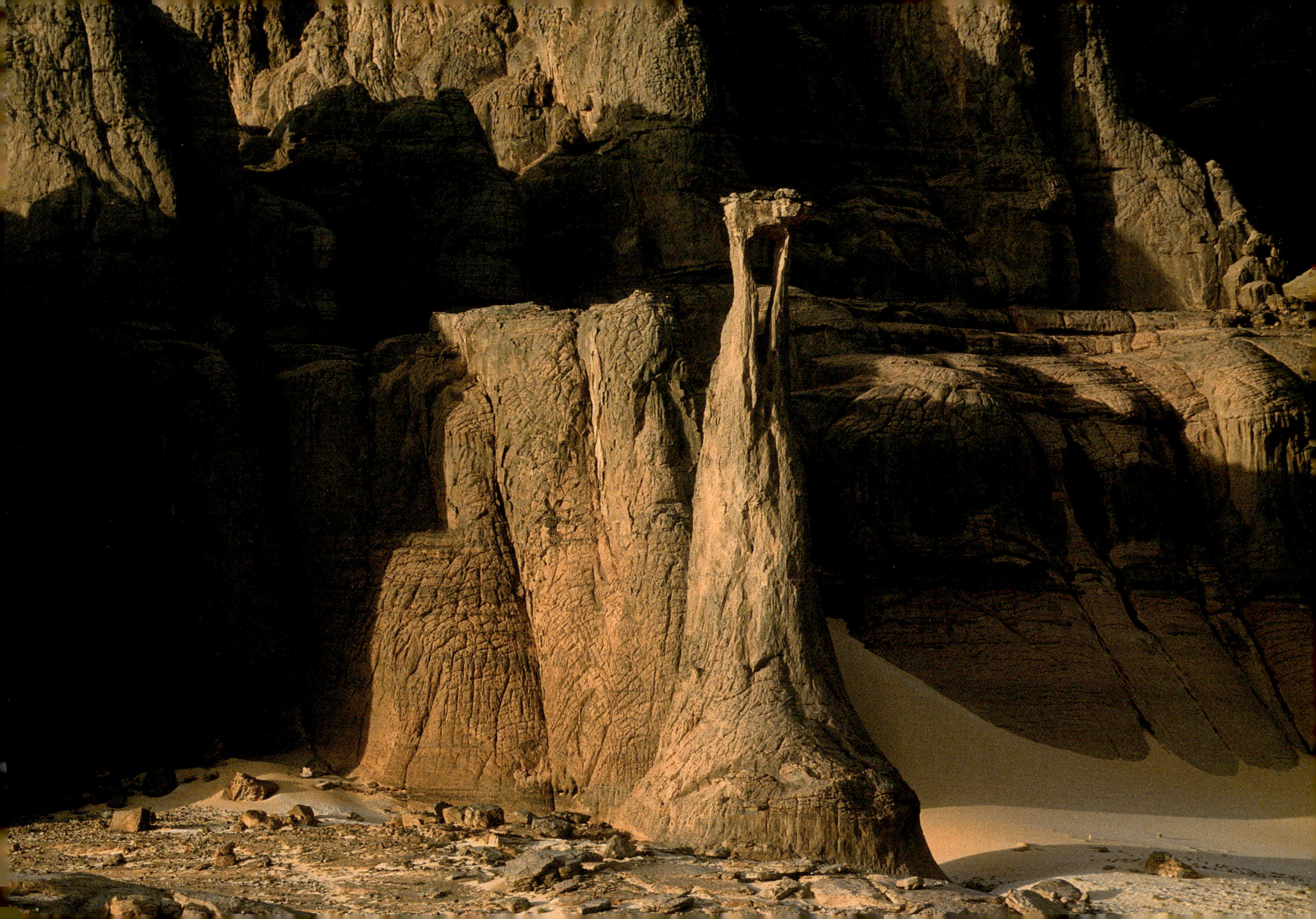

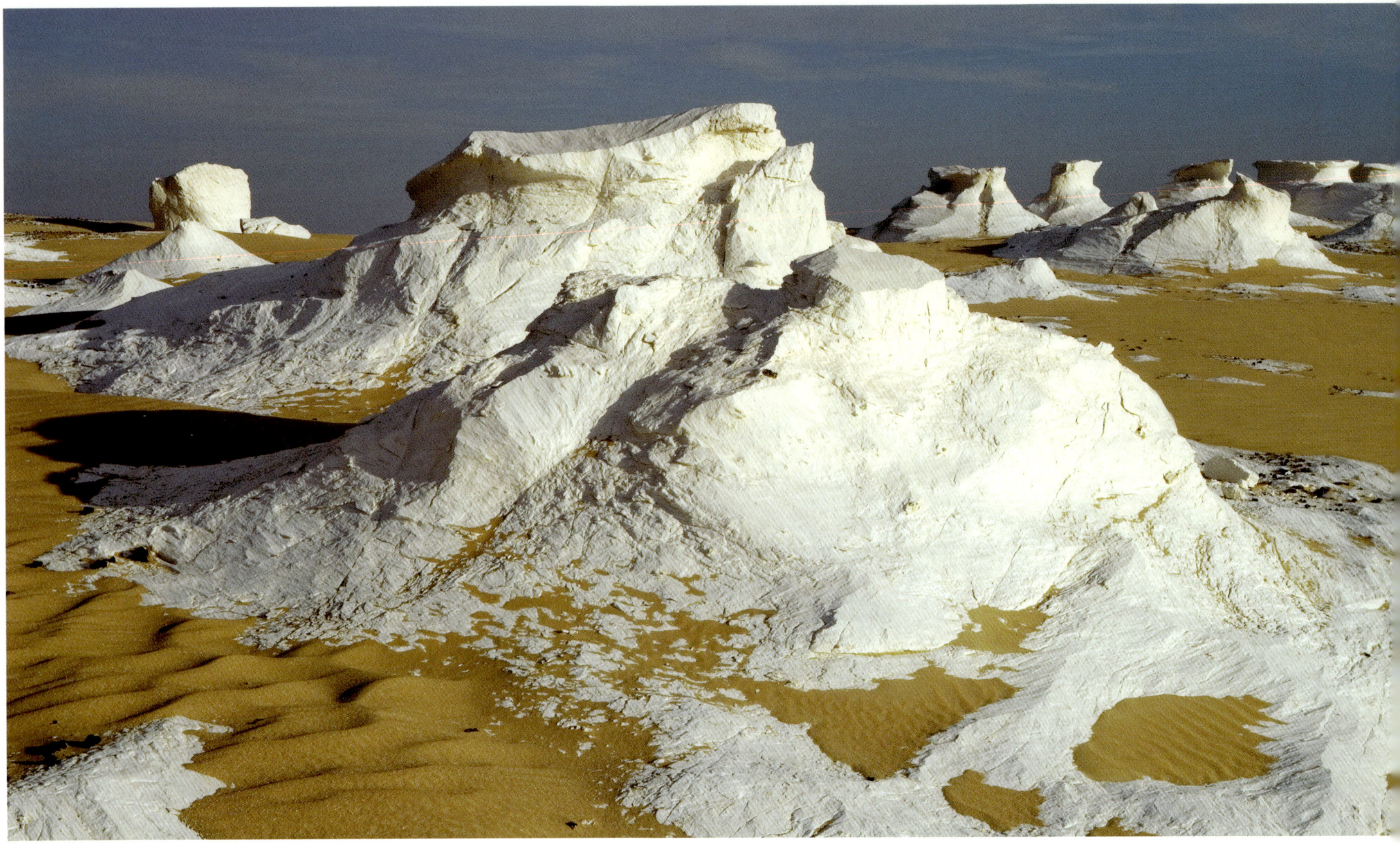

28 White Desert, Egypt

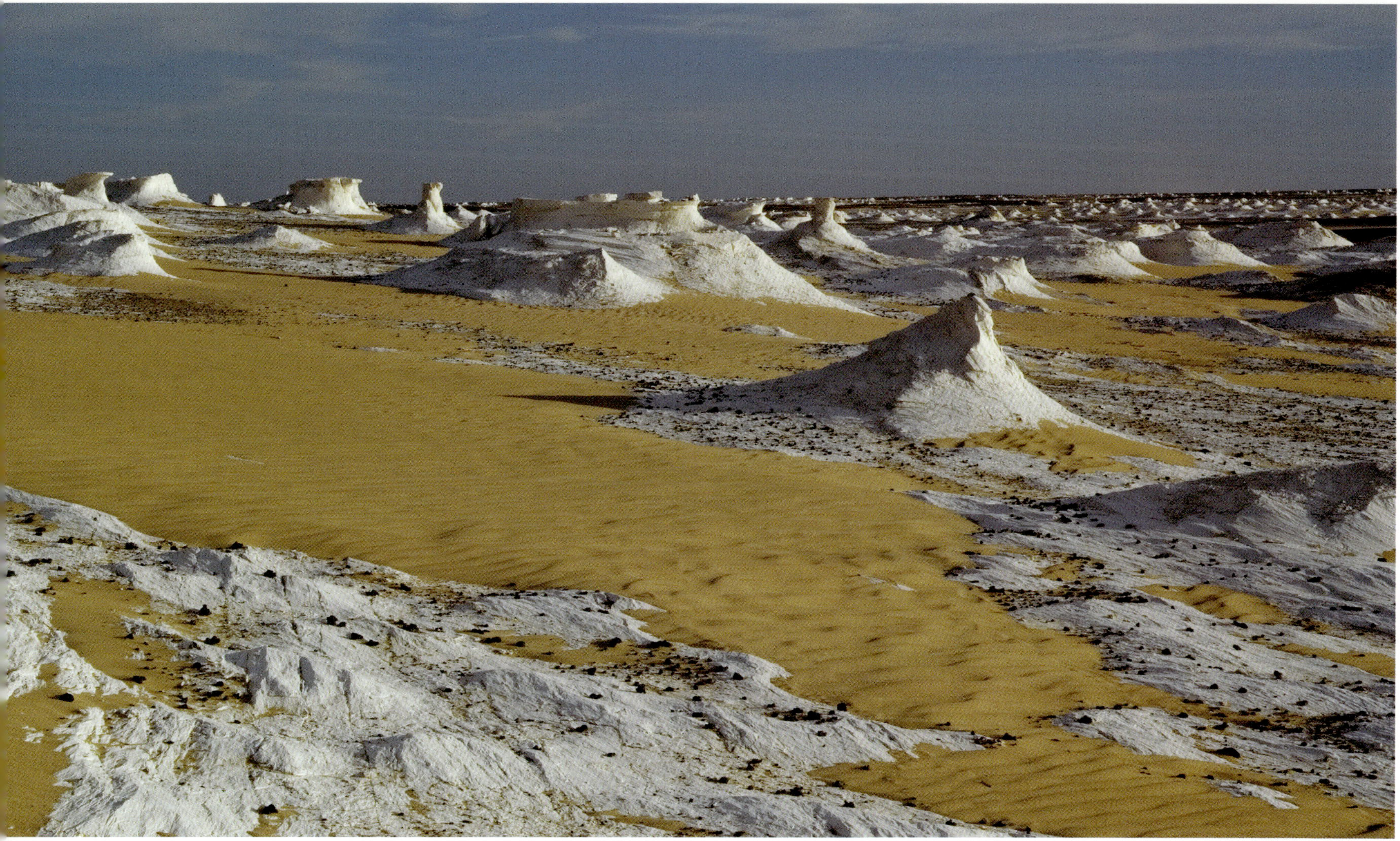

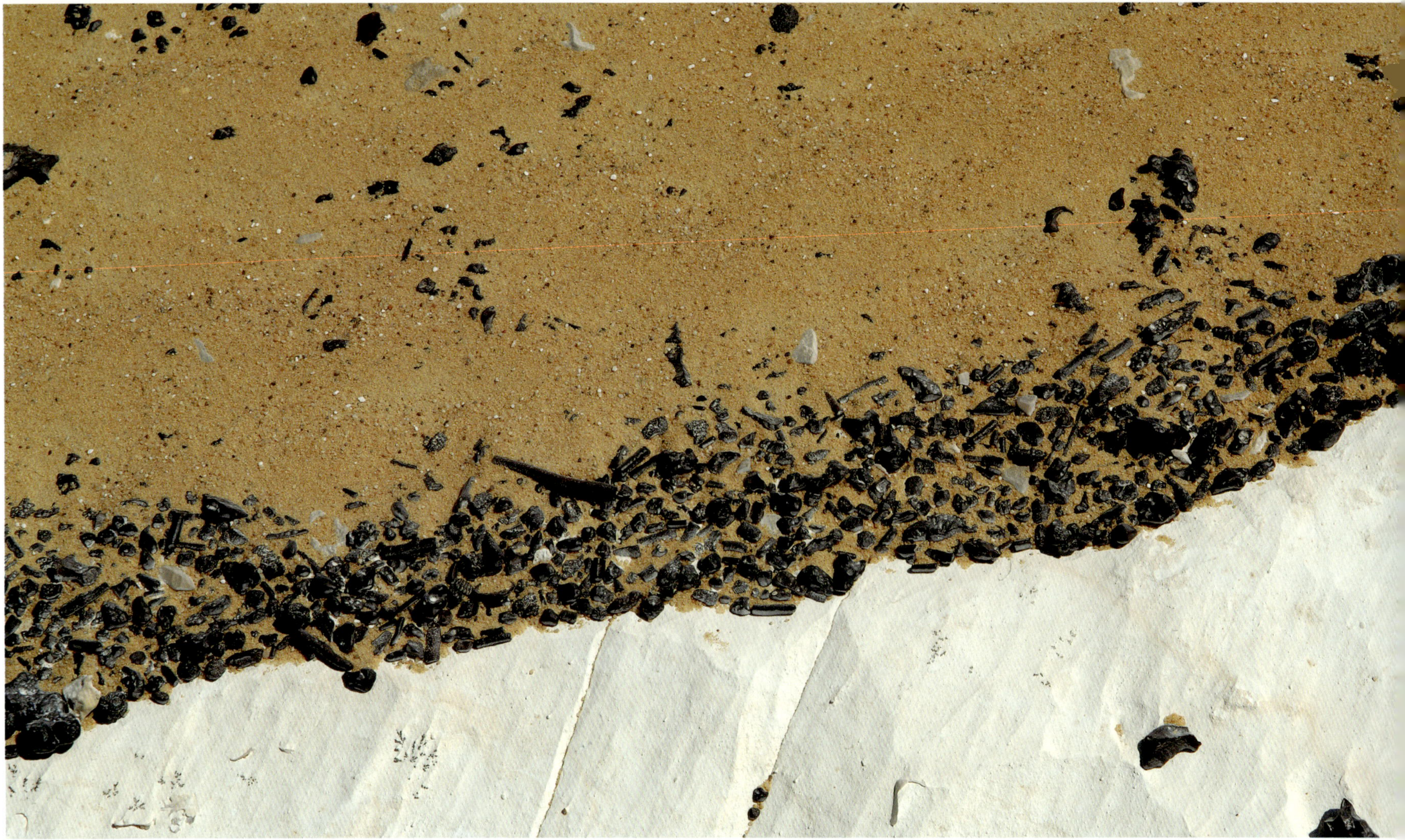

29 White Desert, Egypt

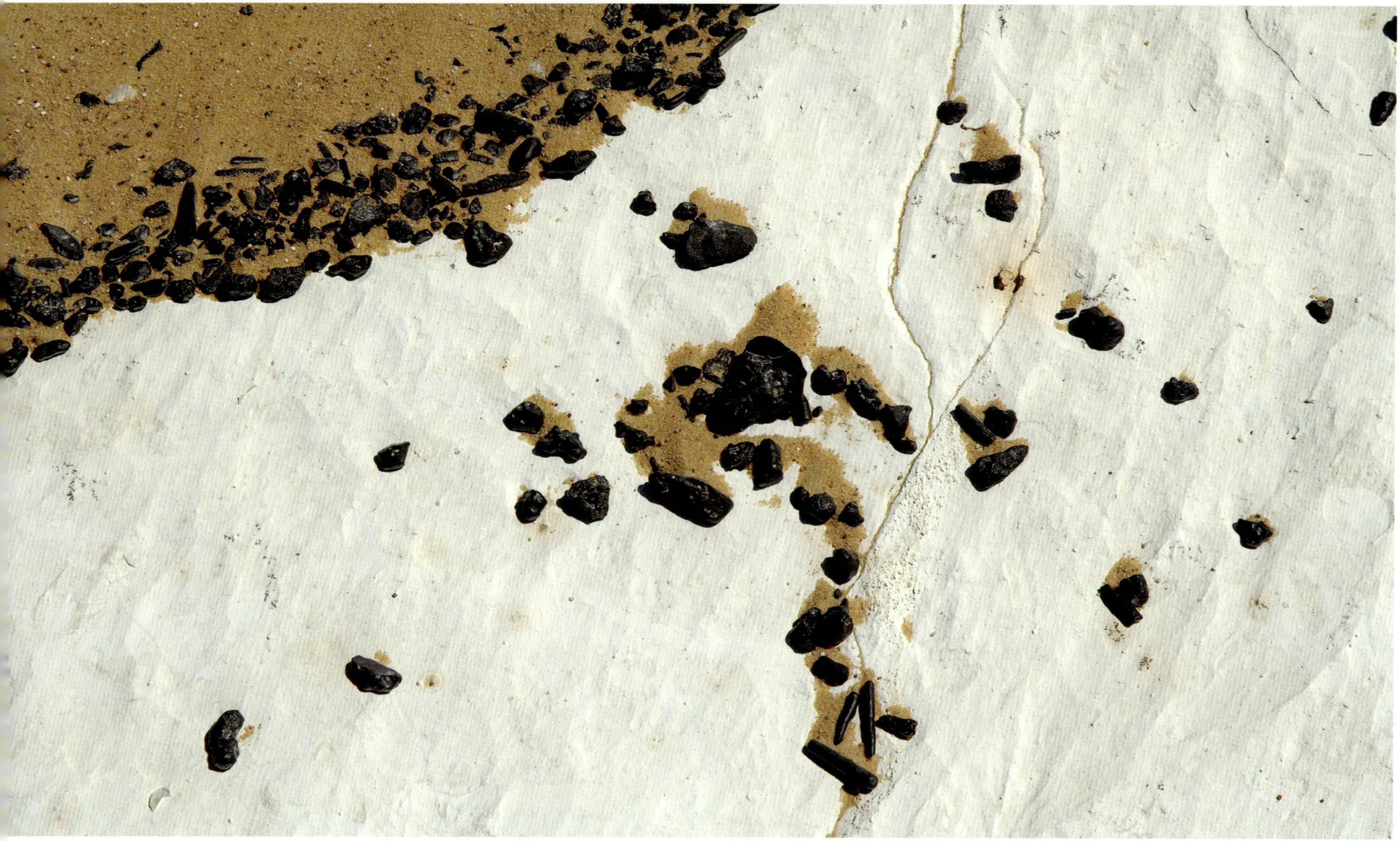

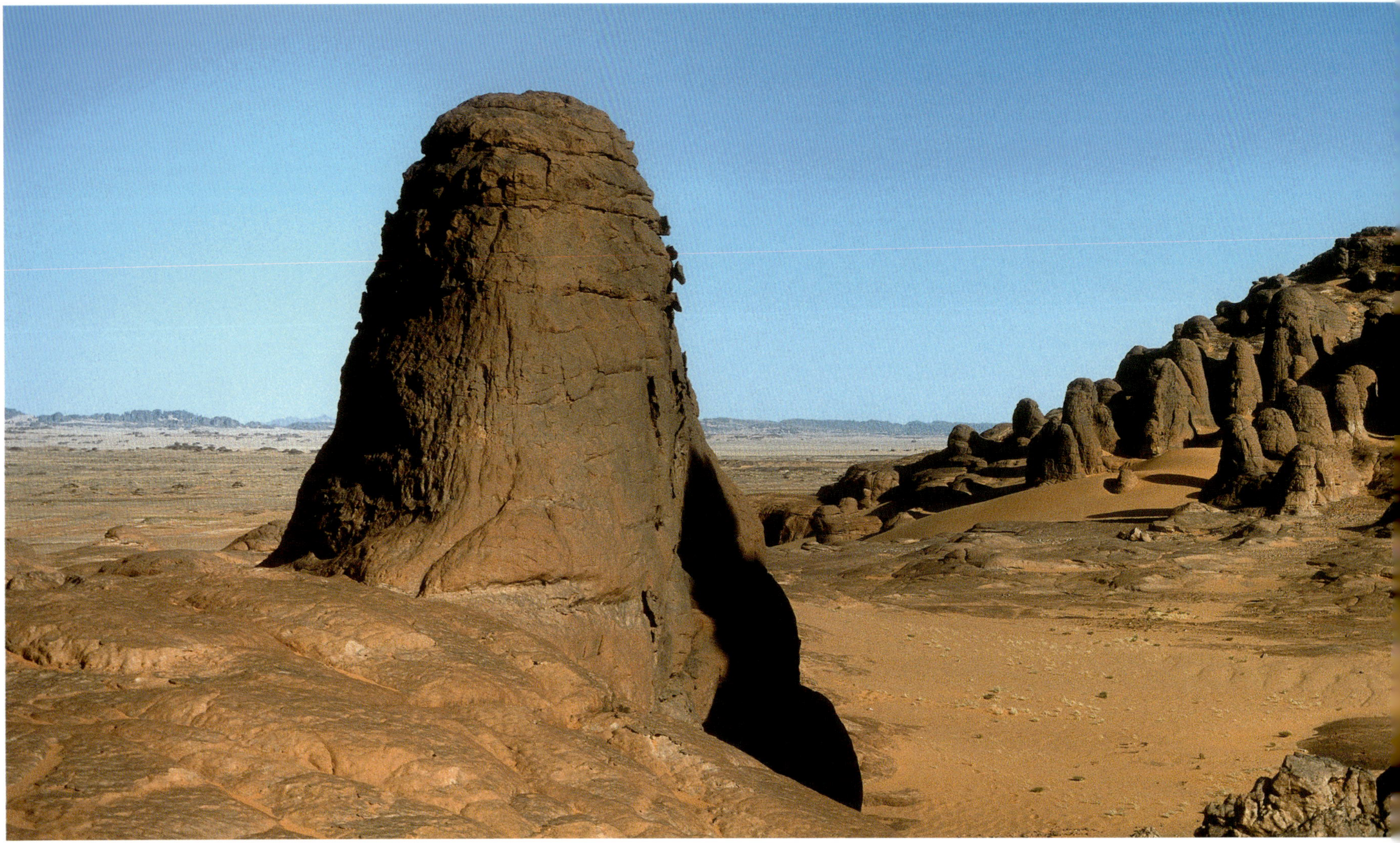

30 Oued Tagrira, Algeria

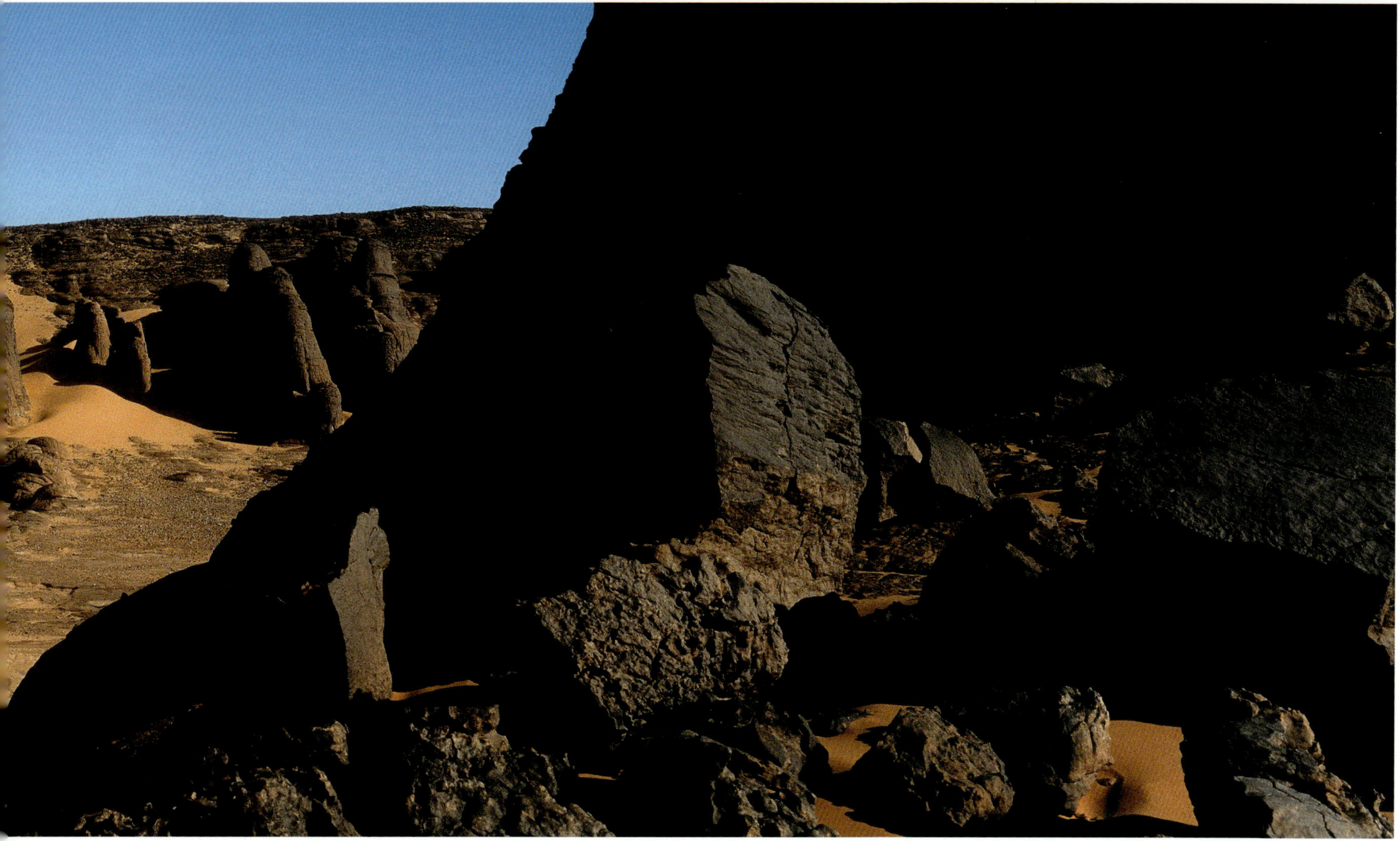

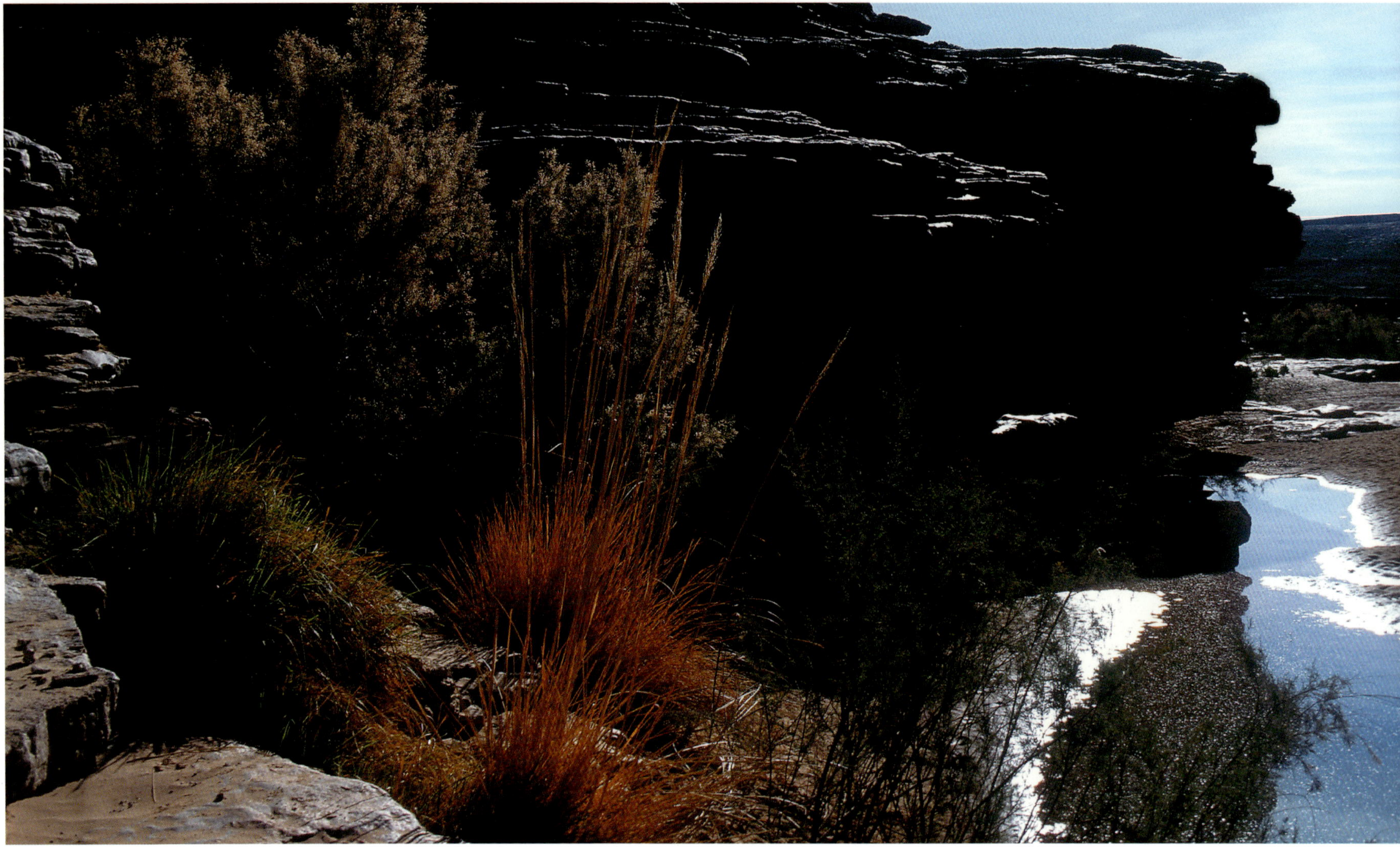

31 Guelta, Algeria

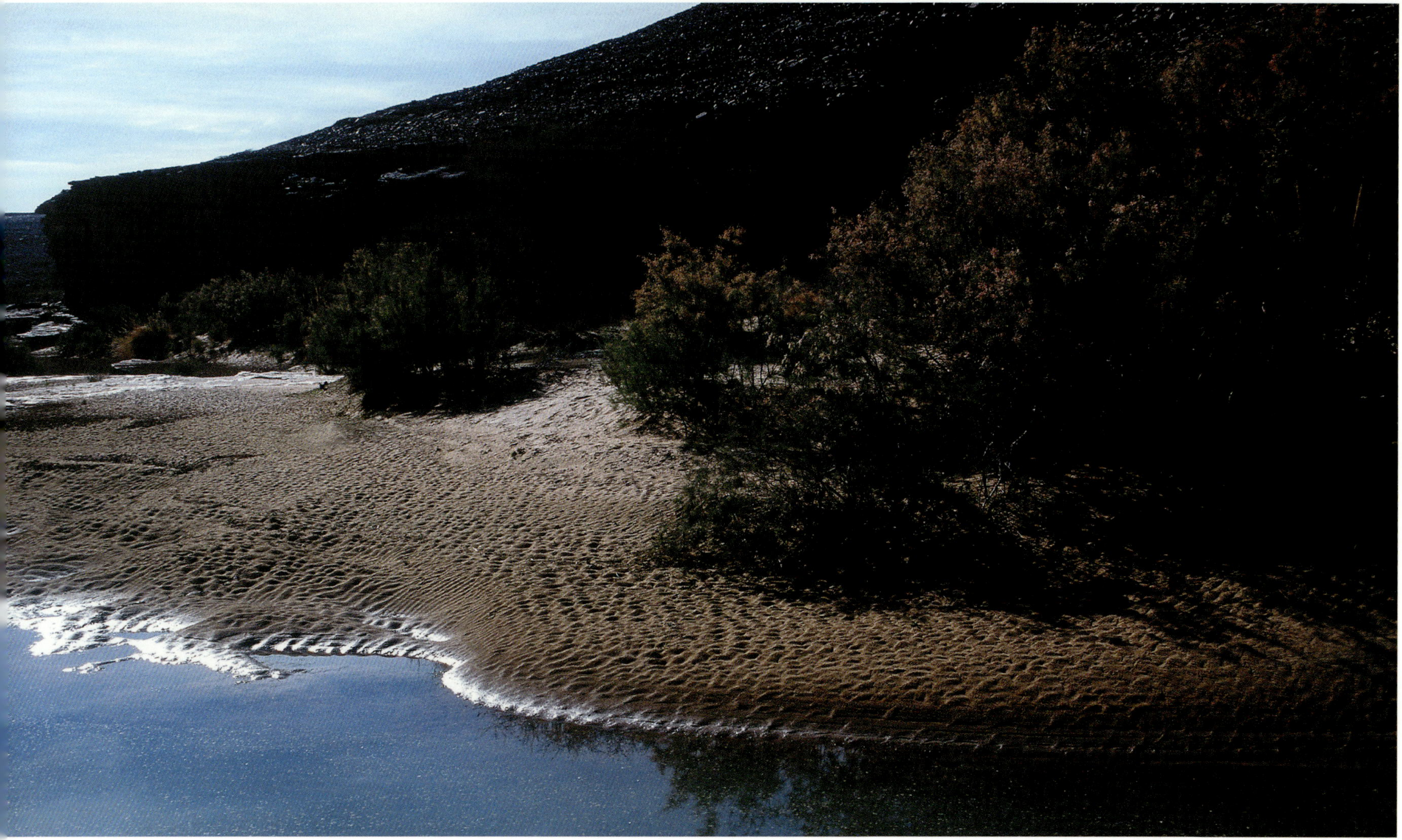

► **32** Near Jabal al Awaynat, Libya

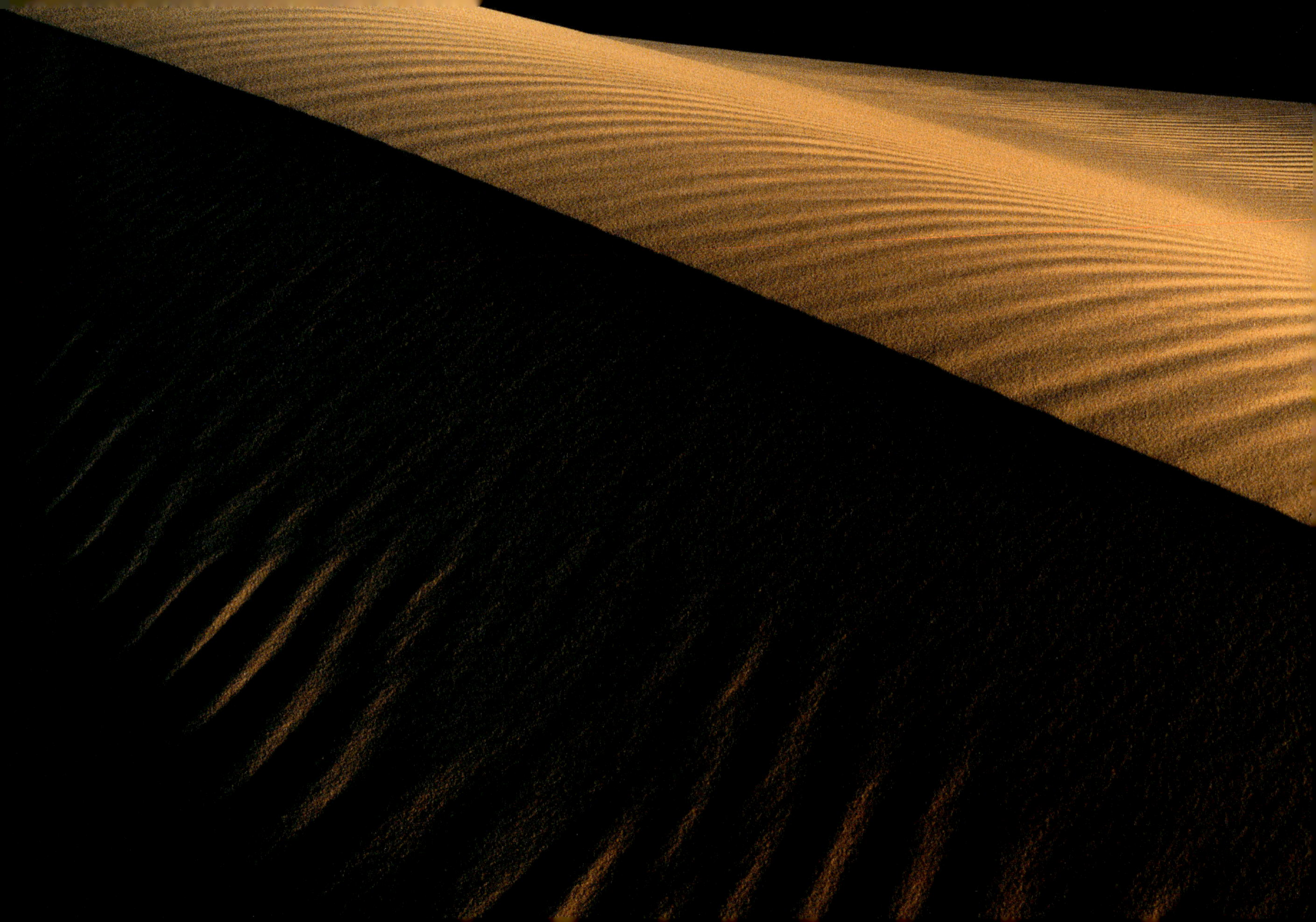

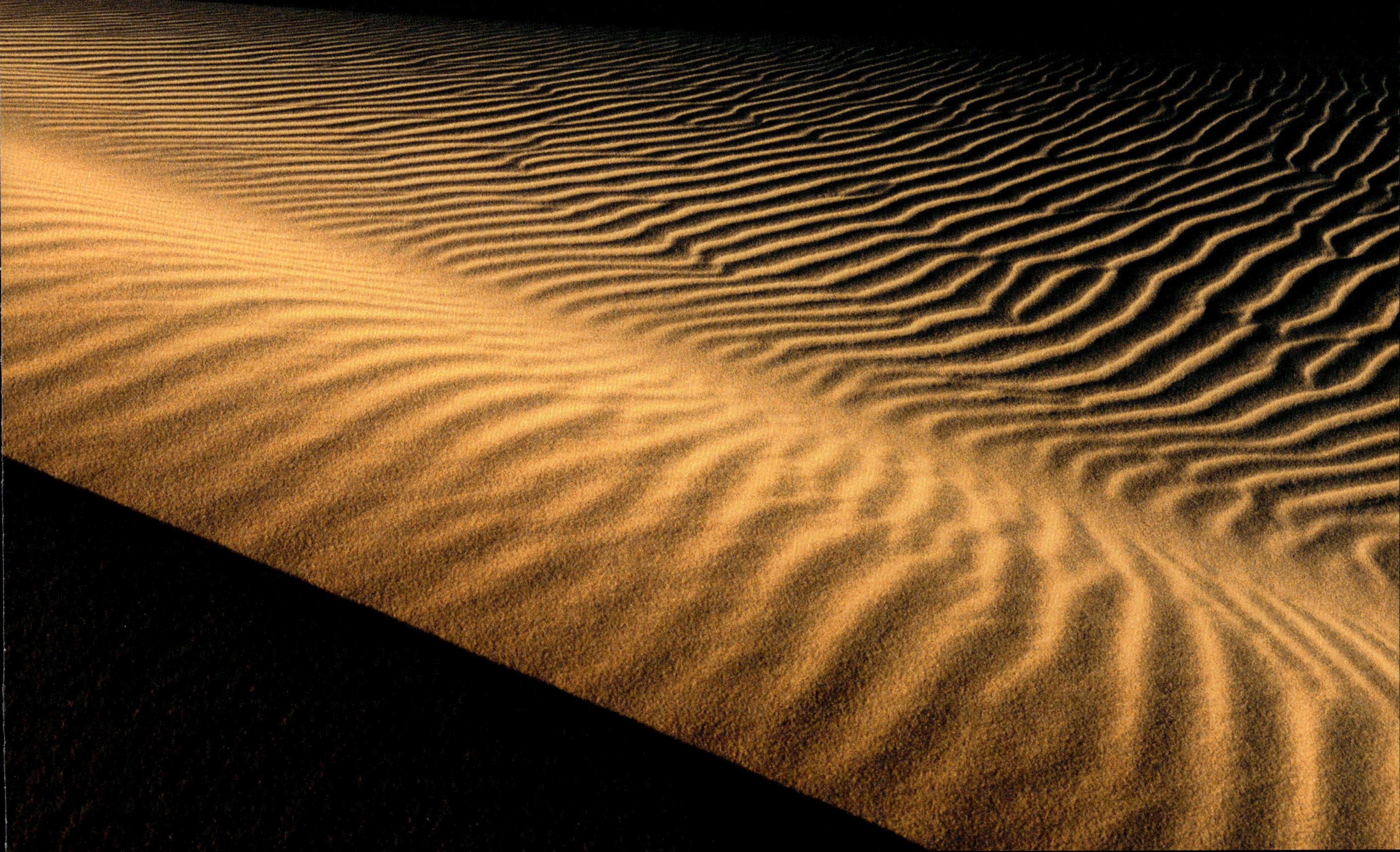

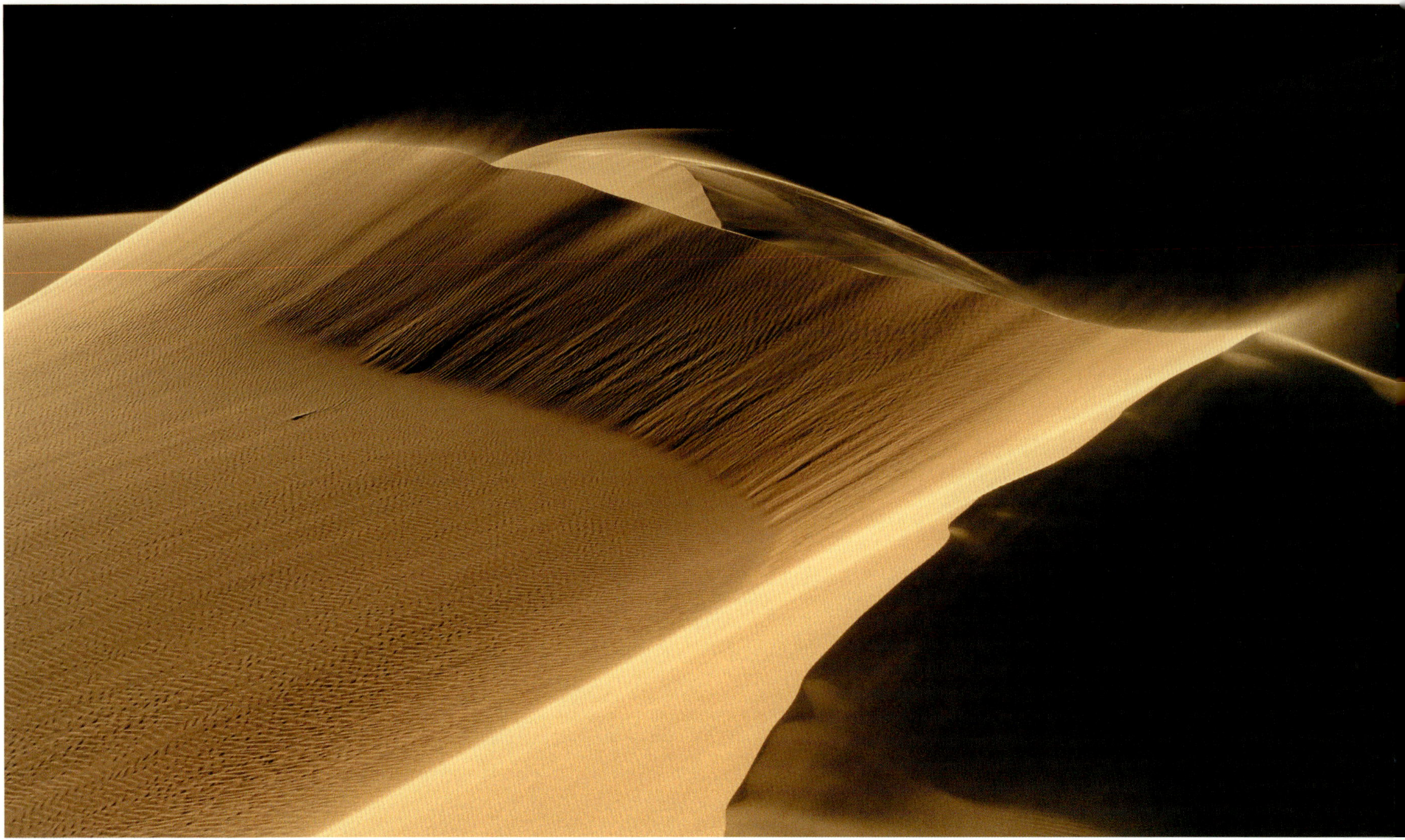

33 Erg Admer, Algeria

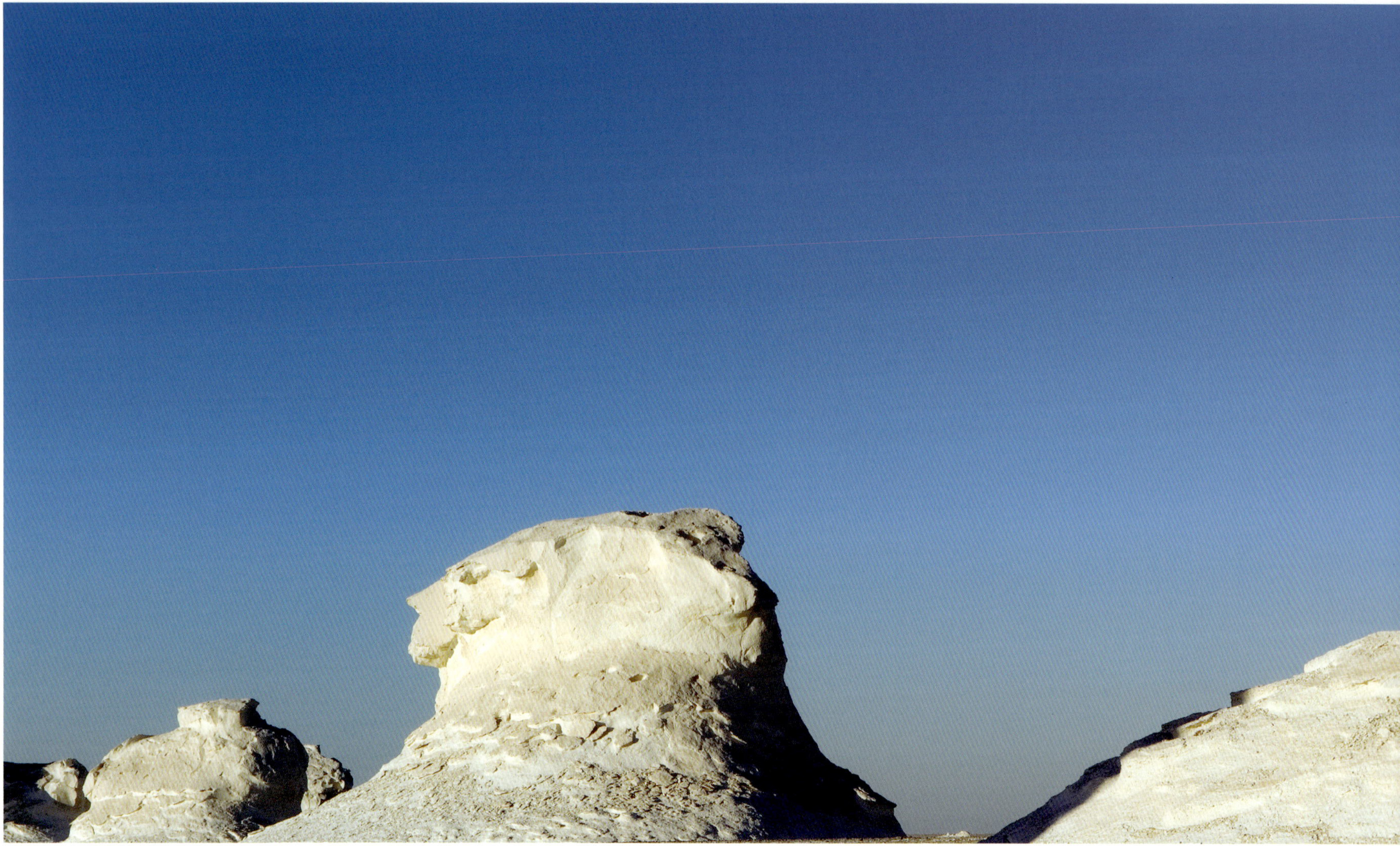

34 White Desert, Egypt

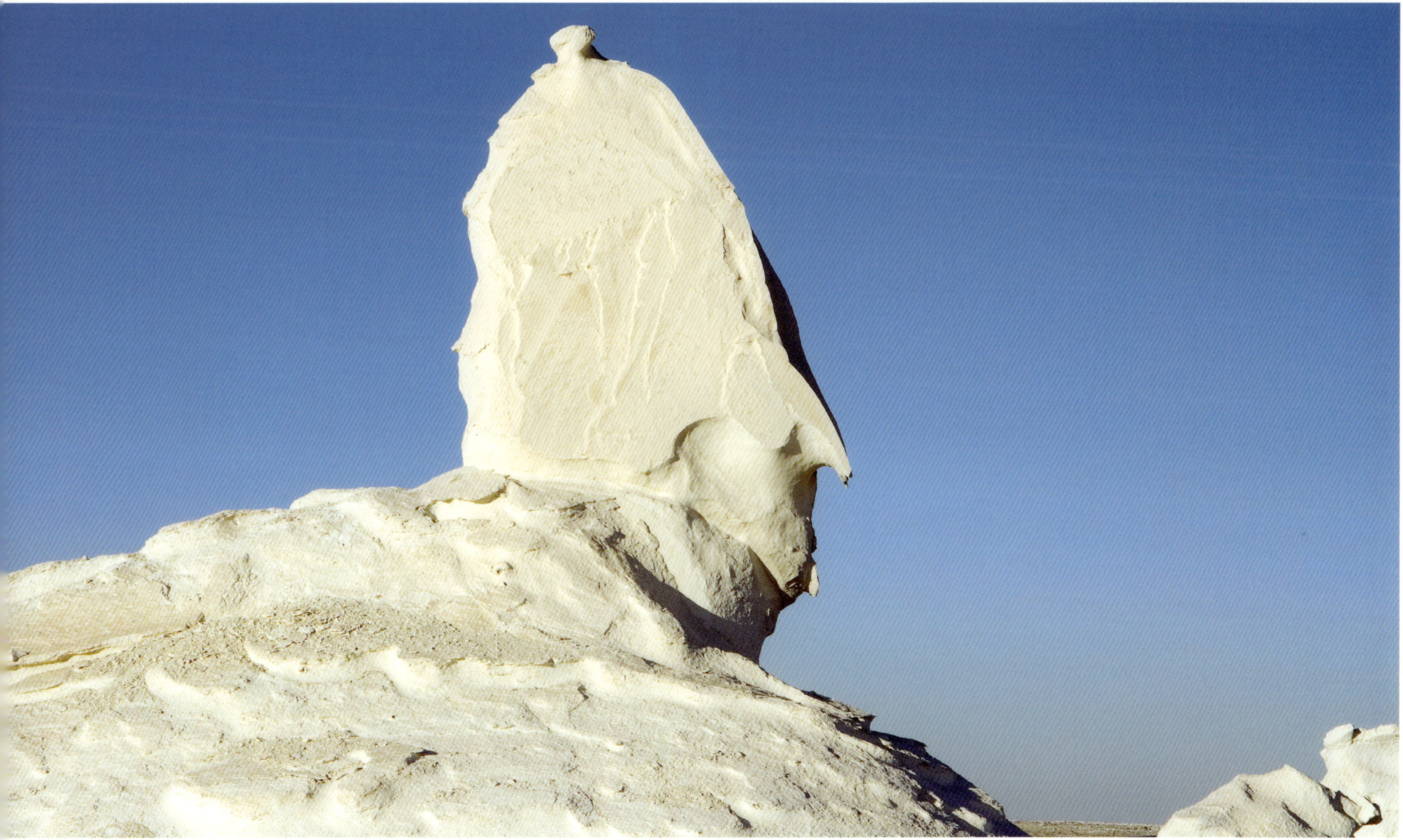

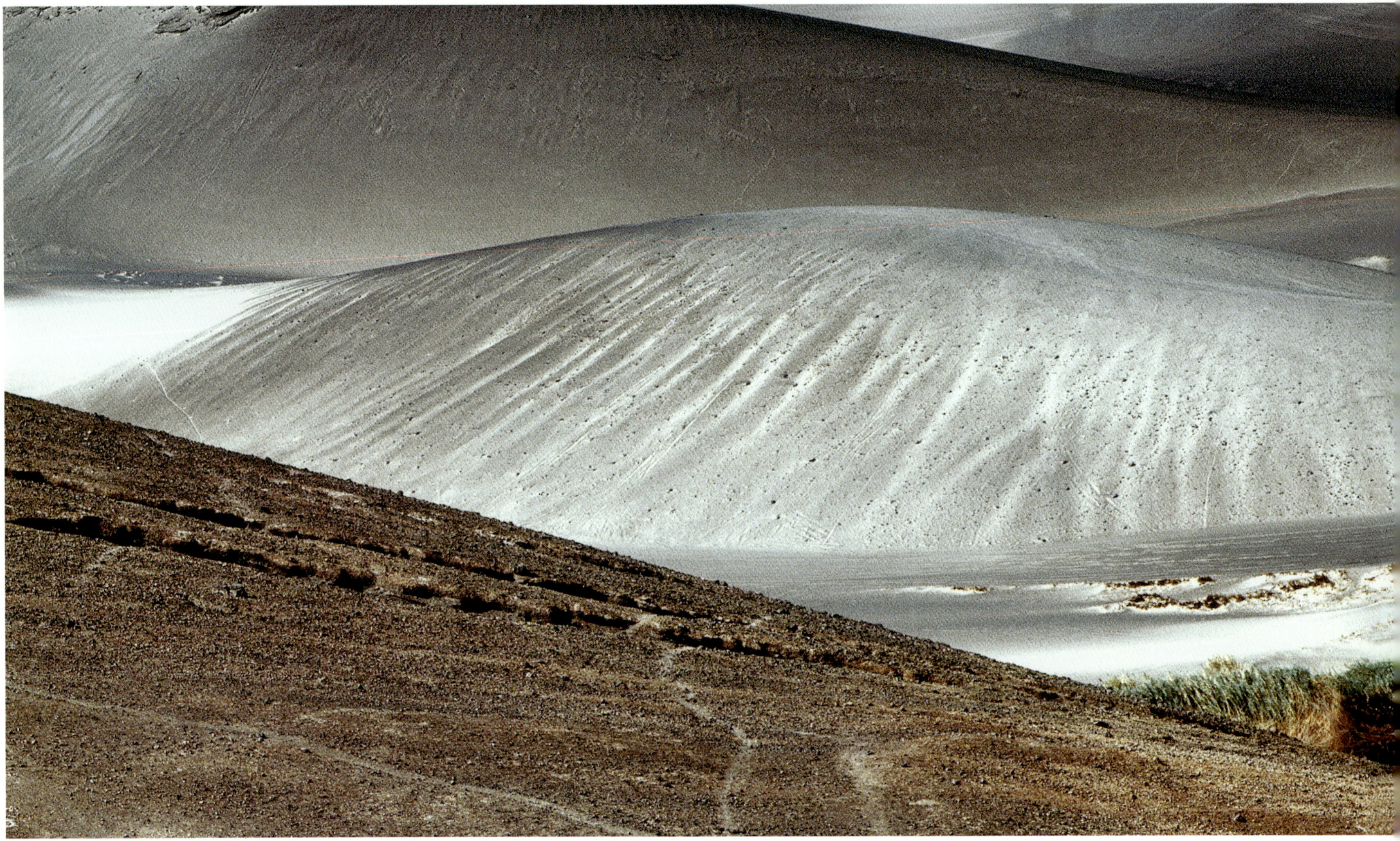

35 Wau an Namus, Libya

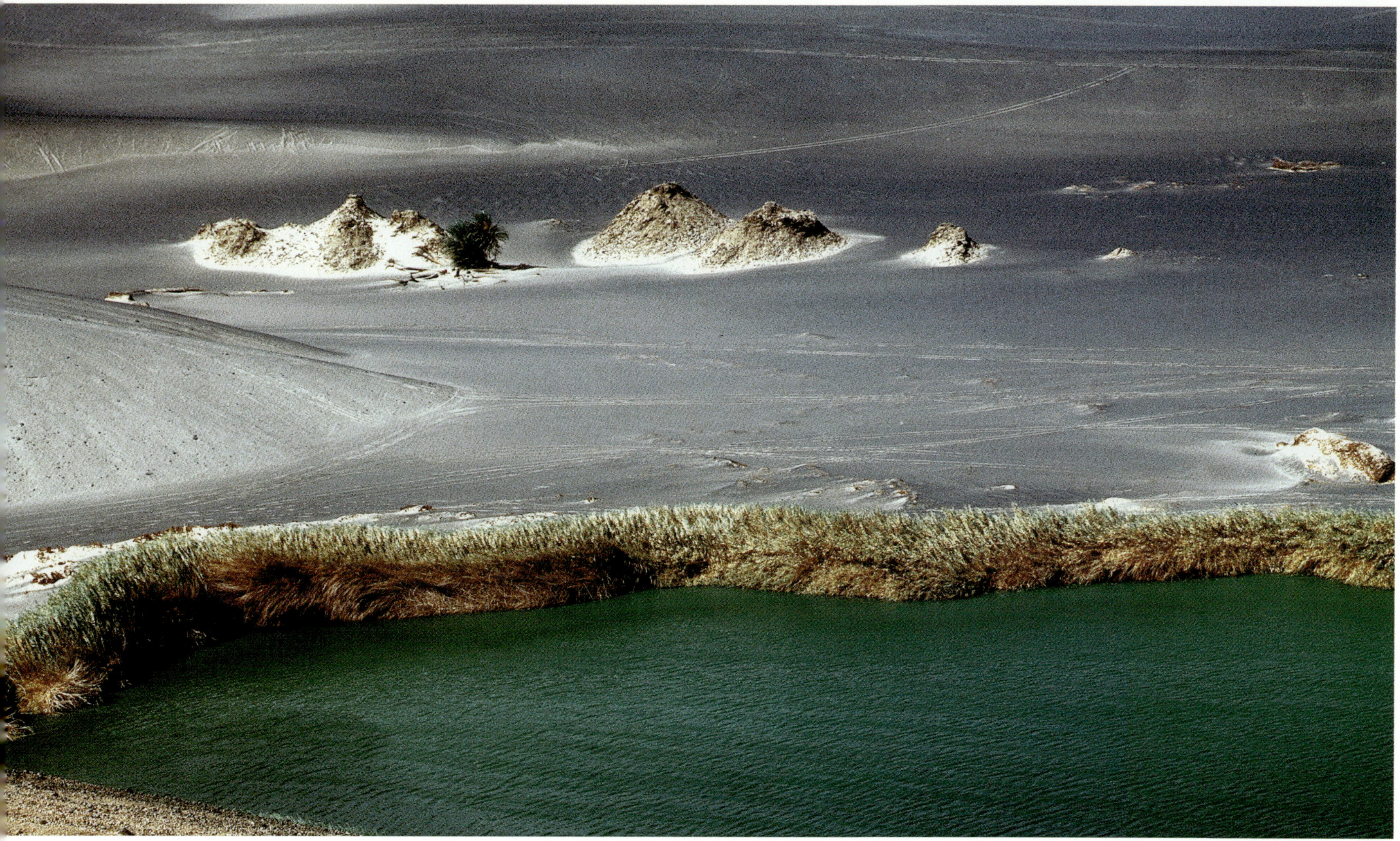

► **36** White Desert, Egypt

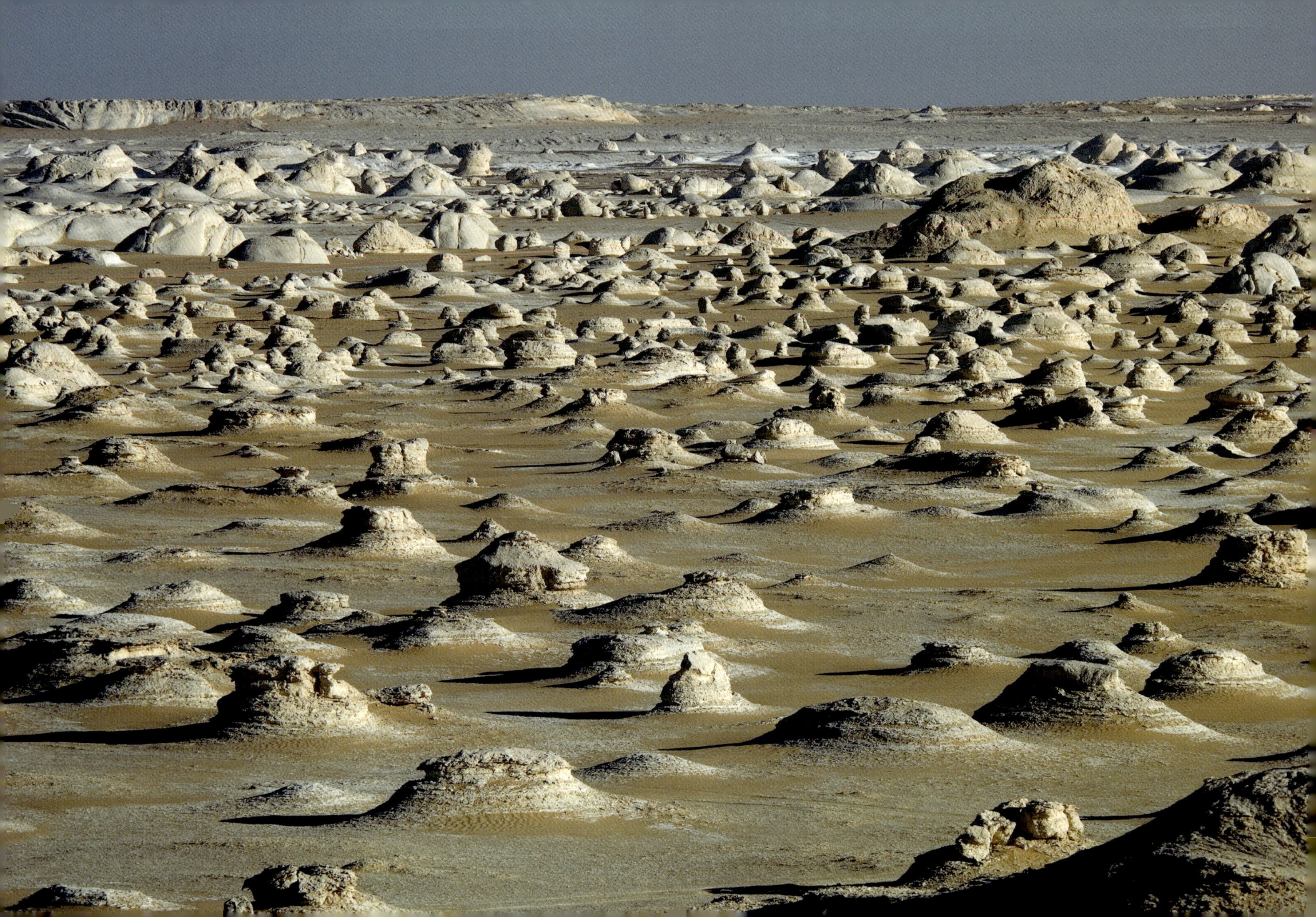

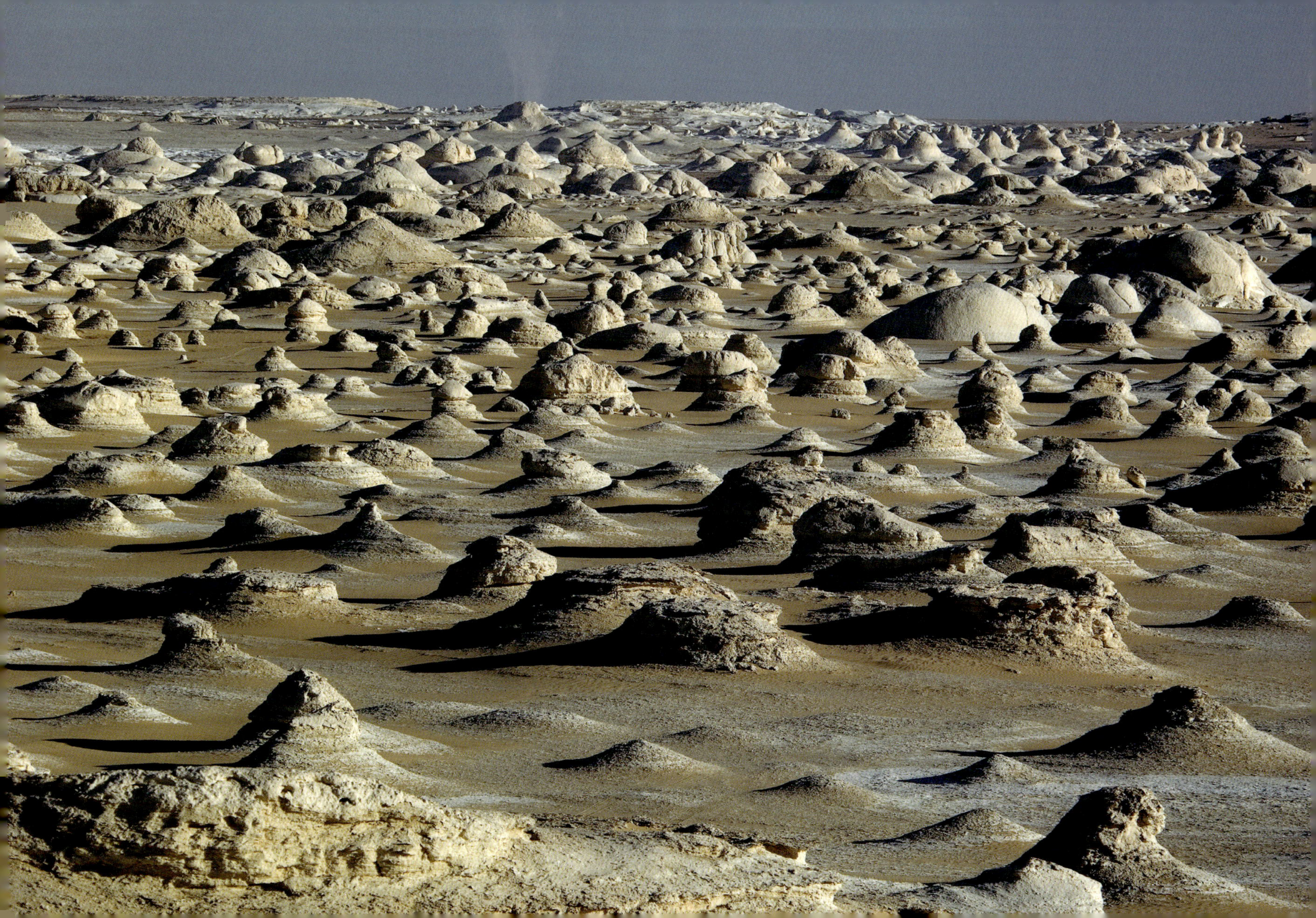

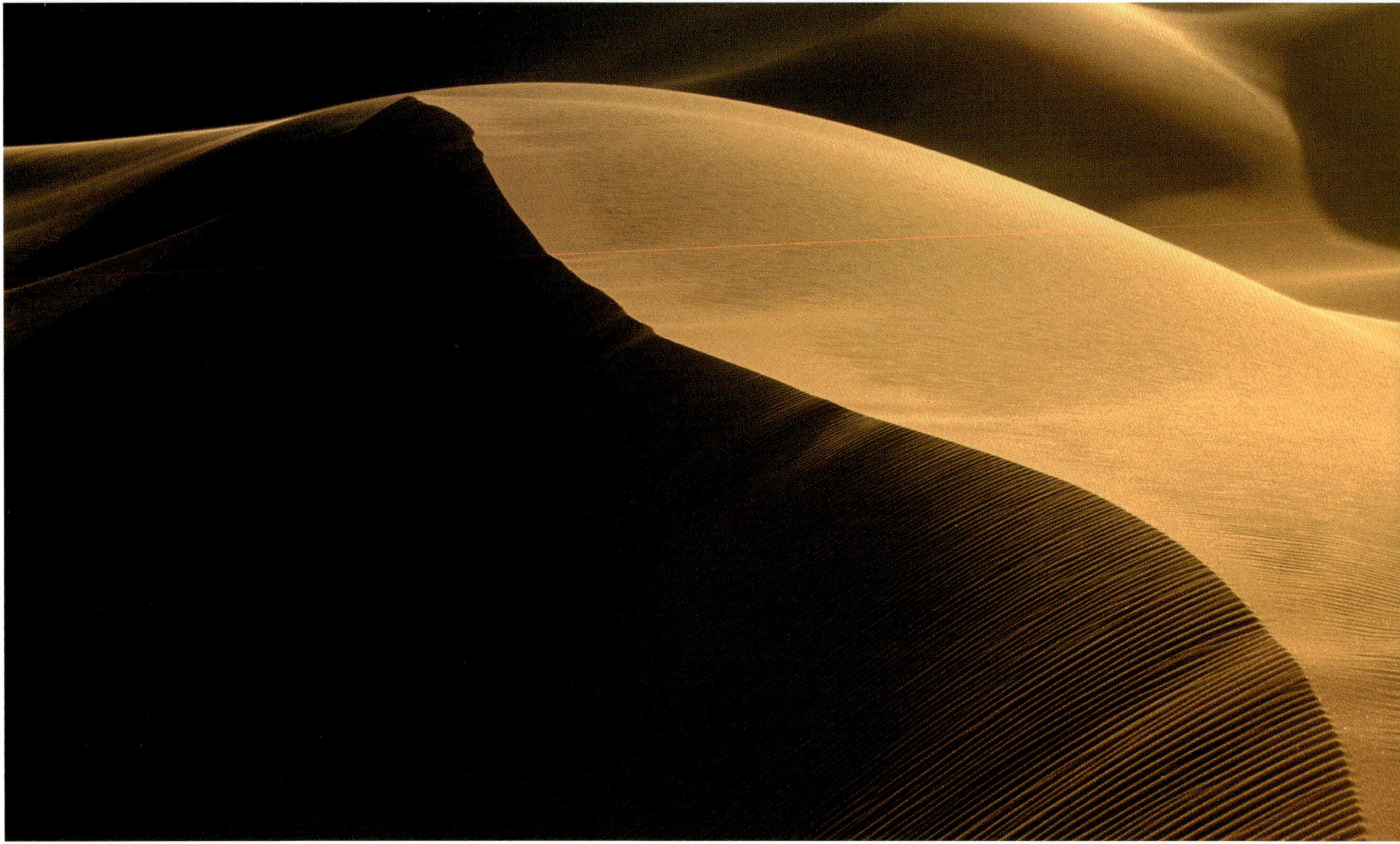

37 Near Serdeles, Libya

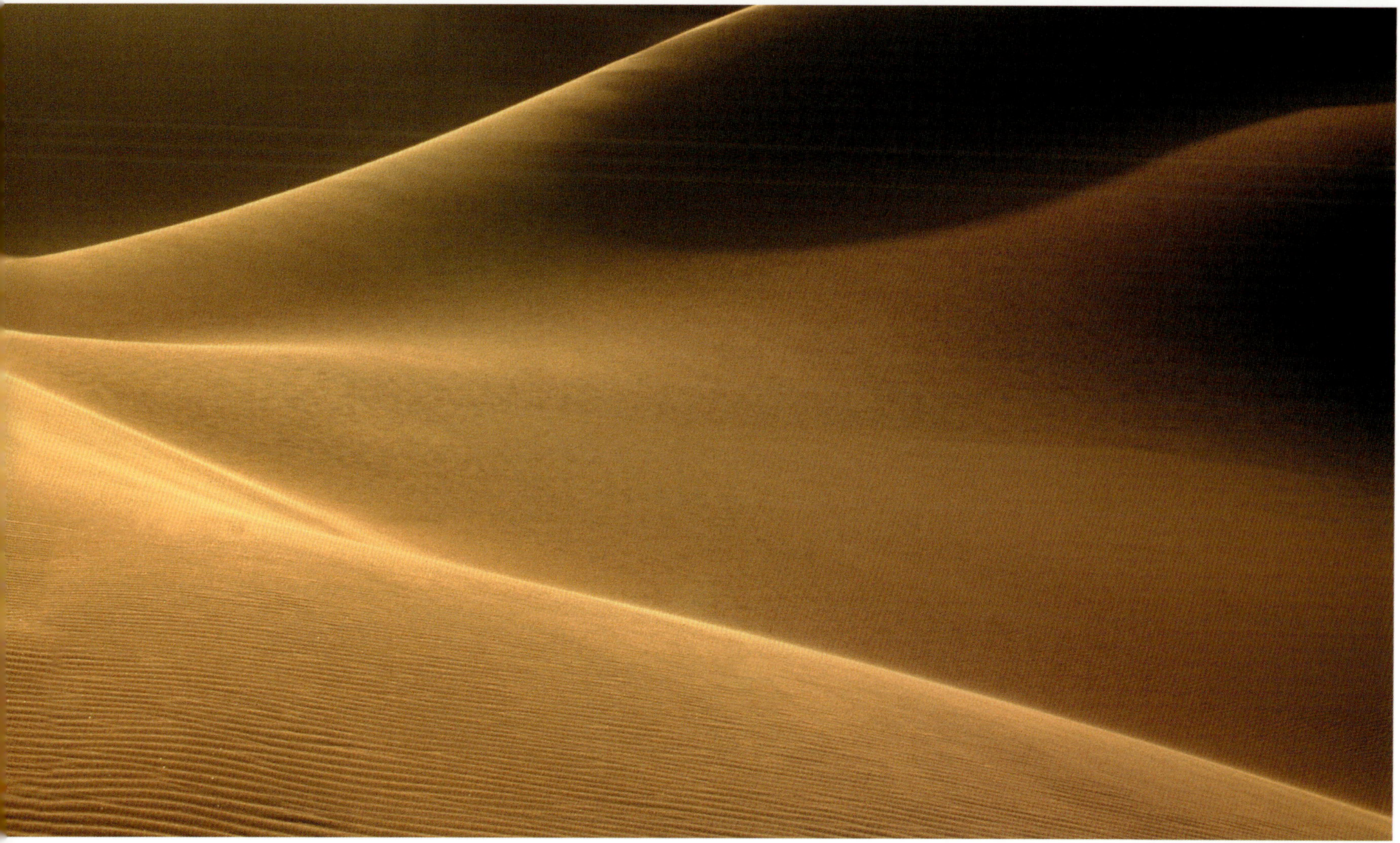

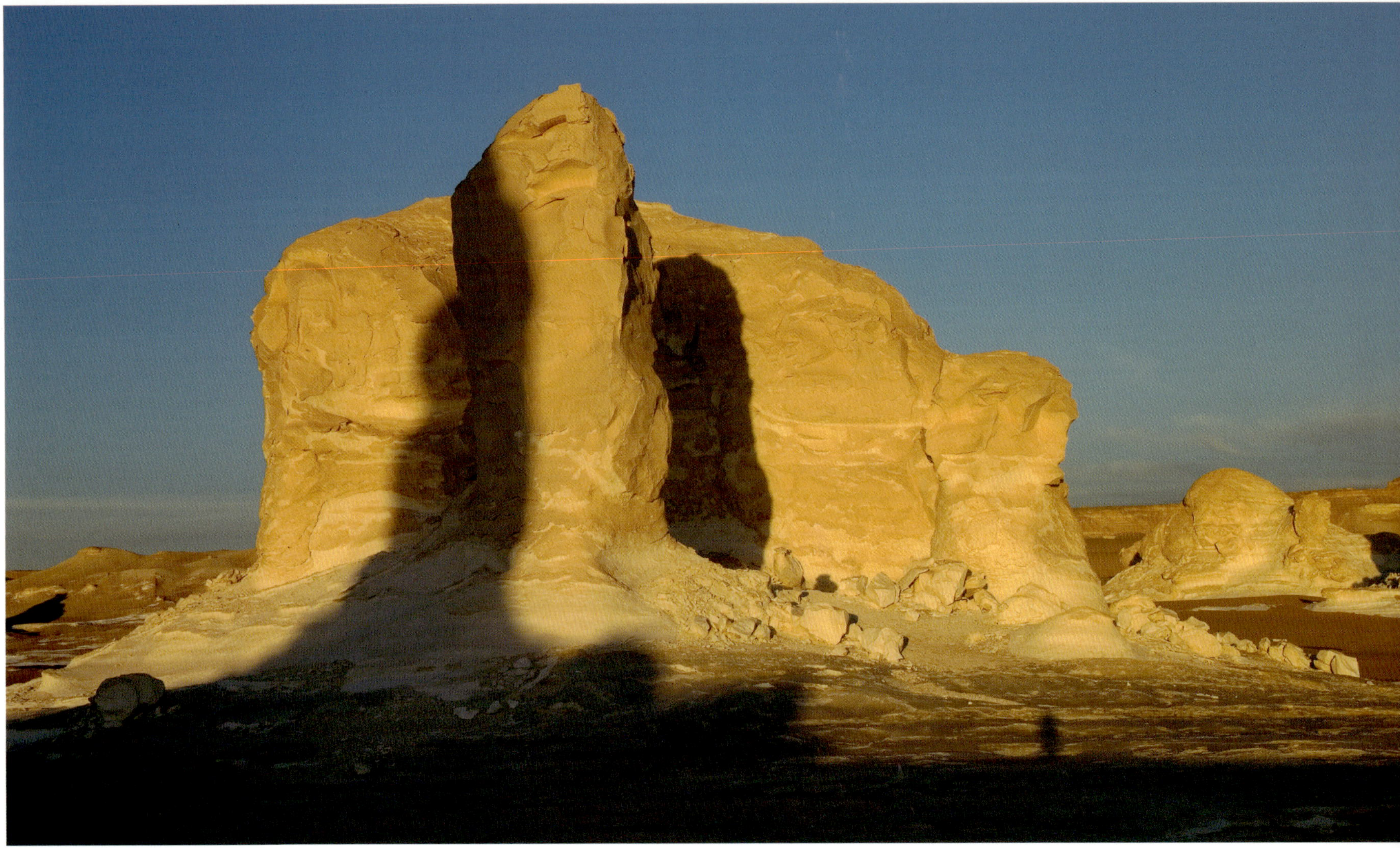

38 White Desert, Egypt

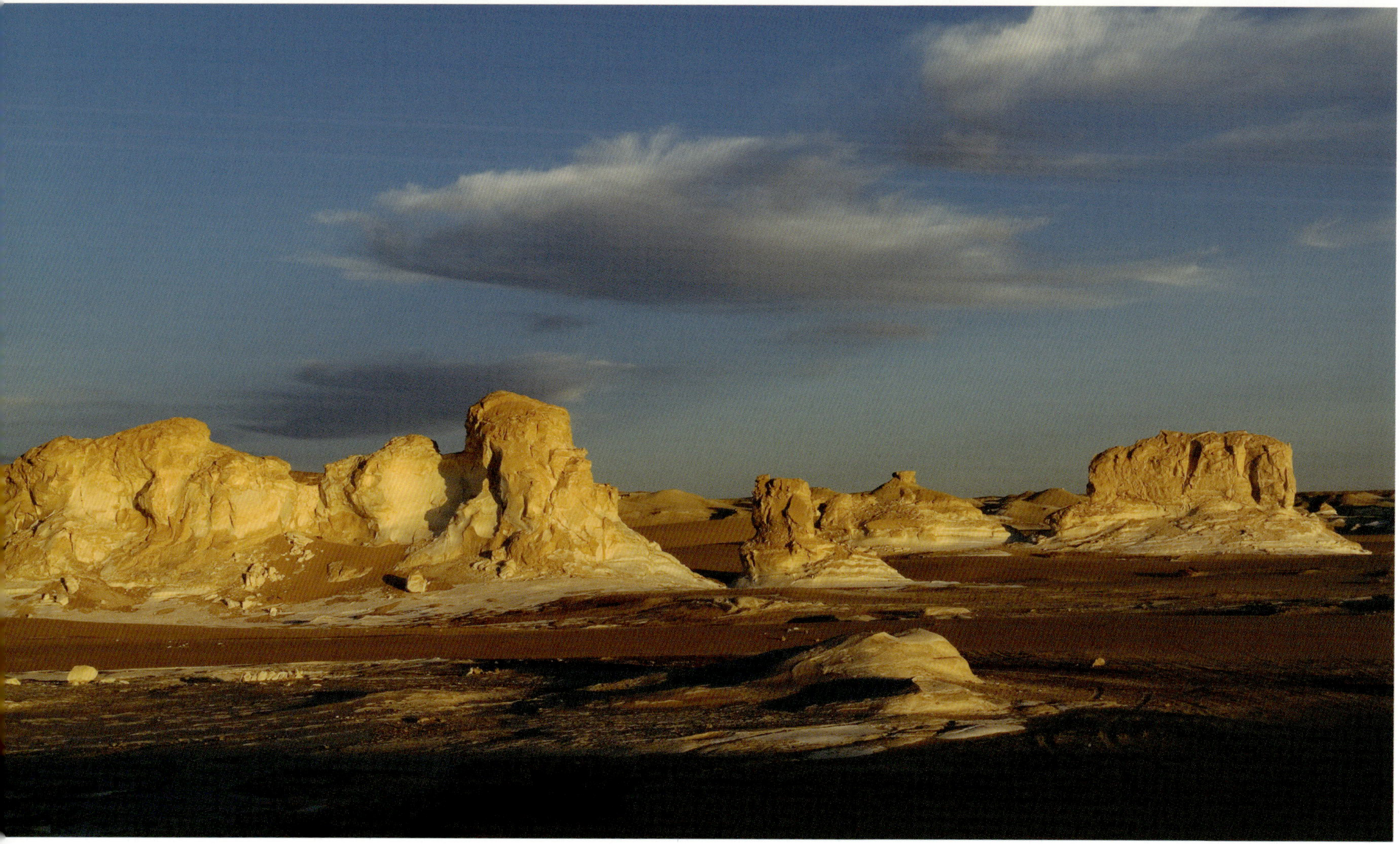

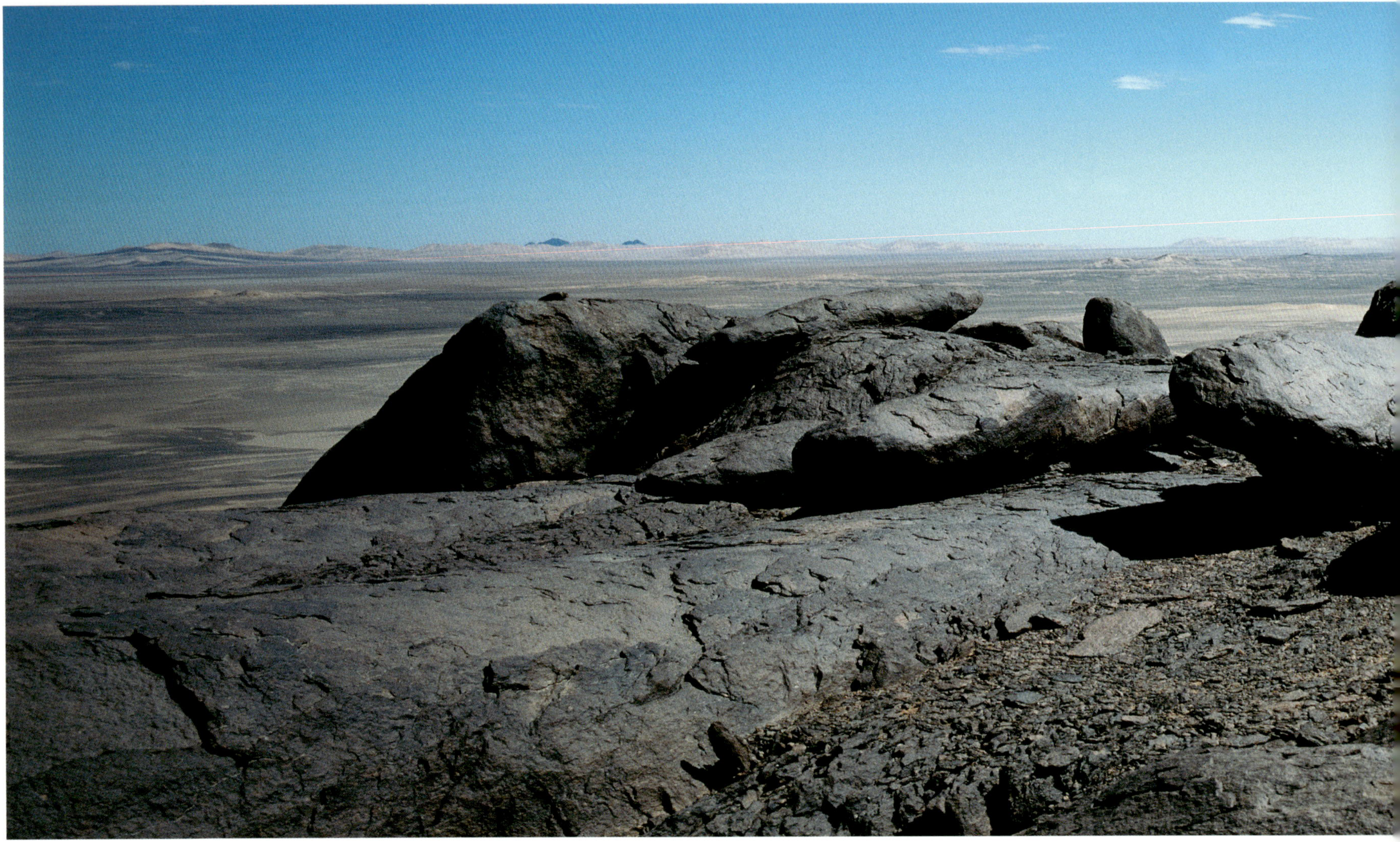

39 Near Erg Admer, Algeria

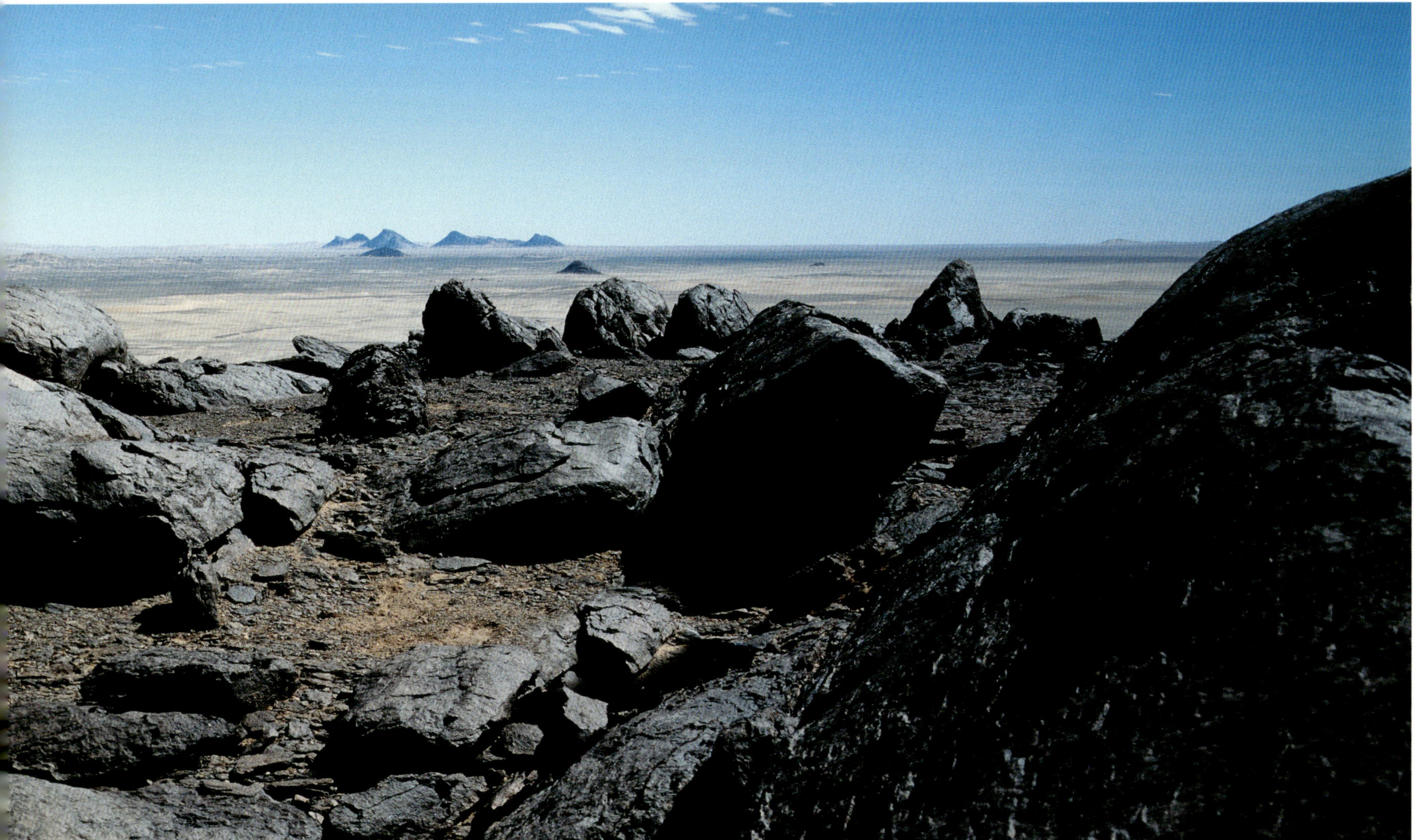

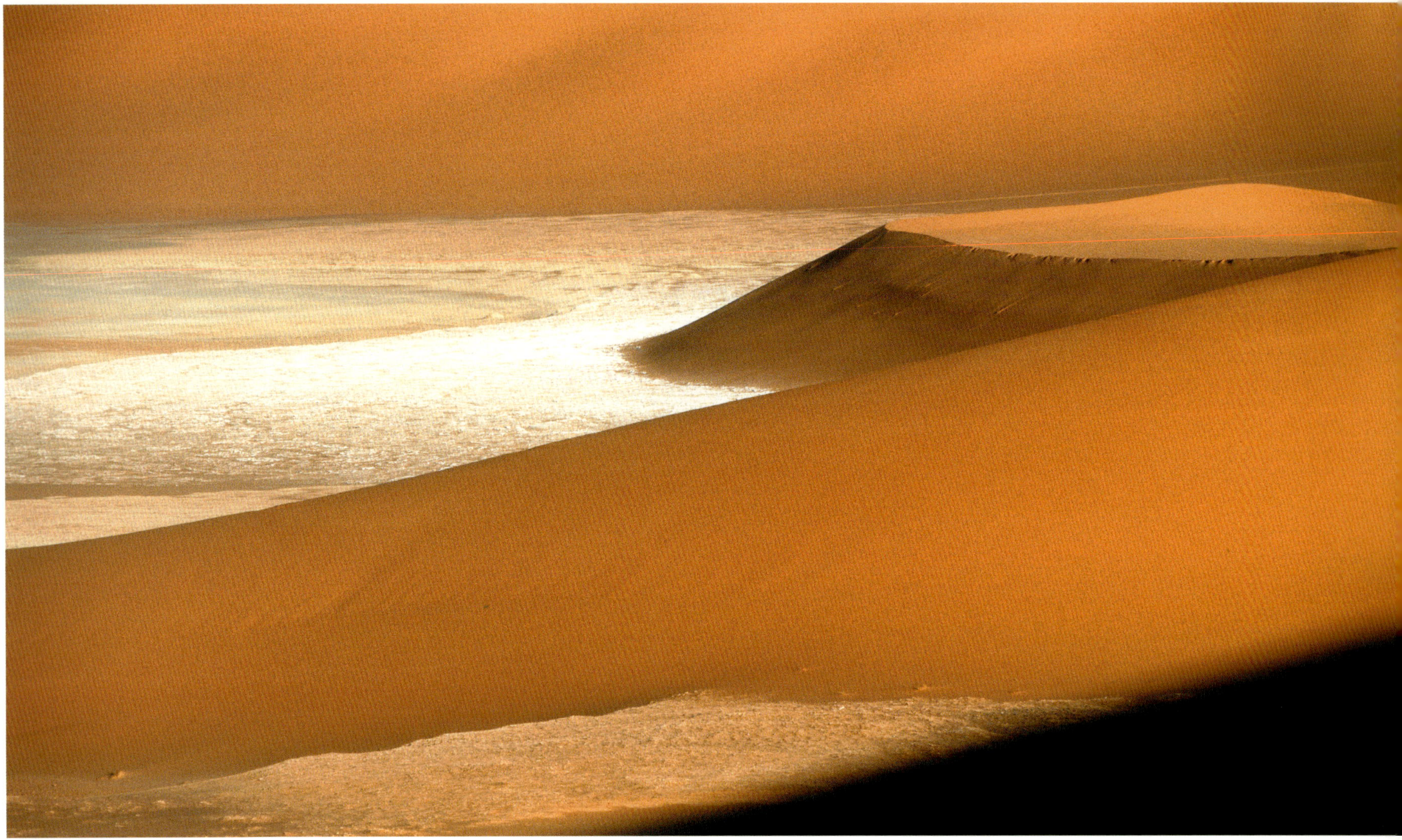

40 Erg Bourarhet, Algeria

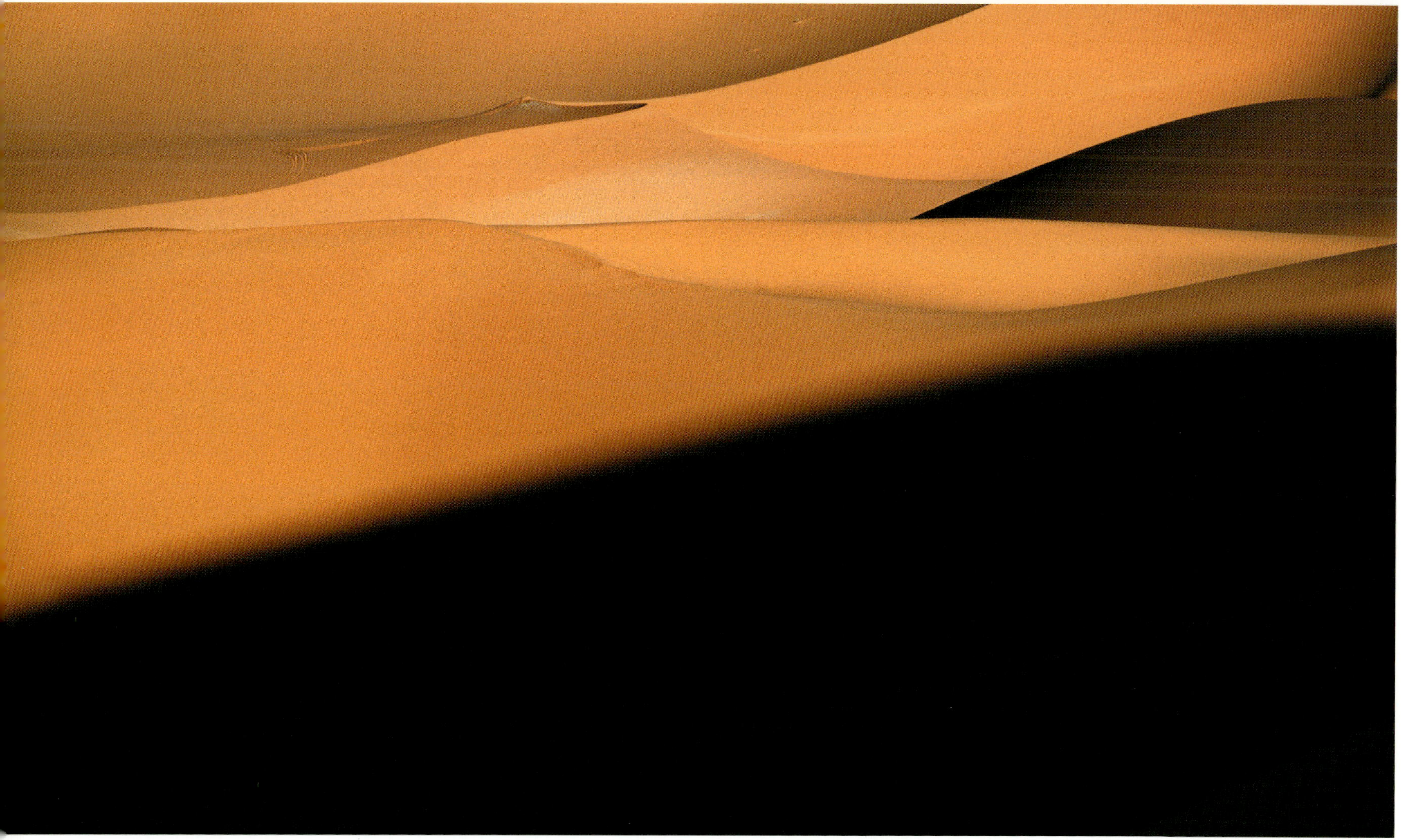

► **41** White Desert, Egypt

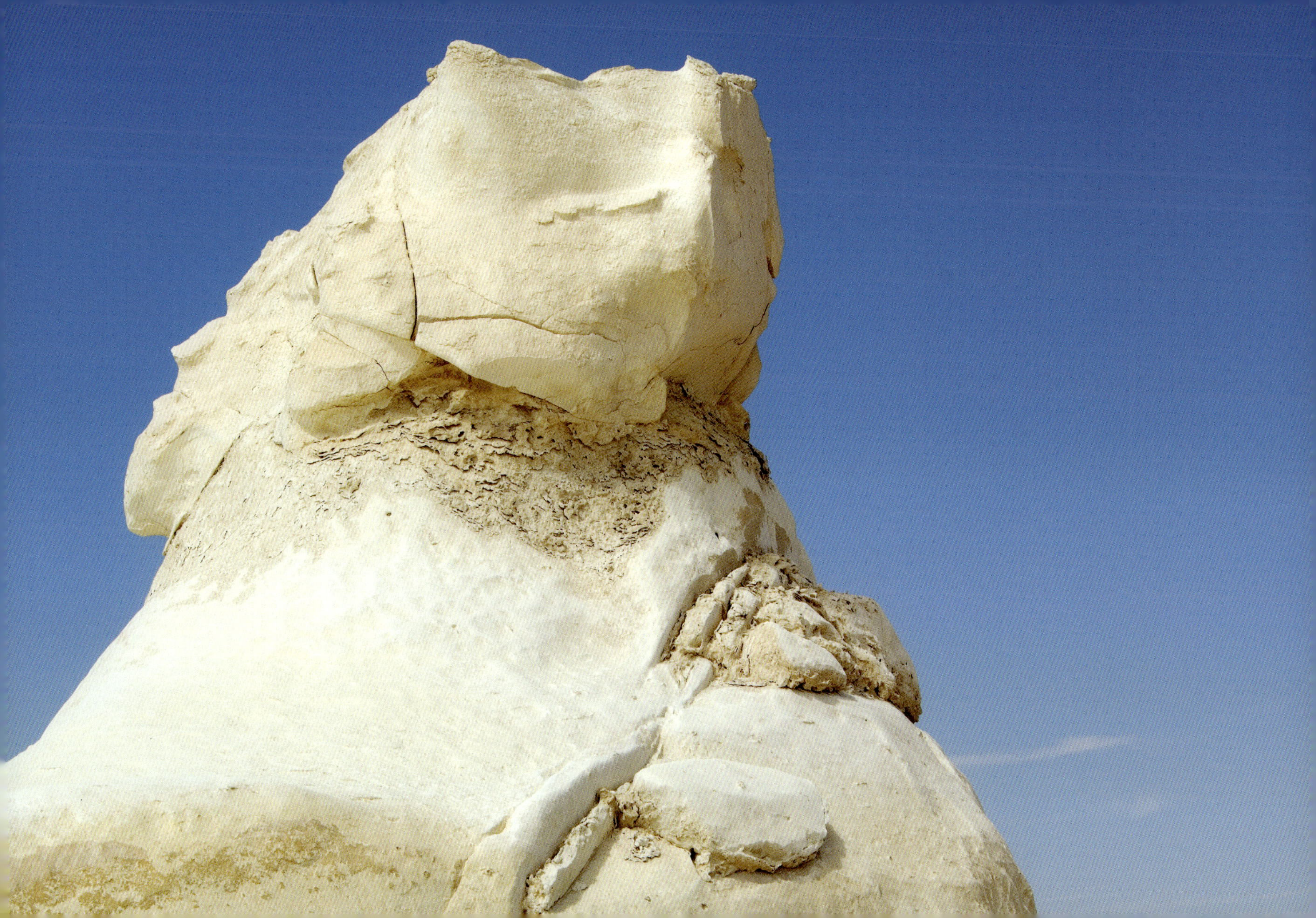

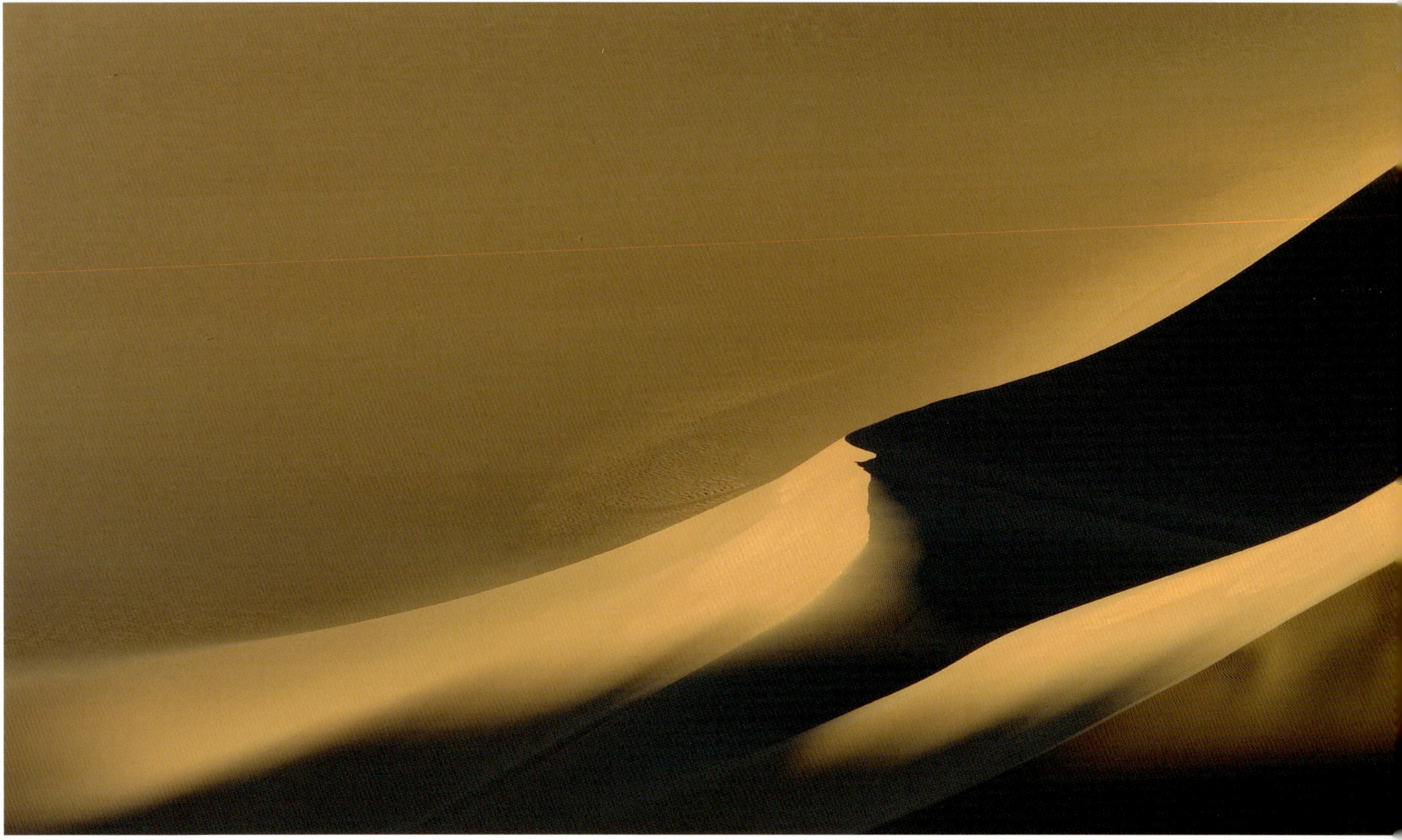

42 Near Ubari, Libya

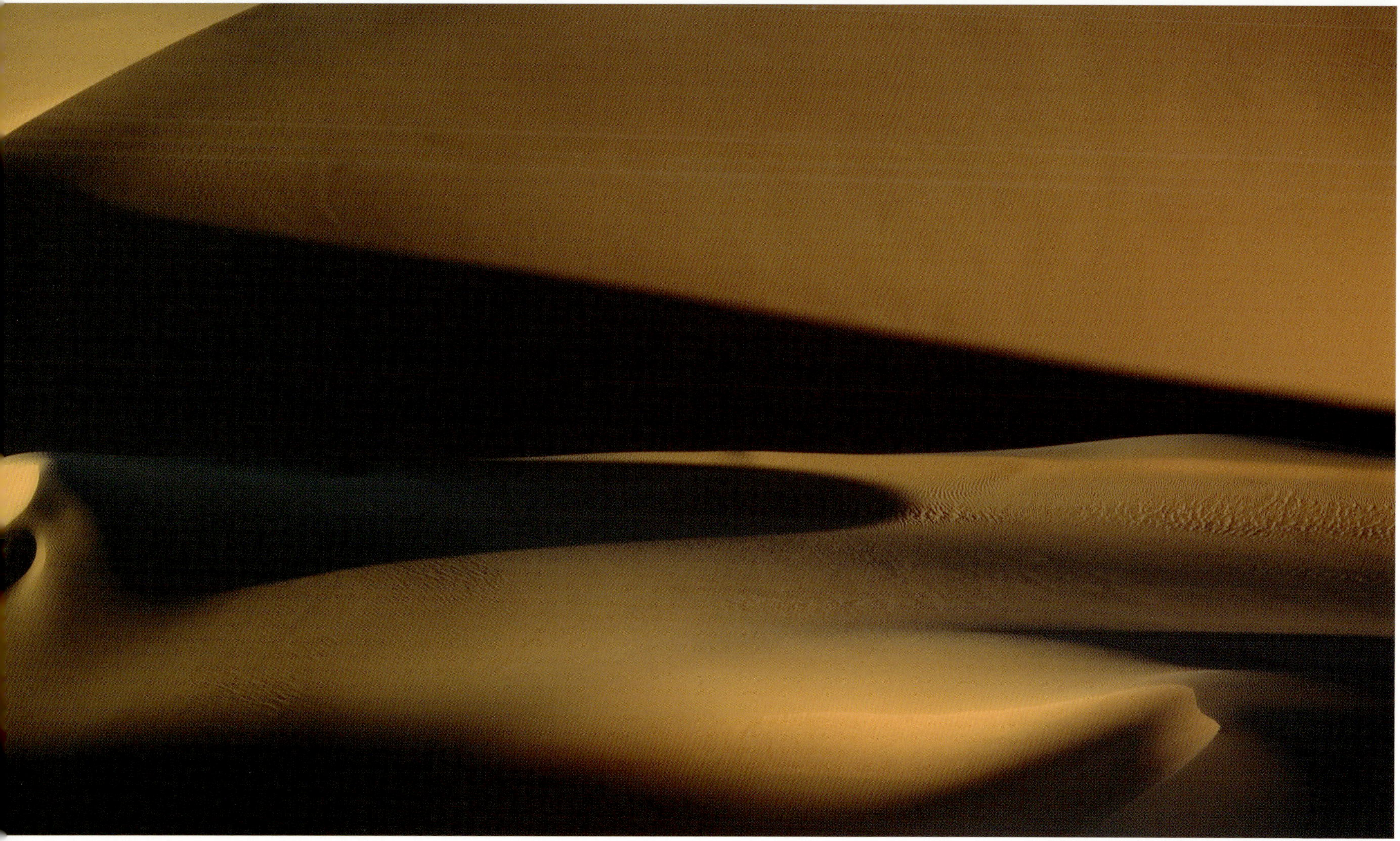

► **43** El Mescheggheg, Al Haruj al Aswad, Libya

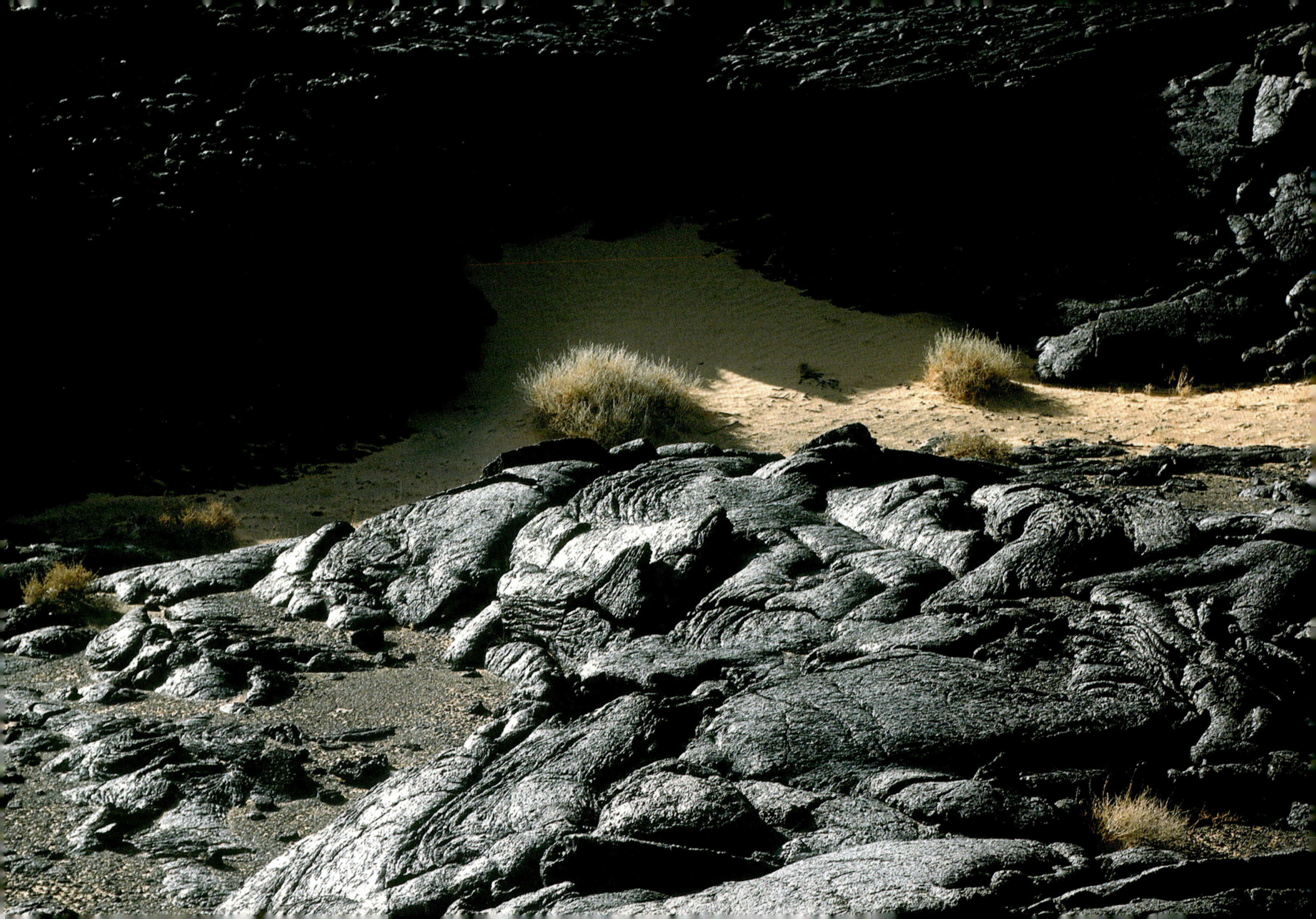

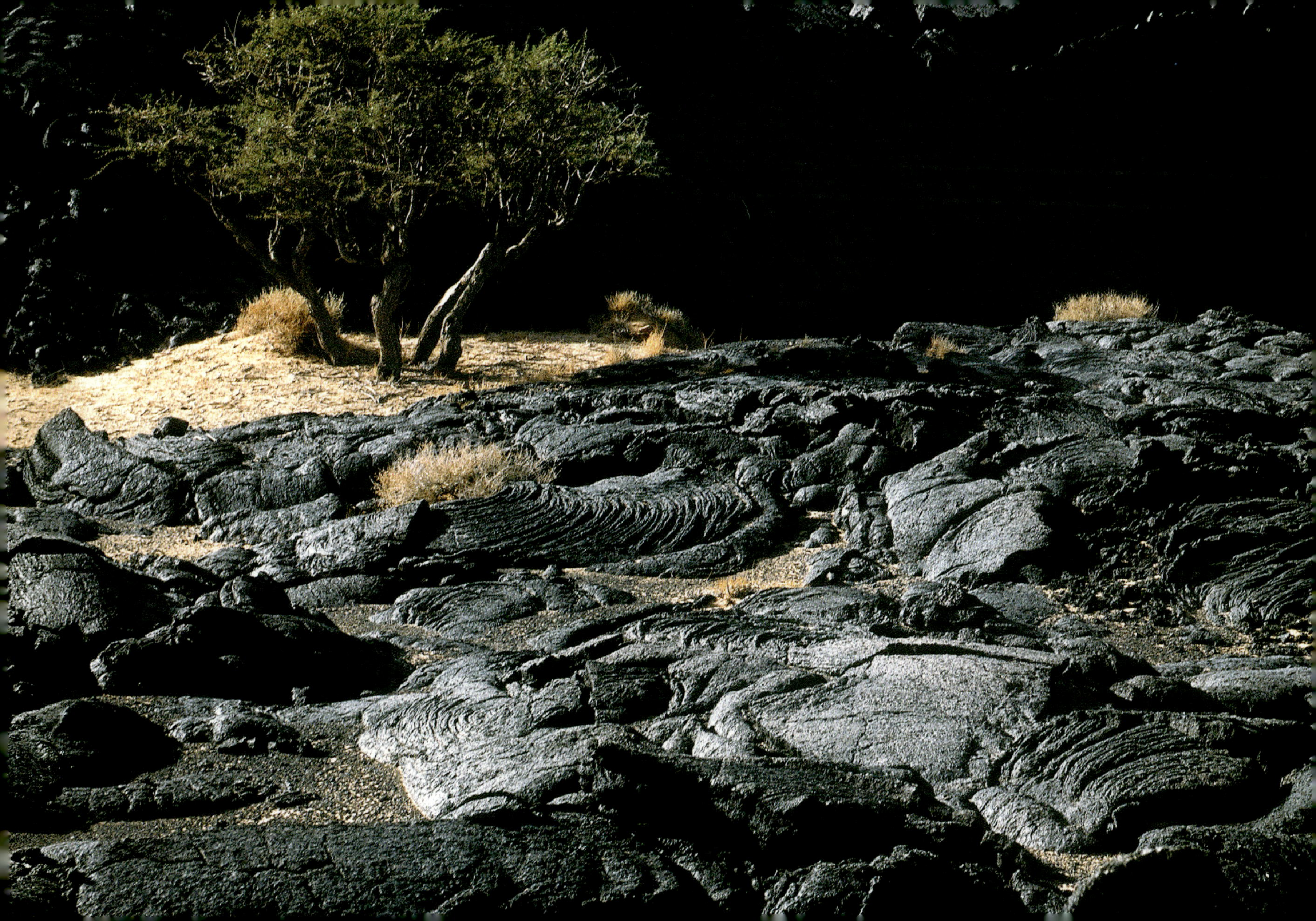

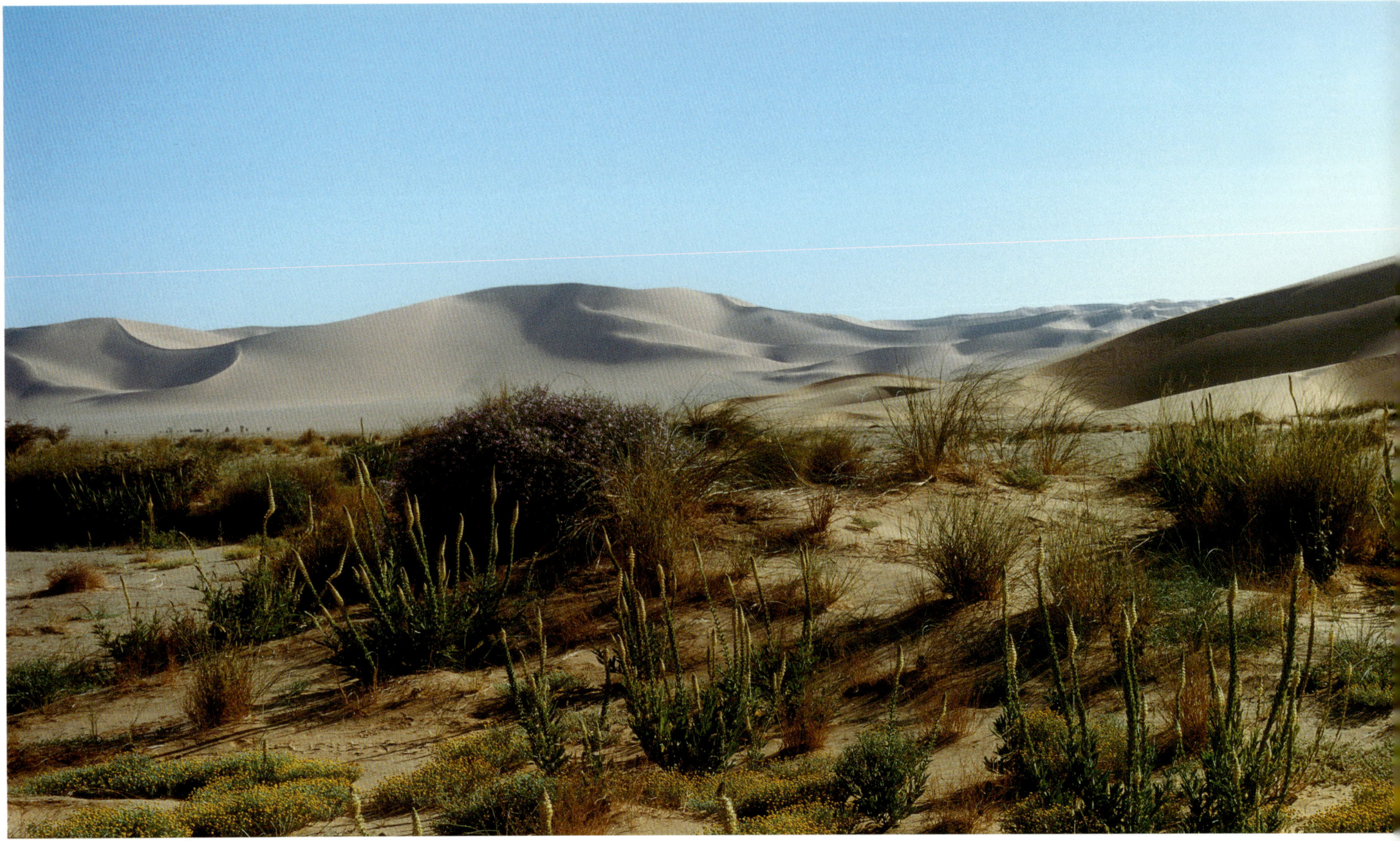

44 Erg Amguid, Algeria

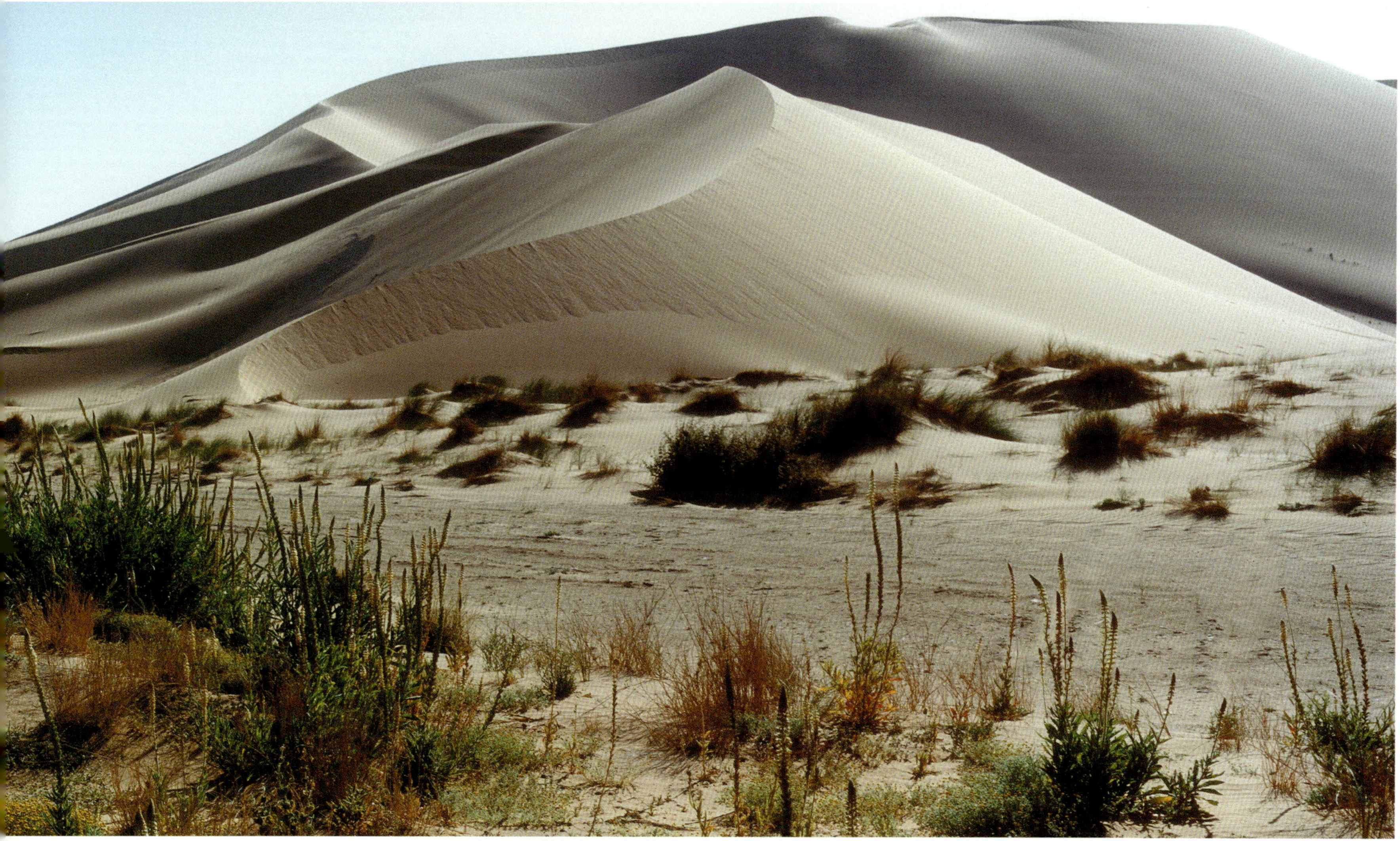

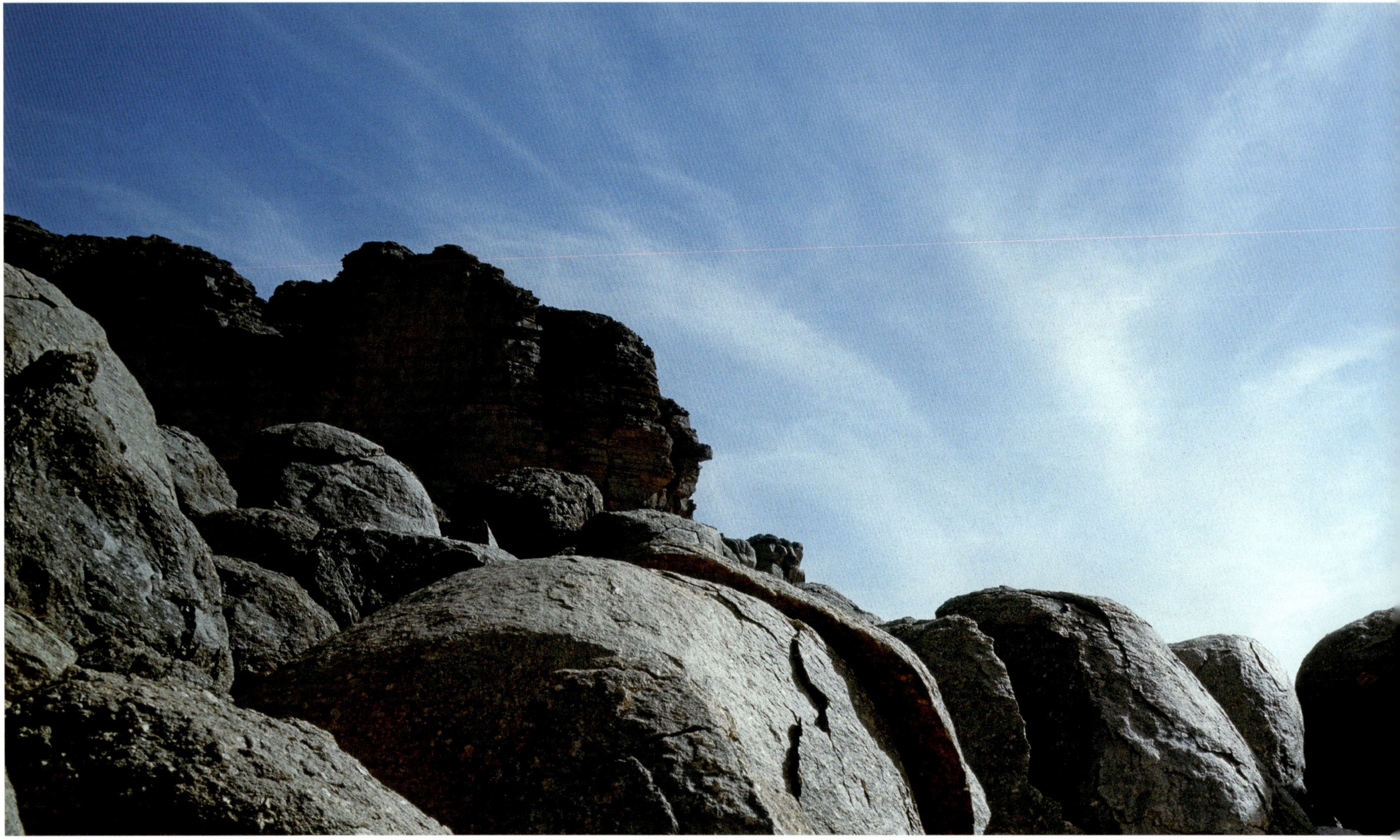

45 Rock balls, Tassili n' Ajjer, Algeria

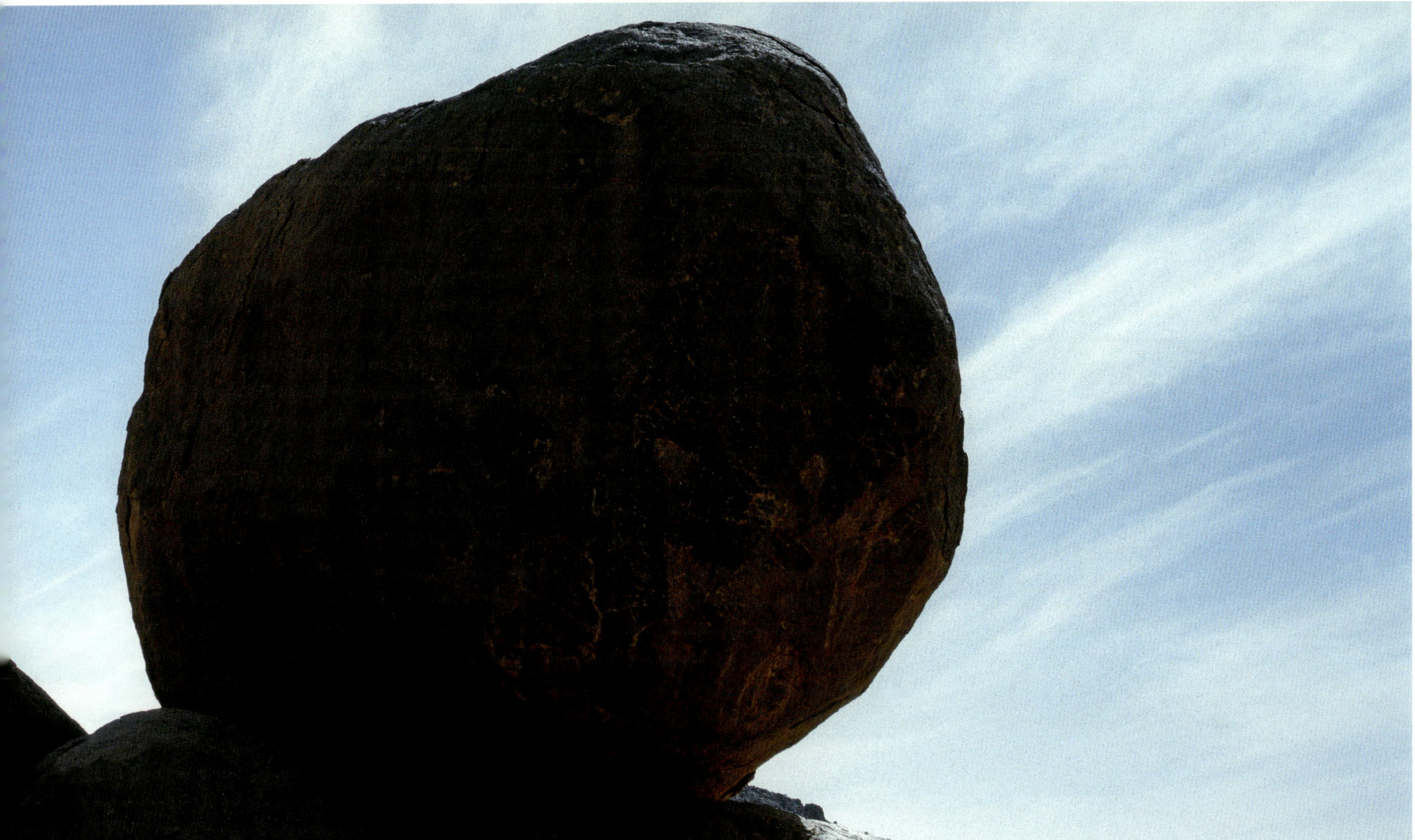

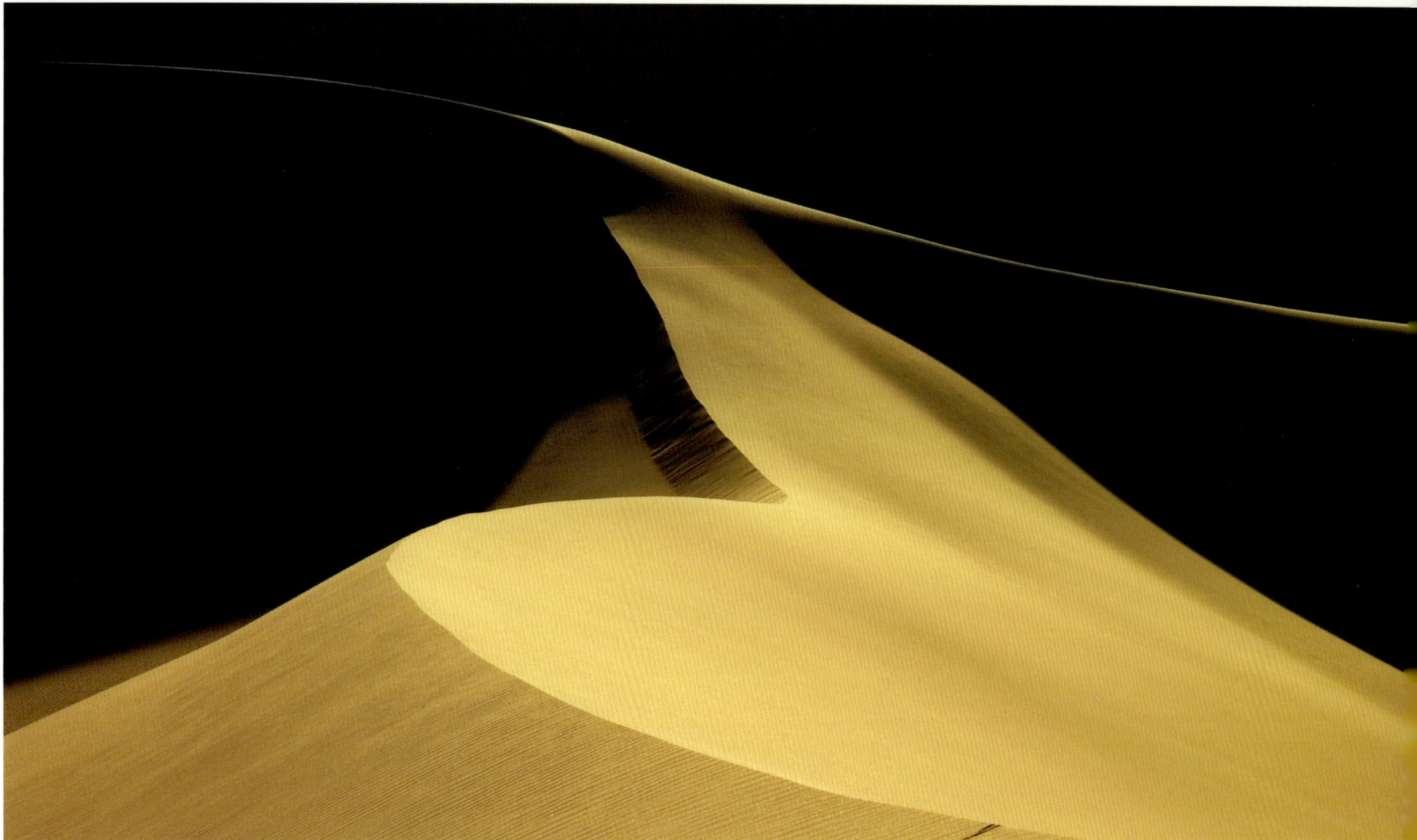

46 Erg Ubari, Libya

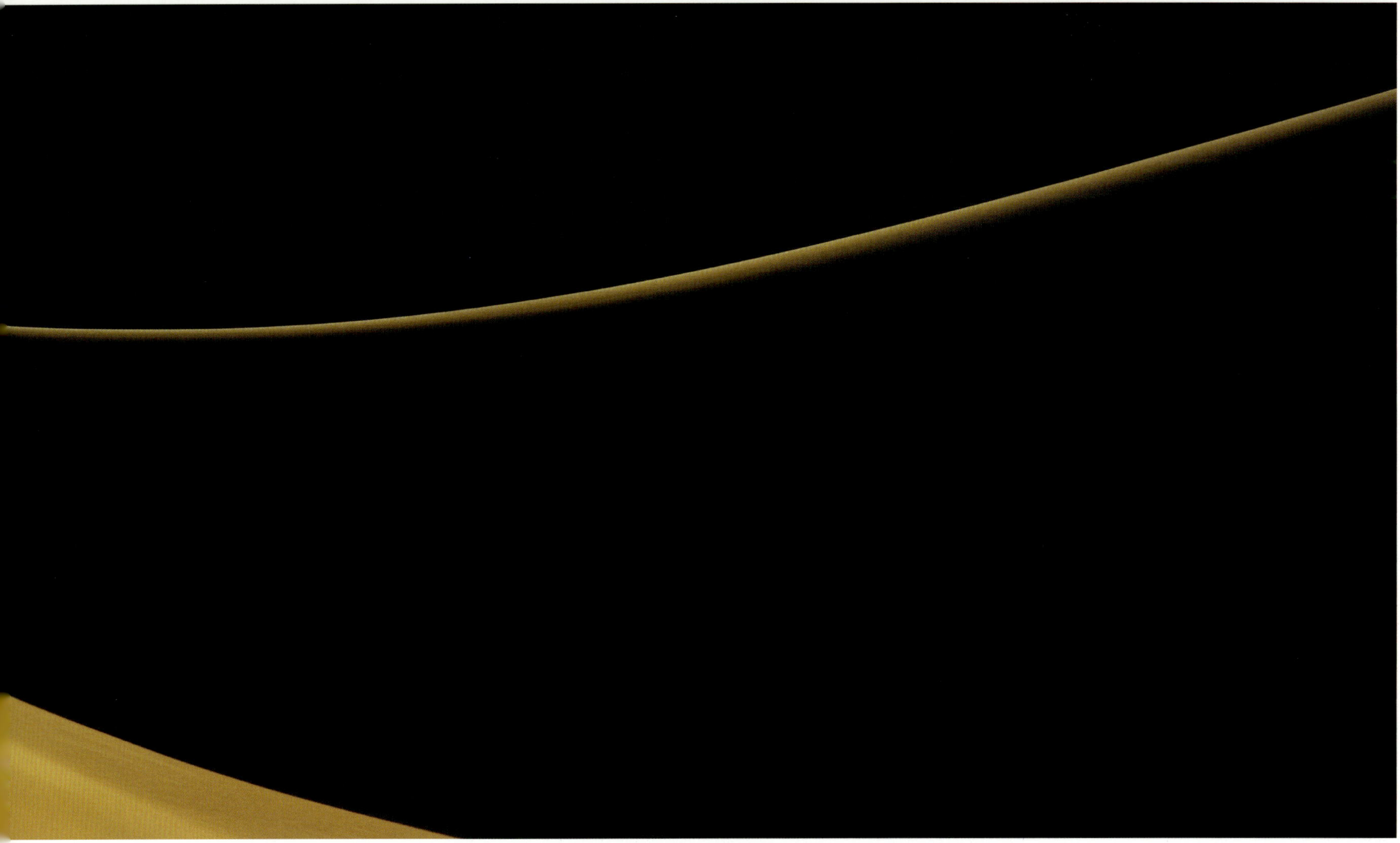

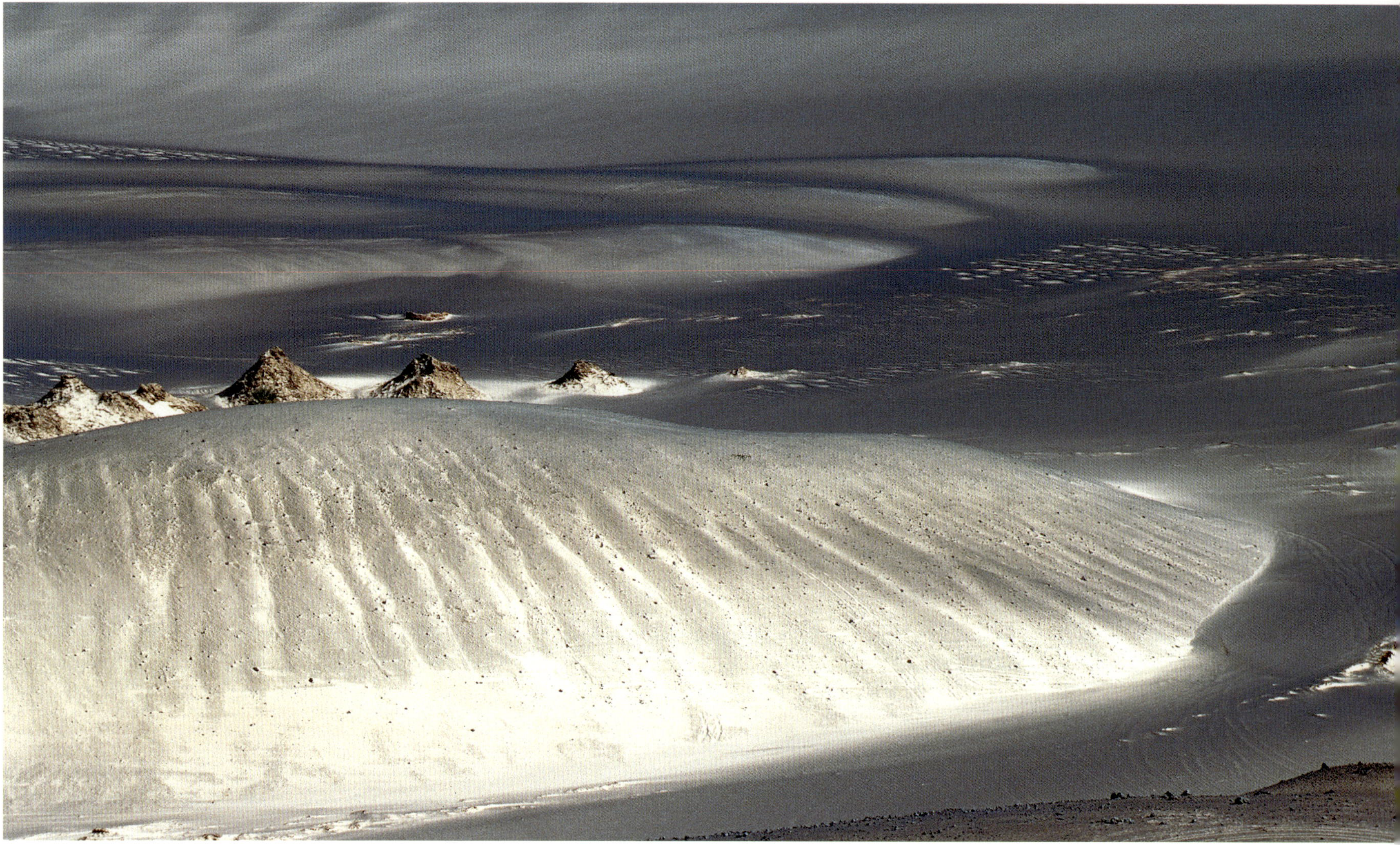

47 Wau an Namus, Algeria

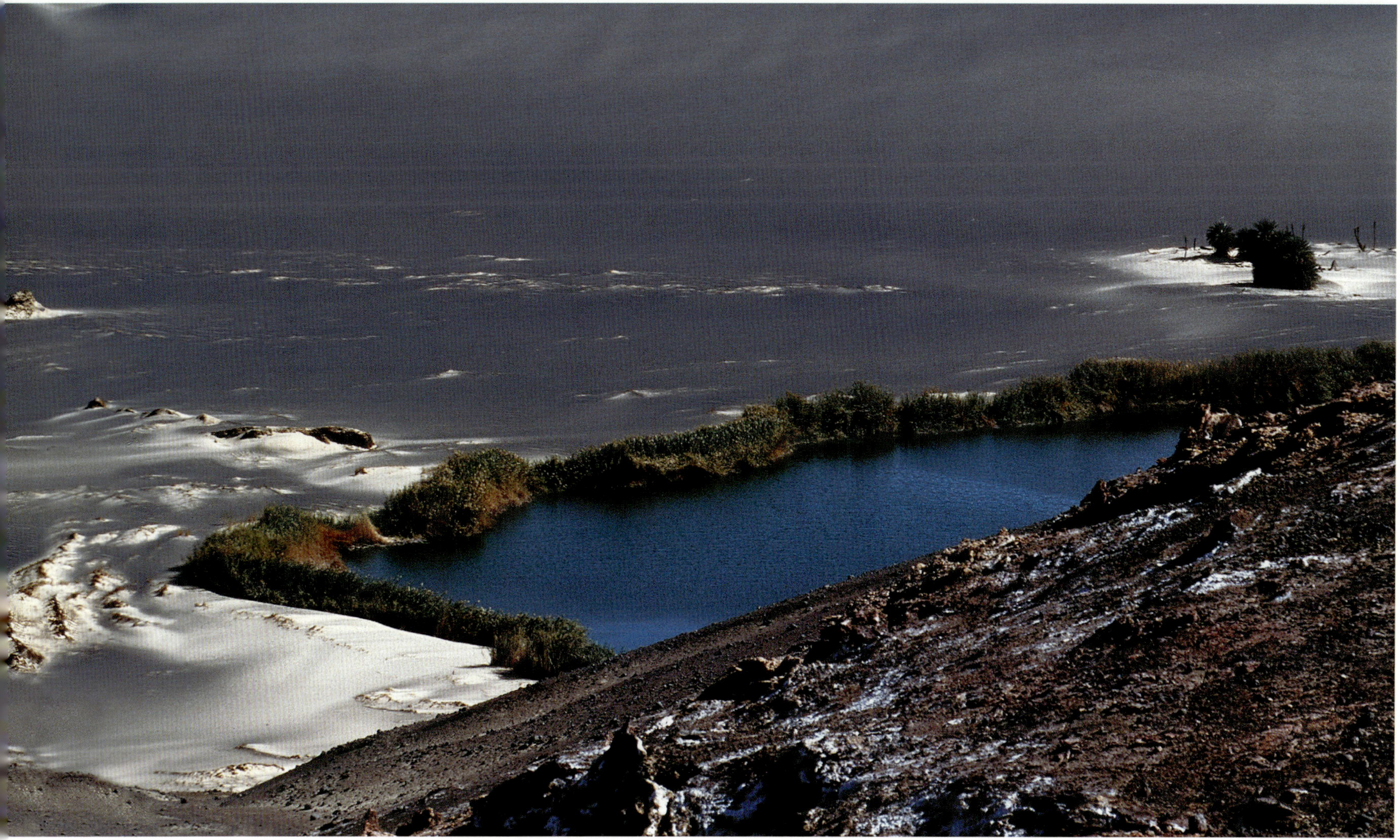

► **48** Erg Amguid, Algeria

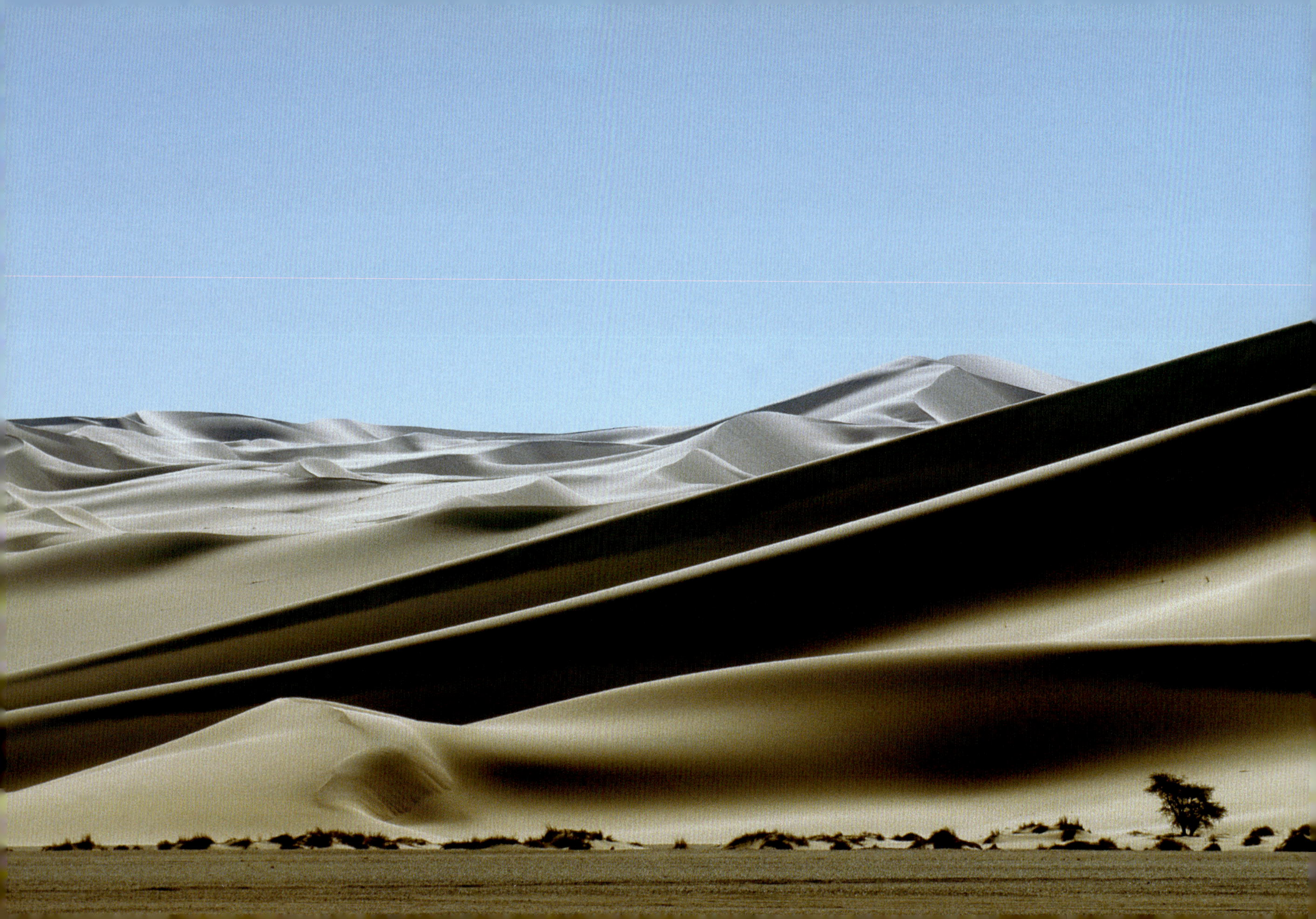

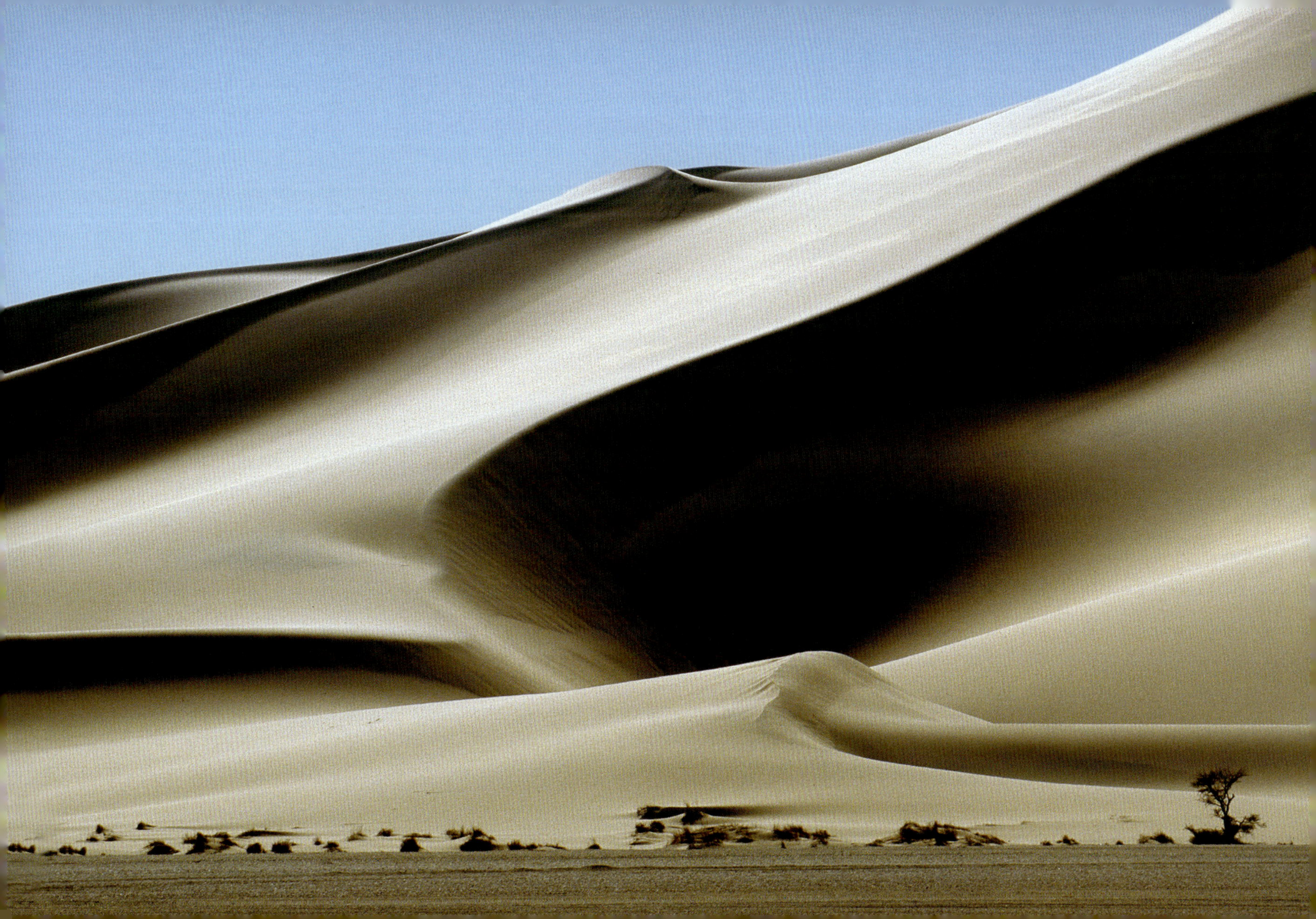

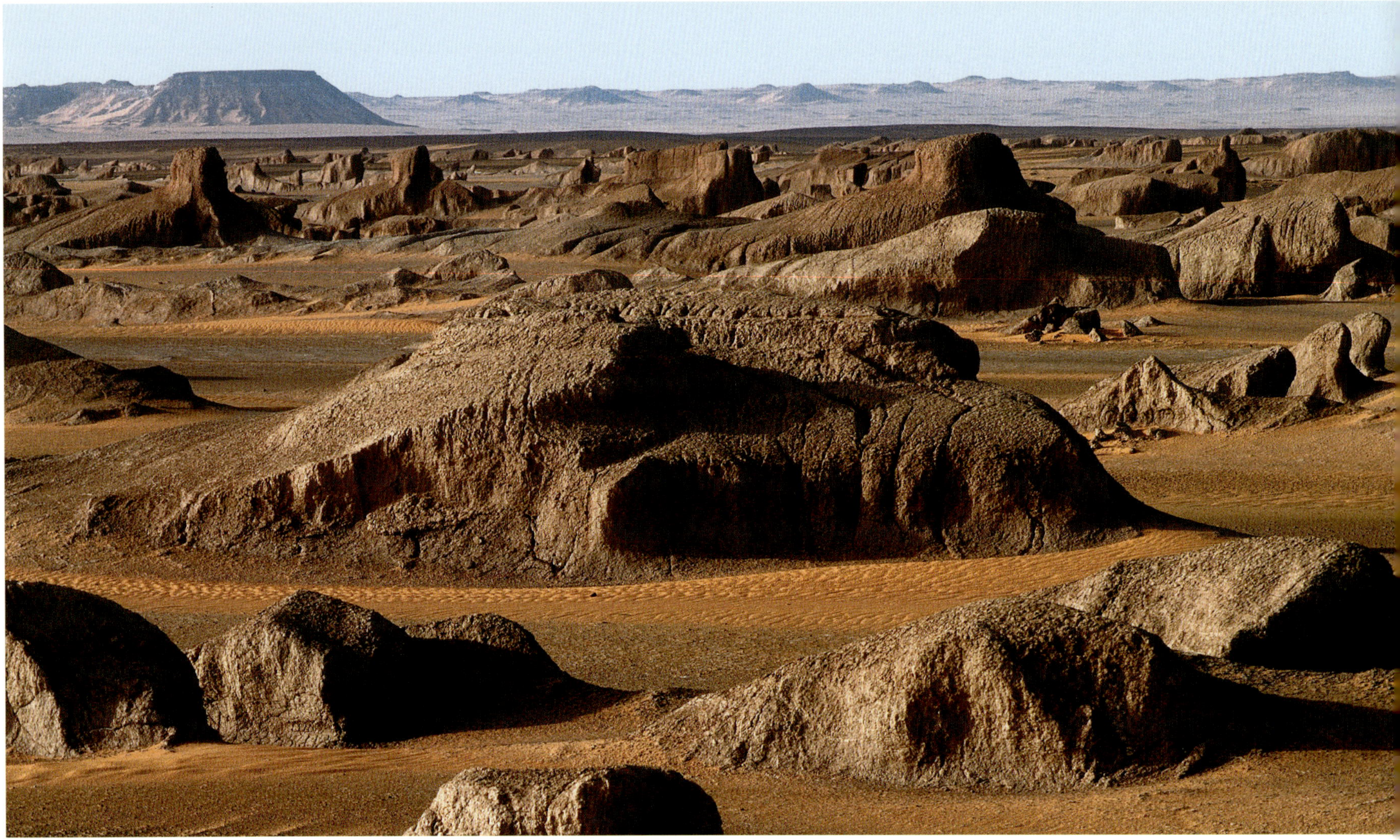

49 Near Al Katrun, Libya

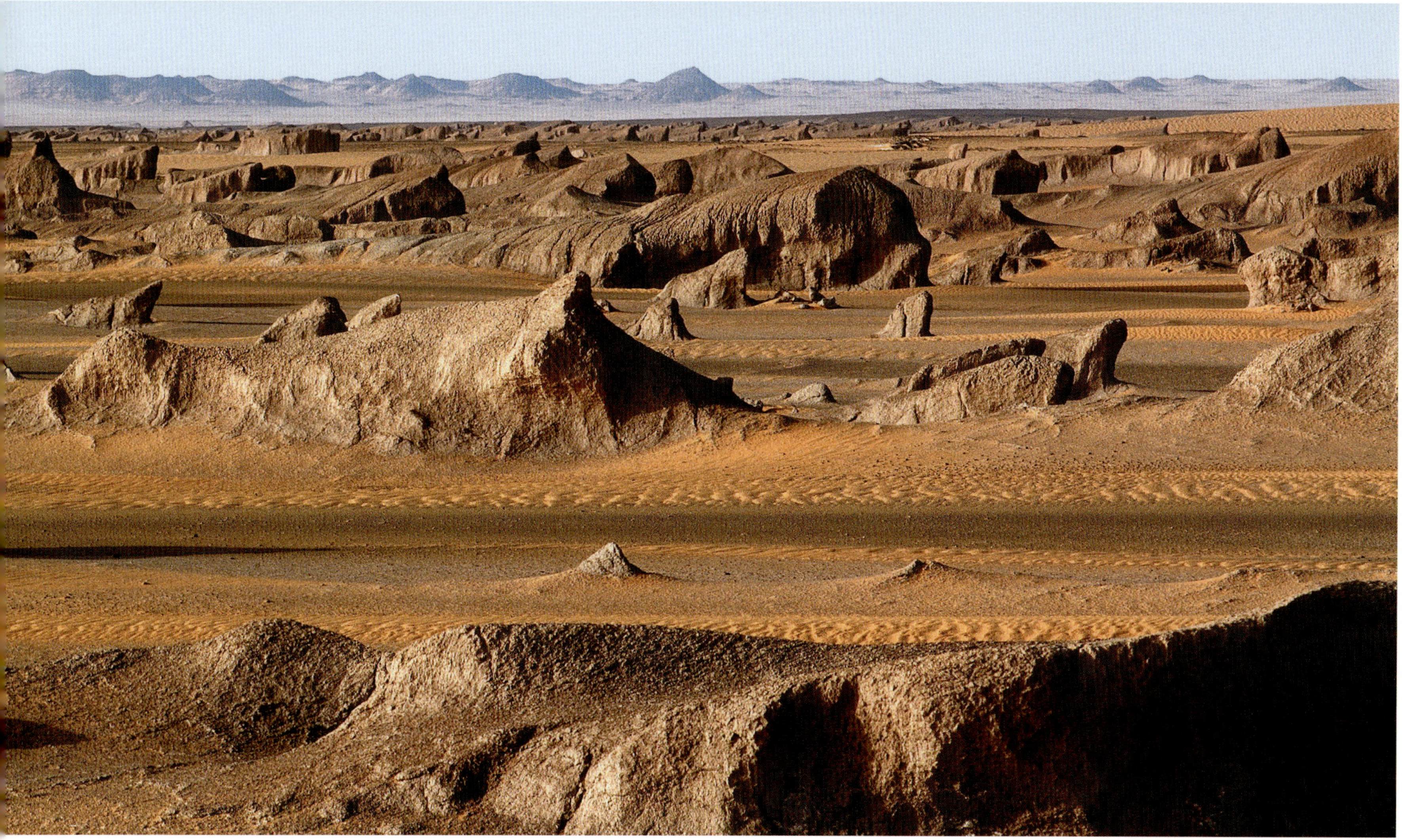

► **50** Oued Tagrira, Algeria

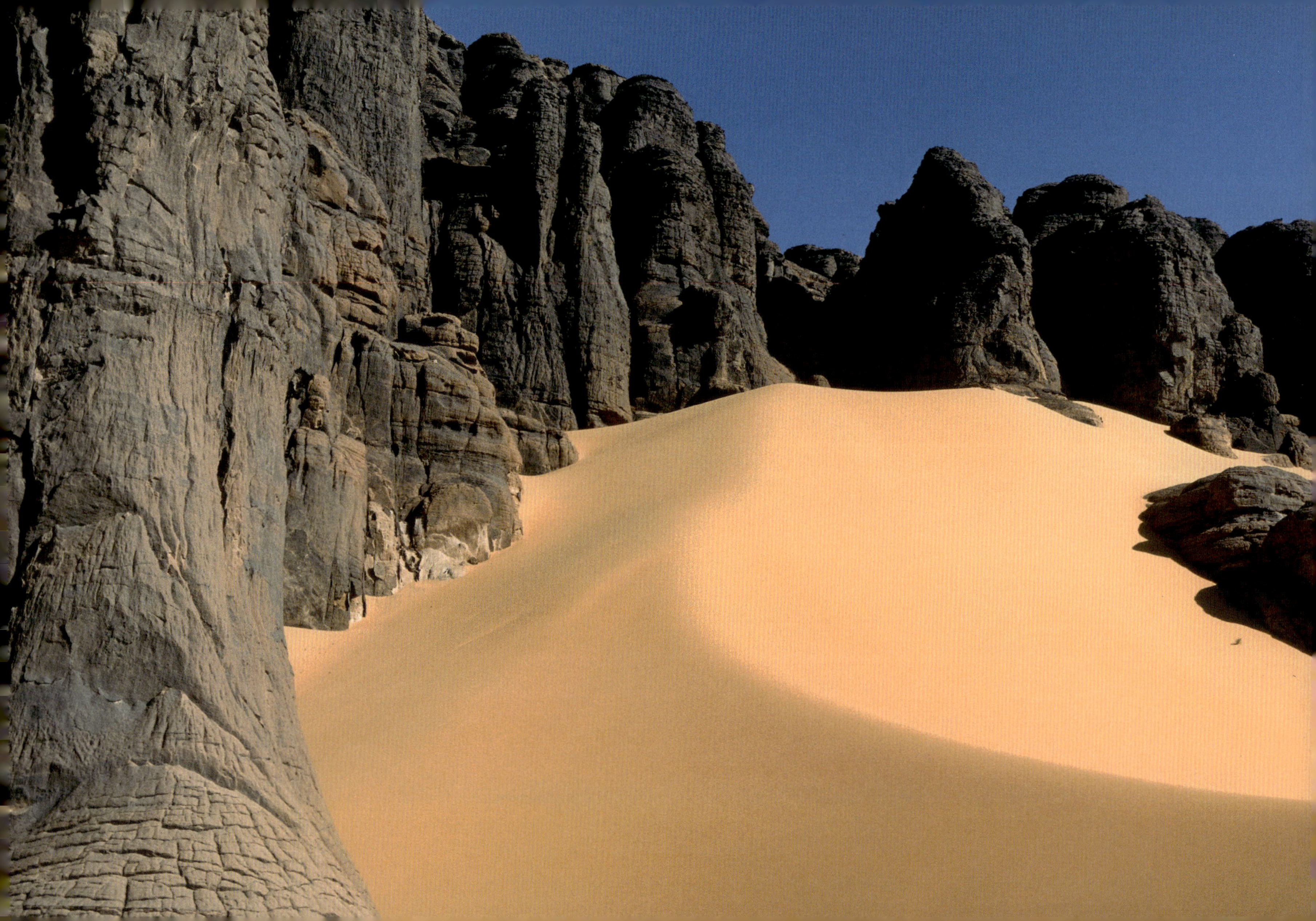

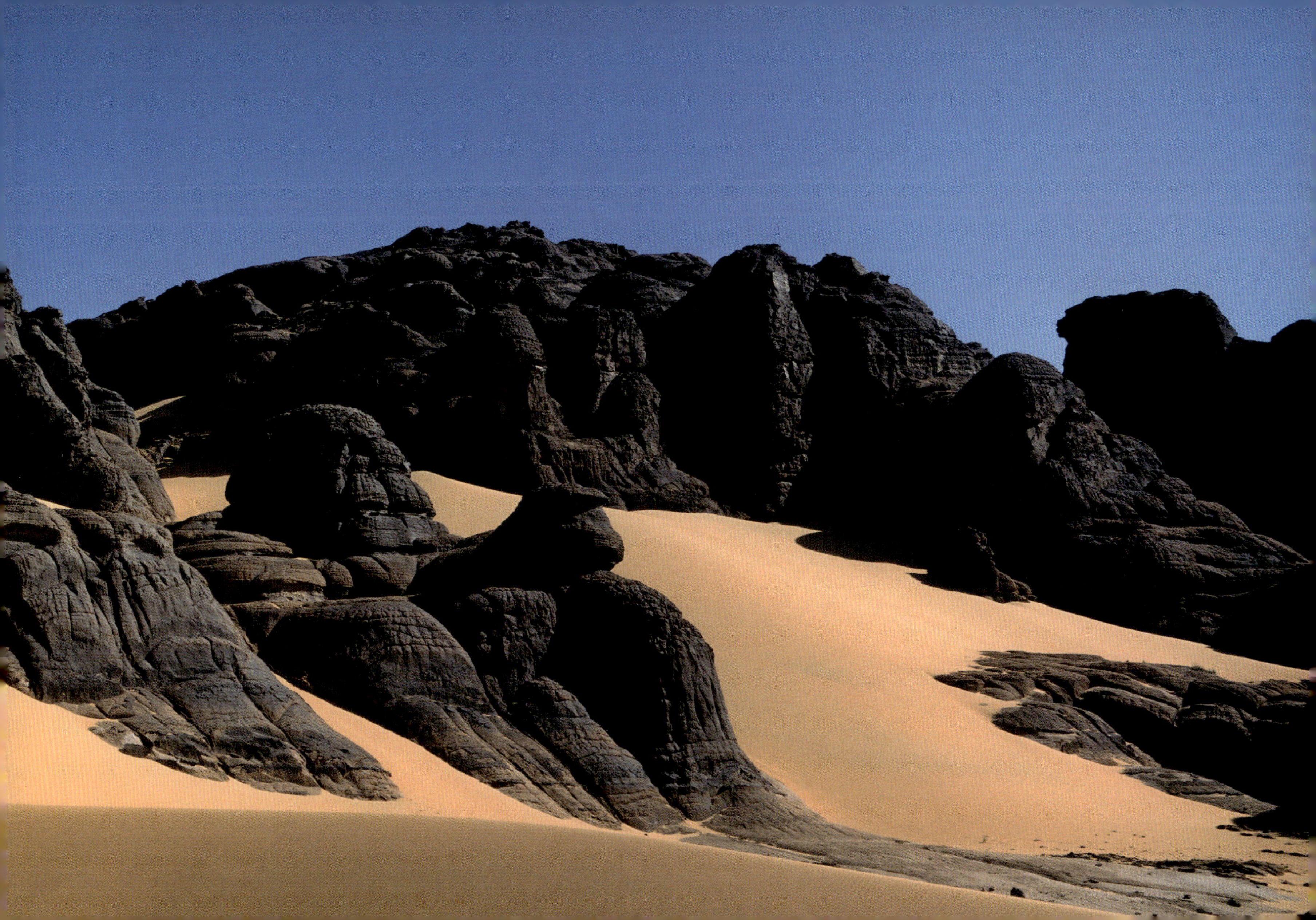

HANS GASSER wurde 1950 in Schwaz/Tirol geboren. Er lebt seit 1967 in Innsbruck/Österreich, wo er seit 30 Jahren als Zahnarzt tätig ist. Als Photograph empfindet er vor allem Wüstenlandschaften als Herausforderung. Die Panoramaphotographie nutzt er als Instrument, um Weite und Faszination dieser Landschaften zu vermitteln und spürbar zu machen. Seit 1990 reist Hans Gasser fast jedes Jahr in die Wüstenregionen der Sahara, zuletzt besuchte er die so genannte „Weisse Wüste" im Westen Ägyptens.

IRIS LEMANCZYK wurde 1964 in Kirchheim/Teck bei Stuttgart geboren. Nach dem Studium der Germanistik und Geographie lockte immer wieder die Ferne. Sie reiste um die Welt, schnupperte eine Zeit lang Zirkusluft, lebte in Namibia und besuchte für ein paar Monate Australien und Neuseeland. Dazwischen arbeitete sie als Zeitungs-Redakteurin bei der „Südwest Presse" in Ulm. Seit 1997 ist sie freiberuflich tätig, schreibt Kinder- und Jugendbücher sowie Sachbücher, verfasst Reiseberichte und ist als Dozentin für Kreatives Schreiben tätig.

HANS GASSER was born in Schwaz in Tyrol in 1950. He has lived in Innsbruck, Austria, since 1967 and has now worked there as a dentist for some 25 years. As a photographer, he constantly finds himself challenged by desert vistas. He makes use of panorama photography as an instrument for conveying a tangible sense of the breadth and fascination of such settings. Ever since 1990 Hans Gasser has been repeatedly travelling to the desert regions of the Sahara and most recently he visited the "White Desert" in western Egypt.

IRIS LEMANCZYK was born in 1964 in Kirchheim/Teck near Stuttgart. After studying German and geography, she gave way to the call of far-distant places. She travelled around the world, experienced the circus life for a time, lived in Namibia and spent several months in Australia and New Zealand. In between, she also learnt something more conventional: newspaper editing with the "Südwest Presse" in Ulm. Since 1997 she has worked as a freelancer, writing children's books and non-fiction and compiling travel reports, and also works as a lecturer on creative writing.

HANS GASSER est né en 1950 à Schwaz dans le Tyrol mais il vit depuis 1967 à Innsbruck en Autriche où il est dentiste depuis plus de 30 ans. Photographe amateur, il considère les paysages désertiques comme un véritable défi. La photographie panoramique est pour lui un instrument dont il se sert pour rendre palpables et perceptibles l'immensité et la fascination de ces paysages. Depuis 1990, Hans Gasser parcourt presque chaque année les régions désertiques du Sahara, la dernière en date le « Désert blanc » dans l'ouest de l'Egypte.

IRIS LEMANCZYK est née en 1964 à Kirchheim/Teck près de Stuttgart. Après des études de philologie allemande et de géographie, elle effectue régulièrement des voyages lointains. Elle voyage à travers le monde, séjourne pendant quelque temps dans un cirque, vit en Namibie et passe plusieurs mois en Australie et en Nouvelle-Zélande. Entre toutes ces occupations, elle trouve néanmoins le temps d'apprendre un métier sérieux : rédactrice journalistique au quotidien allemand « Südwest Presse » à Ulm. Depuis 1997, elle travaille comme rédactrice indépendante, écrit des livres destinés à l'enfance et à la jeunesse ainsi que des livres d'essai. Elle rédige également des comptes rendus de voyage et dispense des cours de création littéraire.

HANS GASSER nació en 1950 en Schwaz (Tirol) y reside desde 1967 en Innsbruck (Austria) donde ejerce desde hace 30 años su profesión de dentista. El desafío que más le atrae como fotógrafo son los paisajes desérticos. Habitualmente utiliza la fotografía de panoramas como un instrumento para plasmar la amplitud y la fascinación que irradian estos paisajes. Hans Gasser viaja casi cada año desde 1990 a las regiones desérticas del Sahara. En su última expedición estuvo en el famoso "desierto blanco" del oeste de Egipto.

IRIS LEMANCZYK nació en 1964 en el pueblo de Kirchheim/Teck junto a Stuttgart (Alemania). Tras terminar su carrera de Filología Germánica y Geografía se dejó atraer cada vez más por el encanto de los destinos exóticos: viajó por el mundo, experimentó durante algún tiempo la vida en un circo, residió en Namibia y pasó algunos meses en Australia y Nueva Zelanda. Y entre todas esas ocupaciones todavía encontró tiempo para aprender un oficio serio: redactora de periódicos en la editorial alemana "Südwest Presse" de Ulm. Desde 1997 trabaja como redactora libre y escribe diversos libros: desde literatura infantil y juvenil a libros de texto. Además confecciona relatos de viaje e imparte seminarios de creación literaria.

HANS GASSER è nato nel 1950 a Schwaz / Tirolo. Dal 1967 vive a Innsbruck / Austria, dove lavora come medico dentista da 30 anni. Come fotografo egli avverte sopattutto i paesaggi del deserto come sfida. La fotografia panoramica viene da lui utilizzata come strumento per trasmettere e far percepire la vastità e il fascino di questi paesaggi. Dal 1990 Hans Gasser si reca ogni anno nelle regioni del deserto del Sahara. Ultimamente ha visitato il cosiddetto "deserto bianco" nell'Egitto occidentale.

IRIS LEMANCZYK è nata nel 1964 a Kirchheim/Teck vicino a Stoccarda. Dopo la laurea in Lingua e Letteratura Tedesca e in Geografia ha seguito la sua passione per i viaggi in paesi lontani. È stata in tutto il mondo, per un certo periodo ha respirato l'aria del circo, ha vissuto in Namibia e per qualche mese ha abitato in Australia e Nuova Zelanda. Tra un viaggio e l'altro si è dedicata alla più razionale attività di redattrice presso la Südwest Presse di Ulm. Dal 1997 lavora come libera professionista, scrive libri per bambini e ragazzi e testi di saggistica, redige reportage di viaggi ed insegna scrittura creativa.

ISBN: 978-3-89823-347-7

Concept: Bernhard Wipfler, Sebastian Wipfler, Marcus Bela Schmitt
Design: Designgruppe Fanz & Neumayer | Marcus Bela Schmitt & EDITION PANORAMA | Diana May
Editorial department: Dr. Michael Barchet, Wolfgang Roth
Translations: Global-Text Fachübersetzungen, Heidelberg | Mark Woolfe, Jocelyne Abarca, Dr. Maria Carasi, Sebastián González Mohíno
Printing: abcdruck GmbH, Heidelberg
Bookbinding: Josef Spinner Großbuchbinderei GmbH, Ottersweier

EDITION PANORAMA GmbH
G 7, 14
D - 68159 Mannheim

www.editionpanorama.com

A production by EDITION**PANORAMA**

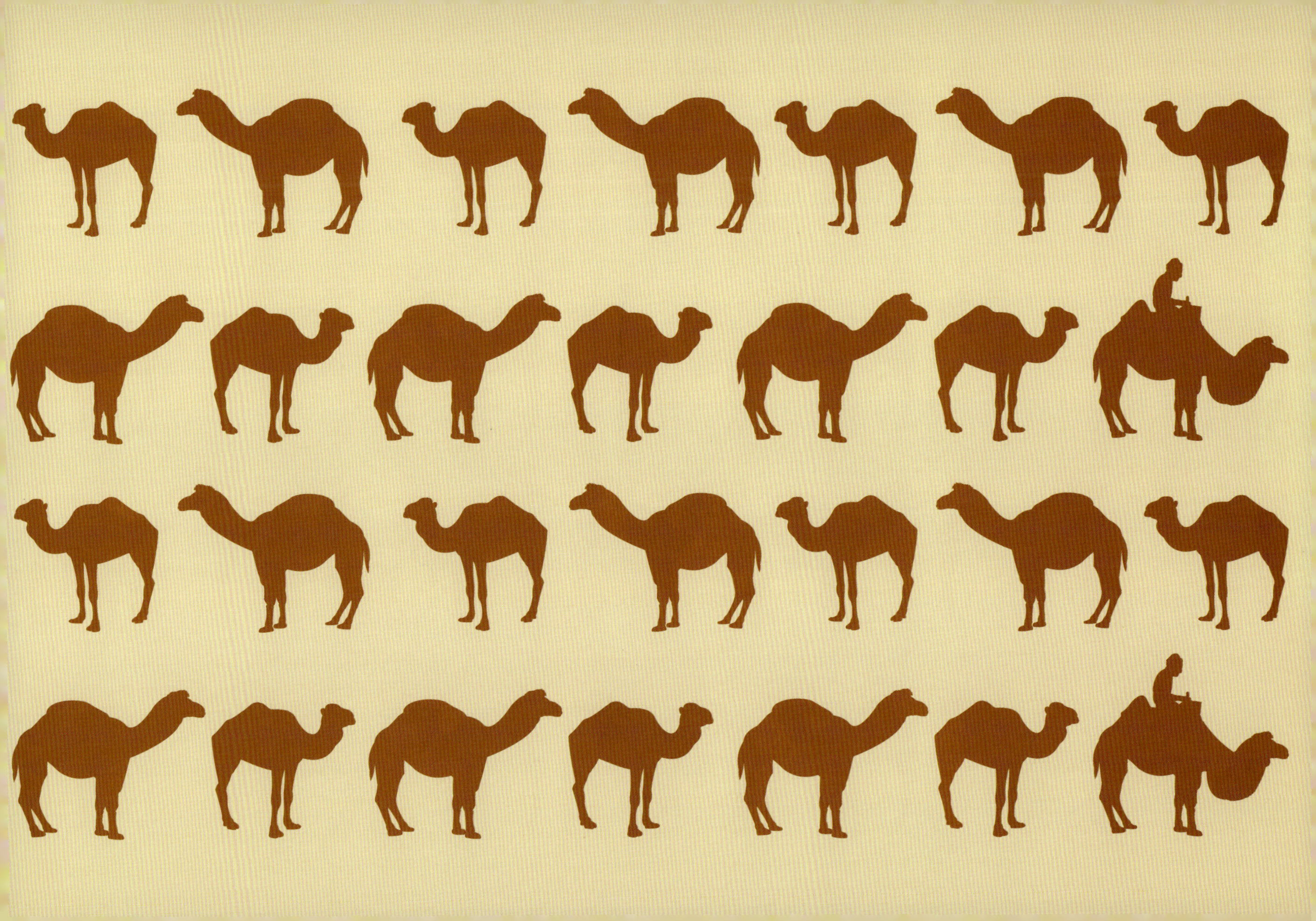

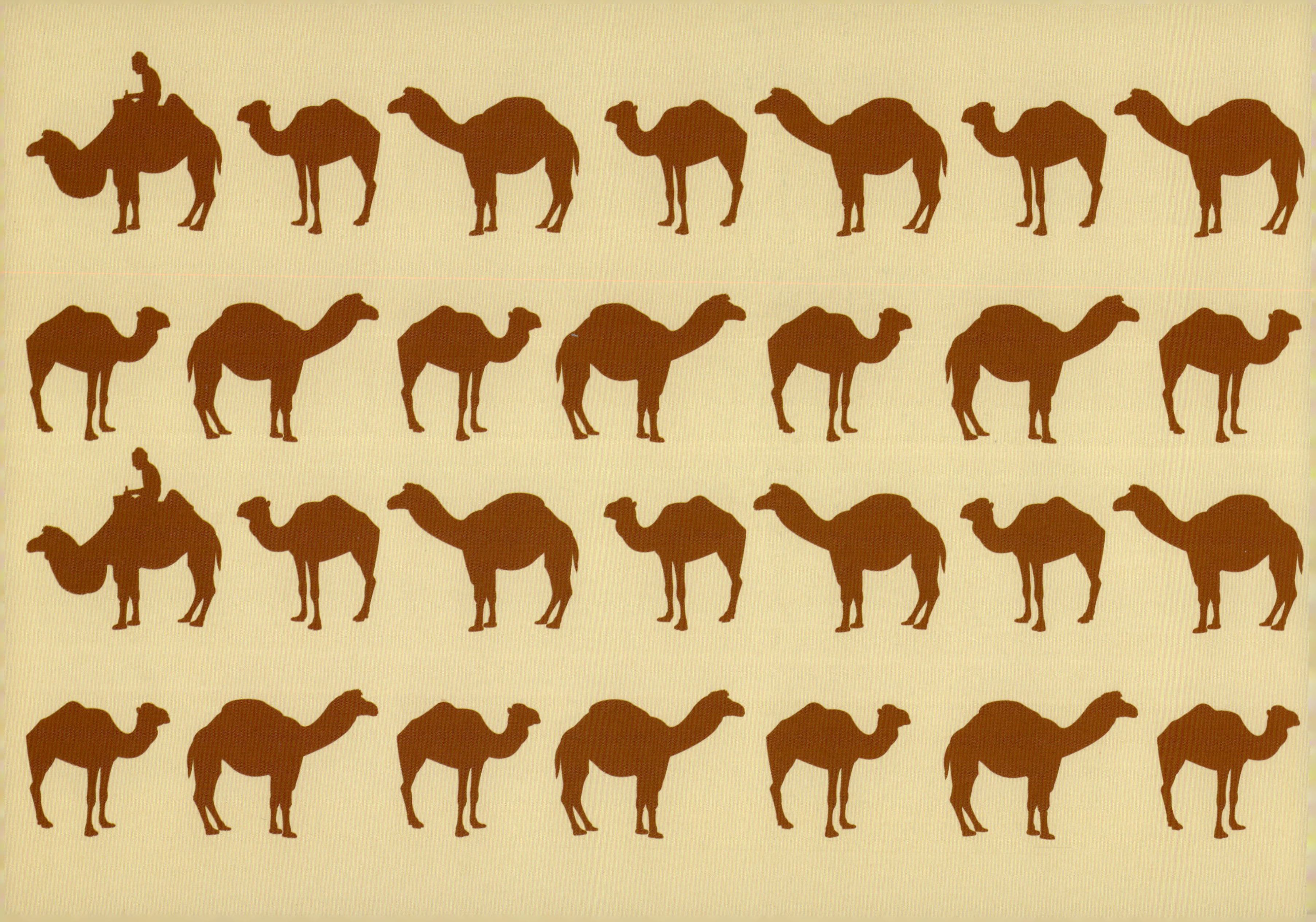